D1452313

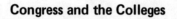

Congress and the Colleges

Lexington Books Politics of Education Series
Frederick M. Wirt, Editor

Michael W. Kirst, Ed., *State, School, and Politics: Research Directions*

Joel S. Berke, Michael W. Kirst, *Federal Aid to Education: Who Benefits? Who Governs?*

Al J. Smith, Anthony Downs, M. Leanne Lachman, *Achieving Effective Desegretation*

Kern Alexander, K. Forbis Jordan, *Constitutional Reform of School Finance*

George R. LaNoue, Bruce L.R. Smith, *The Politics of School Decentralization*

David J. Kirby, T. Robert Harris, Robert L. Crain, Christine H. Rossell, *Political Strategies in Northern School Desegregation*

Philip K. Piele, John Stuart Hall, *Budgets, Bonds, and Ballots: Voting Behavior in School Financial Elections*

John C. Hogan, *The Schools, the Courts, and the Public Interest*

Jerome T. Murphy, *State Education Agencies and Discretionary Funds: Grease the Squeaky Wheel*

Howard Hamilton, Sylvan Cohen, *Policy Making by Plebiscite: School Referenda*

Daniel J. Sullivan, *Public Aid to Nonpublic Schools*

James Hottois, Neal A. Milner, *The Sex Education Controversy: A Study of Politics, Education and Morality*

Lauriston R. King, *The Washington Lobbyists for Higher Education*

Frederick M. Wirt, Ed., *The Polity of the School: New Research in Educational Politics*

Peter J. Cistone, Ed., *Understanding School Boards: Problems and Prospects*

Lawrence E. Gladieux, Thomas R. Wolanin, *Congress and the Colleges: The National Politics of Higher Education*

Dale Mann, *The Politics of Administrative Representation: School Administrators and Local Democracy*

Congress and the Colleges

The National Politics of Higher Education

Lawrence E. Gladieux
Thomas R. Wolanin

Lexington Books

D.C. Heath and Company
Lexington, Massachusetts
Toronto   London

Library of Congress Cataloging in Publication Data

Gladieux, Lawrence E
    Congress and the Colleges.

    Includes bibliographical references and index.
    1. Federal aid to higher education—United States. 2 Universities and colleges—Law and Legislation—United States. I. Wolanin, Thomas R., 1942-   joint author. II. Title.
KF4234.G55   344'.73'074   75-22881
ISBN 0-669-00183-x

Published simultaneously in Canada

Printed in the United States of America

International Standard Book Number: 0-669-00183-x

Library of Congress Catalog Card Number: 75-22881

To Lois and Thompy

Contents

Introduction

This is a study of policy making by the federal government. Specifically, it describes and explains the genesis, enactment, and consequences of the Education Amendments of 1972, an omnibus measure widely characterized as the most significant higher education law since the land-grant college legislation of more than a century ago.

The book is intended to help fill a gap in understanding with respect to an important realm of national policy. Few acts of Congress in recent decades have signalled basic shifts in the role played by the federal government in American society. The Social Security Act, the Employment Act of 1946, Medicare and the civil rights laws of the 1960s fall into this class. Such historic breakthroughs have drawn the interest of political observers and have frequently been the subject of case studies. Other major enactments, however, like the Education Amendments of 1972, have broadened and elaborated the federal role in areas where there is already a consensus on government's legitimate involvement. Such bills, which are the daily fare of national policy-makers, have received less attention.

Billions of dollars, moreover, are expended yearly on federal programs supporting postsecondary education and these programs have an impact on the lives of millions of students, their parents, teachers, administrators and the general public. Yet the literature on federal policy making for postsecondary education is somewhere between slim and nonexistent.

The book also explores the dynamics and results of omnibus legislation as a contemporary approach to domestic policy making. Domestic programs have proliferated and form in many areas a complex web of federal efforts. Large, multiprogram bills have become more common if not typical of policy making in fields like housing, crime control, health, agriculture and energy as well as education. An omnibus bill is a vehicle for aggregating programs and expressing a variety of interests. Many higher education programs and others only tangentially related to higher education were collected in the grab bag that was inelegantly titled, "The Education Amendments of 1972."

The endless vying for governmental power and patterns of change and continuity in legislative-executive relations are another dimension of the book. The formulation and enactment of the Education Amendments of 1972 demonstrate congressional initiative in domestic policy making. While on the basis of this case one is hardly led to proclaim congressional dominance or even resurgence, it suggests that in some circumstances, as when the executive branch abdicates or is passive, Congress can be a reservoir of innovative thinking and constructive action on the domestic front.

The story of the 1972 bill and its aftermath at the same time illuminate the evolution of the Nixon strategy for controlling domestic policy. After an initial period during which the Administration sought to make an imprint through legislative proposals, it then turned inward and tried to guide policy through impoundment and other budgetary controls as well as tight management of bureaucratic rule making. In contrast to domestic policy making in the Johnson years, this side of the Nixon Administration has been relatively little studied.[a] This book adds to the limited body of literature probing dimensions of the Nixon Administration other than Watergate and foreign affairs.

One caveat should be noted on the scope of the study. The federal impact on higher education is far flung, involving scores of agencies and stemming from a variety of national objectives like space exploration, foreign assistance, health care and agriculture. This study does not address the totality of federal activity impinging directly or indirectly on colleges, universities and students. It only touches, for example, on the vast domain of federally sponsored scientific research and development. The focus, rather, is on the core of federal higher education programs and policies centered in the Department of HEW, and the legislation authorizing them.

These are some of the major dimensions of the book. In treating the topic, we blend different types of analysis. There are essentially two approaches to describing and explaining social events. The first approach is from ground level and requires being immersed in, and sensitive to, the texture and stuff of human experience. This approach emphasizes the circumstantial, accidental, unique and disorganized realities of life. The second is an aerial view—detached, analytic and general, placing events in the context of forces, trends, ideas and movements.[b]

Our study draws on both approaches. Part I, "The Environment for Policy Making," provides an intellectual and historical perspective on the proximate political events. In Part II, "The Education Amendments of 1972," we try to capture the reality of an episode in American politics. This is not a personal or intimate memoir of events in which we were both participants.[c] We have extended our information beyond personal knowledge and selected material to form a coherent narrative. Here we try to communicate some of the feel of politics as well as specific insights into the workings of the political process in Washington. Part III, "Impact and Process," puts the case material in the perspective of, first, the development of federal higher education policy and, second, the study of the policy-making process. We have thus broadened the case beyond the formal stages of government decision making by examining the larger background of events and by attempting to generalize from them.[d]

---

[a]A notable exception is Richard Nathan's *The Plot That Failed: Nixon and the Administrative Presidency*, John Wiley & Sons, New York, 1975.

[b]See Isaiah Berlin, *The Hedgehog and the Fox*, Simon and Schuster, New York, 1966.

[c]Gladieux was Associate Director of the Washington Office of the College Entrance Examination Board; and Wolanin was a Congressional Fellow in the office of Congressman Frank Thompson, Jr., during the saga of the Education Amendments of 1972.

[d]Chapter 1 is based in part on material that appeared as "The Political Culture of a Policy Arena: Higher Education," in Matthew Holden, Jr. and Dennis Dresang, eds., *What Govern-*

We have written the book with several audiences in mind—first, a general audience of citizens with an interest in American government and politics. Students and teachers may find the book especially adapted to instruction in this area because it deals with federal programs that directly affect them. We also hope to reach those with a professional interest in the substance of federal higher education policy—government policy-makers, lobbyists, policy analysts, college and university administrators and students of education. And this work is aimed at social scientists and others primarily interested in the governmental process, the "how" rather than the "what" of federal activity.

Four elements have made this book possible:

The idea: The inspiration to undertake the work came from Lois Rice, Vice President of the College Entrance Examination Board, and Congressman Frank Thompson, Jr. When they said, "You two ought to write a book on the 1972 Act," they set in motion a three-year effort the dimensions of which neither we nor they fully appreciated at the time. We thank them for putting us on the track.

The support: Two generous travel and study grants from the Ford Foundation gave us the freedom and resources to undertake and complete the project. It would have been impossible without this assistance, and our special thanks go to Earl Cheit and Peter DeJanosi of the Ford Foundation. Wolanin also gratefully acknowledges support from the Center for Policy and Administration, University of Wisconsin-Madison, during the fall semester of 1972. In addition, we wish to express our appreciation to the College Entrance Examination Board for its cooperation in facilitating the study.

The interviews: Whatever merit this work has is due in large part to the 65 men and women in the Congress, in the U.S. Office of Education and Department of HEW, in the White House, in educational associations and in colleges and universities who generously gave their time and candid comments in off-the-record interviews. Their knowledge and insights about higher education and federal politics enriched us and this work. Quotations and other material drawn from the interviews are not attributed by footnotes because of the confidentiality of the sources.

The partnership: Neither of us could have accomplished this work alone. It is, we believe, better as a result of the division of labor and especially the sharing and testing of ideas. This was in every way a joint effort from planning and outlining to critical review, redrafting and editing.

Valuable comments and assistance were received from Stephen Bailey, Mary Budd, William Cable, Pamela Christoffel, Christopher Cross, Cheryl Evans, David Fellman, Chester Finn, Jean Frohlicher, Richard Fulton, William Gaul,

ment Does, v. 1, Sage Yearbooks in Politics and Public Policy, Sage Publications, Inc., Beverly Hills, California, 1975; Chapter 10 is based in part on material that originally appeared in 4 Journal of Law and Education 301 (728 National Press Bldg., Washington, D.C., 1975); and Chapter 11 is based in part on material that originally appeared in Viewpoints, v. 51 (May, 1975), published by the Indiana University School of Education. All reprinted with permission.

xiv

Julia Gordon, Robert Hartman, Matthew Holden, Ralph Huitt, Clark Kerr, Edward Kimball, Lauriston King, Darrell Mensel, James Mooney, Moshe Shani, Ira Sharkansky, Richard Smith, and Verne Stadtman. We thank them all. The responsibility for this work is, of course, ours alone.

Finally, our beloved wives, Paula and Barbara, tolerated with good humor and patience our absences from home, late night hours, and long arcane discussions. They provided invaluable support and assistance. Our children, Kenneth and Michele and Peter and Andrew, prodded us on with the insistent question: "When is the big book going to be done?"

Lawrence E. Gladieux
Alexandria, Virginia

Thomas R. Wolanin
Washington, D.C.

August, 1975

Part I
The Environment for Policy Making

Mankind are influenced by various causes: by the climate, by the religion, by the laws, by the maxims of government, by precedents, morals, and customs; whence is formed a general spirit of nations.

Montesquieu
The Spirit of the Laws (1748)

1

Historical Legacies

Government action in every major area of public concern takes place within broad boundaries formed by the historical and social environment. This environment is not a neutral medium but rather an important influence on what is done.

We begin with these two premises: (1) Growing out of the American historical experience, there is a basic consensus on the proper federal role in relation to higher education. (2) New policy is usually not made by uprooting wholesale what already exists; federal programs already in place will be the starting point for action. These conditions limit and shape new federal policy making for higher education.[a]

This chapter briefly examines the historical development of higher education in the United States and its relationship with the federal government. This legacy as it existed in the 1960s comprised certain fundamental assumptions and characteristics that to a significant degree established what could and should be done.

The Primacy of the States

In the support and control of public higher education, the states have the primary responsibility. This is the most durable assumption concerning the relationship between the federal government and higher education. At the Constitutional Convention of 1787, several proposals were advanced to give the federal government authority to establish institutions of higher education, or at least a national university as the "cap of the system." All were rejected.[1] The federal service academies, beginning with the establishment of West Point in 1820, for all practical purposes represent the extent of the federal government's direct management of institutions of higher education. Instead, the federal role in higher education has always been one of supplementing the states. "Of all the services that are supported by state funds," one scholar has written, "the state governments have most clearly taken command of higher education."[2] This

---

[a]We do not intend to suggest a determinism that limits change in higher education policy to the gradual and incremental. Instead, we think that change in this area has occurred in this way and that there is a high probability, but not a certainty, that it will continue as such in the future.

division of governmental responsibilities is strongly supported by the attitudes of state and federal policy-makers and the general public.[3]

The Instrumental View of Higher Education

Scholarship, research, and creativity for their own sake have never enjoyed great favor with the American public or with federal policy makers. Higher education instead has historically had the support of the general public as well as the federal government because it is "useful."[4]

This attitude has roots deep in the American historical experience. America has never had an aristocracy or class structure in the European sense. The consequence, to quote de Tocqueville, is that "there is no class. . .in America, in which the taste of intellectual pleasures is transmitted with hereditary fortune and leisure and by which the labors of the intellect are held in honor."[5]

Second, survival was the preoccupation of Americans in the formative years of the nation. As the Handlins have notes, "The important tasks in America were the establishment of settlements, the advance upon the frontier, and the development of a viable economy. Comparatively little energy went to education at any level. . . ."[6] The value of education was measured against its contributions to these basic tasks.

Third, from the point of view of the individual, given the dominant American ethos of "democratic capitalism" and "rugged individualism," higher education has had a value insofar as it has helped each Horatio Alger get ahead in the economic and social system.[7]

The national goals for which higher education has been considered useful have changed over time.

Leadership Training

During the colonial period the dominant mission of higher education was the training of leadership—initially religious leadership, but gradually secularized by the mid-nineteenth century to include political, economic and military leadership.[8] Leadership training remains a theme in federal support but is no longer the keystone of public policy.

Public Land Development

The federal government first became concerned with higher education as an aspect of federal land policy. The proceeds of land sales were a major source of federal revenue and it was desirable to promote settlement of the frontier to insure its defense against hostile Indians and foreign nations, so the federal government sought to promote the sale of public lands. Beginning as early as 1787, part of the proceeds from the sale of public lands was rebated to the developer for the support of a university. Thus support for higher education was indistinguishable from federal support for road construction or river and harbor improvements. The object in each case was to make public lands more attractive to prospective buyers.[9]

Manpower for Economic Prosperity and National Defense

The Morrill Land-Grant College Act of 1862 gave public land, or its equivalent, to each state for "the endowment, support and maintenance of at least one college." At such colleges the Act specified that the "leading object shall be. . .to teach such branches of learning as are related to agriculture and the mechanic arts." This marks the first expression of a major federal objective in advancing higher education, the production of skilled manpower. Federal policy has supported this objective on the grounds that investment in higher education produces economic returns to society—that the availability of highly trained individuals is important to general economic prosperity. In addition, a strong economy has been considered vital to national defense and to effective international competition. Thus the objectives of economic prosperity and national defense are closely related. Producing trained manpower for national security is most clearly seen in the National Defense Education Act of 1958, which states, "The Congress hereby finds and declares that the security of the Nation requires the fullest development of the mental resources and technical skills of its young men and women."

Educational Opportunity

Because of the importance of higher education for individual social and economic mobility, federal policy has also sought to extend higher education to classes of people heretofore excluded. Over time the target population has changed. In the Morrill Act, education at the new land-grant colleges was for the "mechanics" of the cities and the yeoman farmers, both of whom were felt to need more practical, scientific and technical education. The GI Bill of 1944 focused on veterans who merited special benefits both because they had rendered service to the nation and because they needed to catch up with their peers whose lives were not interrupted by military service. The emphasis of student aid proposals in the 1940s and 1950s was on aiding those with high academic merit and special aptitudes, the meritorious. Developing simultaneously from the 1940s to the 1960s was the objective of assisting the "needy" with federal financial aid. Thus in the 1960s President Johnson enlisted higher education in the War on Poverty.

A Democratic Citizenry

The federal interest in supporting higher education has also been linked to the objective of producing a strong democratic citizenry, skilled and wise in governing itself. This objective was important in the movement for "common schools" in the nineteenth century and in the drive for universal education through high school in the early part of the twentieth century. With respect to higher education, the objective was articulated strongly in the report of President Truman's Commission on Higher Education titled, *Higher Education for American Democracy*. This objective has been a general rationale for federal efforts rather than the motive force behind specific programs.

Since the 1940s, this democratic-citizenry objective has sometimes been turned on its head, the concern of policy makers shifting from educating students in the principles of democracy and liberating the students' critical ability, to making certain that higher education, particularly when supported by the federal government, does not harbor disloyal, un-American, and radical ideas or people. Thus, as in the McCarthy era, there has been at times a loss of faith in the marketplace of ideas and a desire to selectively pack the market shelves of higher learning.

International Understanding

Finally, the promotion of international understanding and world brotherhood has been a federal objective underlying the support for higher education. The acceptance of continuing international responsibilities after World War II, highlighted symbolically by American support for and membership in the United Nations, led to the perception of this new objective.

That the federal government would treat higher education as a means for attaining national objectives rather than as an end in itself is an assumption that derives from the traditionally utilitarian conception of education in American culture. However, it also relates to the division of federal and state responsibilities. The federal government has a supplementary role in supporting higher education; thus federal policy is limited to objectives important from a federal standpoint; it is not concerned with the entire range of objectives of higher education.

The instrumental view underlying federal higher education policy has an important consequence for the structure of federal efforts in this area. A major emphasis has been on categorical programs, funds earmarked for specific purposes, rather than general aid for the support of higher education.

Public-Private Nondiscrimination

Since the federal thrust has not been to support higher education per se but rather to use it as an instrument to accomplish other purposes, the benefits of federal programs have been extended alike to public and private institutions that can accomplish the federal objectives.

Nondiscrimination between the publics and the privates also stems from early historical developments. In the colonial era, higher education was almost exclusively private in its origins and its governance. Yet from its very beginnings it received public support. For example, in the year of its chartering, 1636, Harvard University, the first institution of higher education in America, received a grant from the Massachusetts legislature. By the time the federal government became concerned with higher education in a major way with the Morrill Act of 1862, two basic premises had been established: higher education in America is a dual public-private system in its governance, and private higher education receives public support in its financing.[10] Beneficiaries of the Morrill Act included Cornell University, Massachusetts Institute of Technology and Yale University, all private institutions.[11] All of the federal student aid programs have been open to students in both public and private institutions.

The Fragmentation of Federal Higher Education Policy

Another historical assumption of federal higher education policy is that there is *no* policy in the sense of an integrated, coordinated and comprehensive blueprint. The federal government has had a profound influence on the development of higher education in the United States, but this influence has come about through a complex of federal activities lacking in central direction or vision.

No coherent philosophical or administrative strategy characterizes the federal role in this area because higher education has been approached as a means to attain diverse federal policy ends. The programs are scattered among those agencies responsible for goals for which higher education is in some measure the means: veterans readjustment, medical research, space exploration or atomic energy development.

Also, because the federal role is supplementary to that of the states, an aspect of the consensus is that a comprehensive federal policy is unnecessary. Indeed, if such a comprehensive policy were formulated, it might violate the understanding of the proper federal and state roles because it would imply a primary federal responsibility.

In the Shadow of Elementary and Secondary Education

Higher education has not been the jewel in the crown of federal education policy. The first priority of federal policy, and indeed public policy at all levels, has been basic education for the mass of the citizenry. At the state level, until quite recently, higher education in "normal" schools was viewed primarily as the training ground for elementary and secondary teachers and therefore an extension of the concern for education through grade twelve. At the federal level, the movement for broad federal aid to elementary and secondary education was deadlocked until 1965 by the issues of race and religion and fears of federal control. Yet the dominant focus of federal education policy, before and after 1965, has been elementary and secondary education.

As higher education has come to be viewed as an aid to individual mobility and economic success and as it has become more broadly available, it has gradually edged into a position of more prominent concern for federal policy makers— that is, insofar as higher education has become like mass education through the secondary level, vital for individual and social progress, its status in federal policy has risen. The federal concern for higher education represents an upward extension of the national thrust toward universal elementary and secondary schooling.

These dimensions of the relationship between the federal government and higher education formed the broad context within which new policy would evolve in the late 1960s and early 1970s. In addition, policy making usually proceeds by building on existing legislation. Thus a series of federal enactments in higher education between 1958 and 1968 provided the concrete precedents, the foundation, upon which the 1972 Act was erected.

Legislative Foundations, 1958-1968

When news of the launching of the first man-made earth satellite by the Soviet Union reached the United States in October, 1958, federal commitments in higher education were modest. The most extensive programs were in research, and the National Science Foundation (1950) was the landmark of a permanent federal role. The support of land-grant colleges and the corollary programs of experiment stations and extension services were firmly in place and noncontroversial. Precedents had been established in student aid—a Depression era work-study program and a World War II loan program for students in disciplines with manpower shortages. But in 1958, federal student assistance consisted of the Korean War extension of the GI Bill and graduate training and fellowship programs serving a limited number of students. In the decade following, the federal commitment in higher education mushroomed to include grants to undergraduates, federal direct and guaranteed loans, work-study and graduate fellowships, construction assistance, and a plethora of new categorical programs.

The National Defense Education Act (1958)

Shortly after Sputnik President Eisenhower was questioned, point-blank, at a news conference, "I ask you, sir, what are we going to do about it?"[12] The Eisenhower Administration cast about for a response to the Soviet challenge.

Putting aside its conservative reservations about broadening the federal role in education, the Administration hit on a program to strengthen American schooling, particularly in the sciences. Since Sputnik was a product of Soviet scientific manpower and research, the United States would meet the challenge by doing better in these areas.

The President advanced two proposals, an expansion of the National Science Foundation and, more importantly, a collection of new education programs, billed as temporary emergency measures, that became the National Defense Education Act of 1958 (NDEA). In an unusual display of comity, the differences between the Administration's bill and a bill introduced by congressional Democrats were rapidly compromised without partisan rancor. Assistant Secretary of HEW Elliot Richardson led the collaboration from the Administration side. The almost ritualistic clash over race and religion that had long characterized congressional debates on education was temporarily suspended for this emergency "national defense" measure.

The only major controversy concerned federal scholarships for undergraduates. The scholarship provisions, featured in both the Administration's bill and the Democratically sponsored measure, ran into a deep congressional suspicion of giving students a "free ride" to attend college—no matter how meritorious or needy they might be. Scholarships were deleted on the House floor and cut back in the Senate, then abandoned entirely in the House-Senate conference, leaving only a student loan program. The final bill nonetheless authorized a wide array of programs for elementary and secondary as well as higher education, including federal loans to college students, with partial cancellation of the loan if a student taught in elementary or secondary school; fellowships for graduate students preparing to teach in higher education; and support for foreign language and area studies.

Although the Act did not include scholarships, which Eisenhower considered the keystone of his recommendations for higher education, it was a landmark in federal higher education policy. The loan program constituted the first broad federal student aid since the work-study program of the 1930s. NDEA was styled a temporary, emergency program, and a program specifically aimed at producing scientific manpower. However, it became in fact a permanent and broader program well before its initial four-year authorization expired. NDEA represented a quantum leap in the acceptable size and scope of the federal role in supplementing the states in the field of higher education. It was also the first omnibus education bill, grouping together a variety of only loosely related titles that could have been separate bills.

The Higher Education Facilities Act (1963)

Federal aid to education was a major item in President Kennedy's domestic program. Kennedy proposed massive aid to elementary and secondary schools, federal loans for higher education facilities construction, and undergratuate scholarships awarded to students on the basis of academic ability as well as financial need. The scholarship program also included a cost-of-instruction allowance to the schools enrolling the federal scholarship holders, foreshadowing a major policy option in the 1971-1972 debate.

The Kennedy strategy followed the NDEA precedent of including programs for federal aid to all levels of education in one large package. However, without the crisis atmosphere of Sputnik and the accompanying national defense argument, the Kennedy proposals foundered in the treacherous cross-currents of partisanship and religious controversy. Most of the conflict centered around the issue of federal assistance to parochial elementary and secondary schools. Student aid and assistance for academic facilities construction were controversial in their own right because of the scholarship provisions and the construction aid to church-related colleges. When the House Rules Committee killed the school aid bill in 1961, the higher education bill went down with it.

In 1962, efforts to pass a school aid bill were abandoned, but both the House and the Senate passed higher education bills. The Senate measure included scholarships along with a cost-of-education payment to the institution, plus a program of loans for academic facilities construction. The House bill had loans and grants for academic facilities but no scholarships. The Senate strongly favored scholarships and opposed grants for academic facilities that would go to private church-related colleges. The House strongly opposed scholarships and favored grants for facilities construction. After an extended period of maneuvering and bargaining, a House-Senate conference negotiated a compromise.

The bill reported from conference included loans and grants for the construction of only specific categories of academic facilities in deference to the Senate concern to limit the scope of aid to church-related colleges. It also included a program of student loans but no scholarships, in deference to the House position. However, 20 percent of the loans were "nonreimbursable" and were, in effect, scholarship grants. As the 1962 election drew near, partisanship increased, particularly Republican opposition to scholarships. In addition, the religious issue was inflamed by the Supreme Court's decision against school prayer in *Engle v. Vitale* in June, 1962. These factors appeared to be decisive when the House voted in September to recommit the bill to conference, effectively killing it.[b]

[b]On the complex story of the politics of federal aid to education in 1961 and 1962, see: Hugh Douglas Price, "Schools, Scholarships, and Congressmen: The Kennedy Aid-to-Education Program," in *The Centers of Power*, Alan F. Westin, ed., Harcourt, Brace & World, New York, 1964; Hugh Douglas Price, "Race, Religion, and the Rules Committee: The Kennedy Aid-to-Education Bills," in *The Uses of Power*, Alan F. Westin, ed., Harcourt, Brace & World, New York, 1962; Richard F. Fenno, Jr., and Frank J. Munger, *National Politics and Federal Aid to Education*, Syracuse University Press, Syracuse, New York, 1962; and James L. Sundquist, *Politics and Policy: The Eisenhower, Kennedy, and Johnson Years*, The Brookings Institution, Washington, D.C., 1968, pp. 180-205.

In 1963, President Kennedy submitted to Congress a new omnibus bill, the National Education Improvement Act of 1963. For higher education, the bill proposed federal aid for academic facilities construction, expansion of the NDEA loan and fellowship programs, new federal student aid programs of insured loans and work-study, and federal aid for teacher preparation and college libraries.

The higher education provisions were broken out of the Administration bill and the House and Senate committees focused on the area where they had reached agreement in the ill-fated 1962 higher education conference report—federal aid for facilities construction. They ignored the recommendations of the President with respect to student aid and other categorical programs. The divisive scholarship issue was set aside. There was a broadly shared perception of the need for federal assistance to help colleges and universities accommodate the boom in enrollments. Partisan and religious passions had quieted. The bill enjoyed relatively smooth sailing to the President's desk, where it was one of the first measures signed into law by the new President, Lyndon Johnson, in December, 1963.

Another breakthrough in federal higher education policy, the Higher Education Facilities Act (HEFA) created a five-year program of federal matching grants and loans for undergraduate and graduate facilities construction. In the debate, the national defense rationale of federal higher education policy receded, and the goal of equal educational opportunity began to emerge. The bill called for a strong state role in the administration of the facilities grants, and despite some strong opposition in the Senate, the nondiscrimination between public and private institutions was reaffirmed, as both were granted eligibility.

The consideration of the 1963 legislation laid the groundwork for future enactments. Programs for federally insured loans, work-study, teacher training, and college libraries would reappear in the 1965 legislation. The church-state issue with respect to higher education was largely laid to rest. The emerging concern with equal educational opportunity would edge closer to the center of federal policy. And the tradition of omnibus higher education bills considered in an atmosphere of muted partisanship would continue to be the hallmark of higher education policy through the 1960s.[c]

The Higher Education Act (1965)

In 1964, the Great Society's War on Poverty was launched with the Economic Opportunity Act, and a civil rights bill of historic dimensions was passed. Then came the landslide victory of Lyndon Johnson over Senator Barry Goldwater in an election that also produced two-to-one Democratic majorities in both houses of Congress.

---

[c]The discussion of HEFA relies on Lawrence K. Pettit, "The Policy Process in Congress: Passing the Higher Education Academic Facilities Act of 1963," Ph.D. dissertation, University of Wisconsin, 1965; and Sundquist, pp. 195-210.

The year 1965 was the Johnson Administration's honeymoon in domestic policy. It was dominated by historic legislation: Medicare, the Voting Rights Act, and the Elementary and Secondary Education Act (ESEA). In education the focus was on ESEA.[d] Overcoming the church-state issue and the fears of federal intervention in elementary and secondary education was accomplished largely by relating aid-to-education to the War on Poverty.

The Higher Education Act of 1965 (HEA-65), passed in the wake of ESEA and obscured from public view by it, featured the first program of federal scholarships for undergraduates, or "Educational Opportunity Grants." They were to be awarded primarily to students "of exceptional financial need." Thus as with ESEA and the church-state issue, the logjam in higher education policy with respect to scholarships was broken by latching on to the antipoverty theme of the times. The Act also created a program of federal insurance for loans obtained by students from state or private sources. In addition, the work-study program created by the Economic Opportunity Act of 1964 was transferred from the Office of Economic Opportunity to the Office of Education. Under this program, the federal government paid most of the cost of part-time employment for students and a "preference" was given to those from low-income families.

While student aid was the principal thrust, the 1965 Act also contained new categorical programs such as assistance for college libraries and aid for "developing institutions," which meant in particular the predominantly Black colleges of the South.

Consideration of the bill was marked by broad bipartisan agreement and rapid action. In the House, amendments to curtail the scholarship program were easily beaten back. In November 1965, President Johnson signed the Act at his alma mater, Southwest Texas State College.

With the passage of HEA-65, the first federal scholarship program for undergraduates finally became law, following almost two decades of efforts beginning with the report of President Truman's Commission on Higher Education. The controversy over federal aid to church-related colleges and universities was dead. The tradition of categorical programs for specific federal purposes was continued. The beginnings of a federal-state partnership (in addition to a simply supplementary role for the federal government) are seen in the requirements that some types of federal assistance be granted in accordance with state plans.

There was now a national commitment to higher education as an important and continuing dimension of federal policy. In 1956, federal expenditures for higher education stood at $655 million and were largely concentrated in research. By 1966, federal expenditures for higher education had increased over 400 per-

[d]On ESEA, see Eugene Eidenberg and Roy Morey, *An Act of Congress*, W.W. Norton, New York, 1969; and Philip Meranto, *The Politics of Aid to Education in 1965*, Syracuse University Press, Syracuse, New York, 1967.

cent to $3.5 billion and supported a broad variety of programs including student aid, facilities construction and categorical programs in addition to continued support of research.[13]

Administration leadership was a chief characteristic of the policy-making process. Major higher education proposals, beginning with NDEA, emanated from the executive branch. Congress was not a rubber stamp. It clearly had the power to frustrate Administration initiatives as it did in the Kennedy years. Congress also made significant modifications in Administration proposals, as in the substitution of the student loan program for the Eisenhower scholarship program in NDEA. However, through 1965, and indeed through 1968, the dominant pattern of policy making was executive branch initiative followed by Congressional response.

The last three years of the Johnson Administration were a period of consolidation and gradual elaboration in federal higher education programs following the historic initiatives and vigorous controversy in the years 1958-1965. The Higher Education Amendments of 1966 extended HEFA and part of HEA-65. The Higher Education Amendments of 1968 extended and expanded NDEA, HEFA and HEA-65, and added a few new categorical programs. Legislative action during this period only slightly modified what was already in place. In the face of fiscal and political constraints imposed by the Vietnam War, the Johnson Administration was looking to contract rather than expand its Great Society commitments. Moreover, the Johnson honeymoon with Congress was over, and urban rioting soured many people on domestic social programs. Federal policy making for higher education had reached a plateau by 1968 as the new programs of the past decade were allowed to endure the test of experience and as circumstances blunted progress on the domestic front.

But all was not quiet. A backlog of unfulfilled aspirations, unrequited hopes, and new problems in higher education was building.

Notes

1. George N. Rainsford, *Congress and Higher Education in the Nineteenth Century*, University of Tennessee Press, Knoxville, 1972, p. 17.

2. Ira Sharkansky, *The Maligned States*, McGraw-Hill, New York, 1972, p. 82.

3. Donald J. Devine, *The Political Culture of the United States*, Little, Brown and Co., Boston, 1972, p. 172; and Heinz Eulau and Harold Quinley, *State Officials and Higher Education*, McGraw-Hill, New York, 1970, pp. 82-83.

4. Oscar Handlin and Mary Handlin, *The American College and American Culture*, McGraw-Hill, New York, 1970, p. 2.

5. Alexis de Tocqueville, *Democracy in America*, I Random House, New York, 1945, p. 54.

6. Handlin and Handlin, p. 5.

7. Louis Hartz, *The Liberal Tradition in America*, Harcourt, Brace & World, New York, 1955, pp. 62, 203-227.

8. Rainsford, pp. 3-14; and Handlin and Handlin, pp. 11-18.

9. Rainsford, pp. 29-54.

10. Ibid., pp. 3-14.

11. Ibid., pp. 103-104.

12. Quoted in James L. Sundquist, *Politics and Policy: The Eisenhower, Kennedy and Johnson Years*, The Brookings Institution, Washington, D.C., 1968, p. 173.

13. Kenneth Ashworth, *Scholars and Statesmen*, Jossey-Bass, San Francisco, 1972, p. 6.

2

A Backdrop of Ferment and Reappraisal

"Legislation," Woodrow Wilson wrote, ". . .is an aggregate, not a simple production. It is impossible to tell how many persons' opinions and influences have entered into its composition."[1]

Like any far-reaching enactment, the Education Amendments of 1972 were buffeted and shaped by myriad forces and events. Many of the variables were circumstantial and internal to the policy-making process—a change of administrations in 1969, a new chairman of the Senate education subcommittee in the same year, shifting alliances within the House education committee, spill-over effects of other pending legislation, the role of Congressional staff. But there were many less proximate influences as well. Broad trends, events and currents of thinking on the campuses and in the country conditioned the environment of federal action on higher education in the early 1970s.

Legacy of the 1960s: The Drive for Equal Opportunity

The goal of equal opportunity for education beyond high school was not an invention of the 1960s; it is a theme that runs through much of the traditional rhetoric and history of American higher education. Great phases in this history—the land-grant college movement, the GI Bill experience and the explosion of enrollments in the post-World War II period—served to broaden access and extend college opportunities to new groups in the society.

But in the 1960s, the concept and the ideal of equal educational opportunity took on new dimensions, a new urgency, and a central place in public policy making for higher education. At the opening of the 1970s it was perceived as a major part of the nation's unfinished business.

Post-War Growth and Democratization

It is perhaps ironic that recognition of the egalitarian shortcomings of higher education came with full force in the mid and late 1960s, for this period marked the culmination of higher education's great success in post-War expansion. In the twenty years following World War II, higher education faced a monumental quantitative challenge: absorbing the "tidal wave" of students reaching college age and seeking a college education. Growth was phenomenal. Degree-credit enrollment in higher education reached nearly 7 million in 1968, more than double the level of 1958 and over four times the level of 1940.[2]

The expansion stemmed from demography—a burgeoning of the college-age population—and from rising aspirations. Aspirations were fueled by the availability of veterans benefits in the post-War years but were fundamentally related to deepening cultural attitudes about the importance of higher education to the nation and the individual. The postsecondary enrollment rates of college-age youth and high school graduates rose steadily.

The landscape and character of American higher education changed dramatically in this era. Private colleges and universities, while expanding enrollments slowly relative to the public institutions, broadened their student constituency. Earlier customs that tended to skew admissions toward the privileged, the social elite and the children of previous alumni gave way to pressures for selection based strictly on ability and academic performance. The most prestigious private institutions became more exclusive than ever before, but their new elitism came to rest more squarely on considerations of merit rather than social origins or family background.

The public sector of higher education meanwhile expanded and diversified at an astounding pace to accommodate the greater part of the enrollment surge. Enrollments in public institutions jumped from 50 percent of the national total in 1950 to 60 percent in 1960 and 75 percent in 1970.[3] Alongside the established public universities and traditional land-grant colleges in the states, there emerged new and rapidly changing institutions: comprehensive four-year public colleges, most of them outgrowths of former state teachers colleges or public normal schools; and hundreds of two-year community colleges, two-year branch campuses of universities and postsecondary vocational institutes. While the pattern varied widely, in virtually every state there emerged a set of institutions constituting, formally or informally, a "delivery system for mass higher education."[4]

The Truman Commission in 1947 had challenged conventional assumptions about the general proportion of citizens capable of collegiate education. The next twenty years went far toward the democratization called for in the Commission's landmark report. While democratizing influences had been at work for many decades, the fundamental transition was made in these years from a higher education system that was principally the preserve of the well-to-do and the hard-working, intellectually gifted children of the less affluent—to a vastly more open system extending opportunities to a larger segment of the people than in any other country in the world.

Unequal Opportunity

Yet great gaps and disparities remained, across regions and states and particularly by income and race. Major barriers to equal opportunity had not been removed for the lowest economic strata and minority groups.

Census reports of the late 1960s showed that a college-age youth from a family with income over $15,000 was nearly five times more likely to be enrolled full-time in higher education than a college-age youth from a family with less than $3,000 income. Further data indicated that such differences could not be dismissed as a function of differences in ability. Race was also closely linked to chances of college attendance; Blacks and minorities were grossly under-represented on college and university campuses.

Moreover, those low-income and minority youth who gained access to college did not enjoy equality of choice, for they were unevenly distributed among types of institutions and tended to be enrolled in less selective colleges. Once again, the pattern could not be fully attributed to variations in ability.

Spectacular growth of the system had partially obscured the fact that many were still denied opportunity, but major social currents converged in the middle of the decade to stir a new consciousness of the problem and a new effort by colleges and universities and the government to deal with it.

The Mid-1960s Breakthrough in Federal Policy

The mid-1960s were a time of national reawakening, of growing awareness that America was not living up to its promise of social justice. The civil rights movement had dramatized the shameful plight of Blacks in America; and the "rediscovery" of poverty amidst unprecedented affluence sparked the national conscience.

It was a time of great, expansive commitments. One of the most celebrated was the goal of equal educational opportunity. Under the leadership of the "teacher in the White House," the nation seemed to redouble its faith in the potency of education to solve social ills, particularly to break the "poverty cycle." "The answer for all our national problems, the answer for all the problems of the world, comes down, when you really analyze it, to one single word—education," President Johnson said in 1964.[5]

The Higher Education Act of 1965 combined many purposes, but it strongly reflected the rising concern for the problems of the disadvantaged. Of greatest significance, Congress for the first time authorized federal scholarships. In the broad legislative sweep of the times, this breakthrough was little more than a sidelight, but its significance can be understood against the background of long-standing controversy over the principle of outright federal grants (a "free ride") to college students.

The breakthrough was even more remarkable from another perspective. Heretofore, most proposals for federal student assistance had been conceived largely with the aim of helping the ablest students, the academic cream. A great deal of attention during the 1950s and early 1960s was focused on the problem of "talent loss." The nation was suffering, it was feared, from the fact that too many young people of superior aptitude, for whatever reasons, were not going on to college. Sputnik, of course, contributed greatly to the concern. Student aid proposals of the period were thus geared to create incentives for the most promising students.

Among colleges and universities the need criterion was coming into some use for disbursing financial aid resources under the control of the institution. In the mid-1950s the College Scholarship Service was established to begin a program of systematic financial need analysis through the device of a "Parents' Confidential Statement." But the concept and practice of basing financial awards on a need determination took hold slowly and in the early 1960s was far from prevalent.

Thus the measures adopted in the mid-1960s for removing barriers to college opportunity represented a major departure. Not only had Congress for the first time voted a general scholarship program—Educational Opportunity Grants—but eligibility was to be based, above all, on need. No ability screening or cut-off would be imposed, only a loose provision that the applicant "shows evidence of academic or creative promise." The new College Work-Study program likewise was to be based on need rather than merit criteria. Programs were also added to identify and counsel needy youth potentially capable of college work.

A new dynamic had begun to shape the federal role in higher education. In the 1950s and early 1960s, much of the case for the federal support was couched in terms of girding the higher education system to cope with spiraling enrollments, to meet national needs for trained manpower, and to expand research. Now another dimension was added—removing barriers to individual opportunity.

A Moral Imperative for Higher Education

As federal policy evolved to reflect a new commitment, so colleges and universities themselves responded to newly perceived obligations. The tide of national affairs—the civil rights movement and the racial crisis, the focus on poverty and urban strife—affected every sector of the society. Higher education was forced to examine its record and conscience in failing to extend opportunities adequately to ethnic minorities and the disadvantaged. The explanation of the past—that the imbalance of opportunity at the college level resulted largely from the failures of earlier schooling—no longer sufficed. A greater responsibility was laid at the doorstep of higher education to reduce barriers of income and race. And a few years later the women's movement would generate an additional set of pressures on higher education to eliminate inequities based on sex, particularly in university employment and graduate admissions.

A major part of the responsibility focused on two segments of higher education with established roles in extending access for minority and low-income youth.

1. Predominantly Black Colleges. The contributions, the plight, and the special needs of the colleges founded for Negroes finally came into the light of governmental and public attention during the 60s. Historically neglected and isolated, products of the "separate-but-equal" doctrine, the more than one hundred public and private, predominantly Black colleges struggled to serve a student population disadvantaged by the effects of racism, poverty and poor schooling. In the 60s, these institutions continued to offer the principal opportunity for Blacks to gain a college education. While their share of total Black enrollment in higher education was declining (to less than half in the late 1960s), they still accounted for an overwhelming majority of baccalaureate degrees earned by Blacks.

2. Community Colleges. Public two-year colleges originated in the early part of this century as an extension of the free public high school. Their openness and community orientation made them the "people's colleges." But the great expansion of these institutions really began in the late 1950s. By 1969 there were over one thousand two-year community and junior colleges, and their students—who were more representative of the college-age population in terms of economic background and ethnic composition than students in any other segment of higher education—accounted for nearly 30 percent of all undergraduate enrollments. The community colleges were shouldering a growing responsibility for providing access to the postsecondary system. They were the most accessible institutions because of their free or nominal tuition, low admission requirements and geographical coverage, though a number of states lagged behind in community college development.

But equity demanded more than access to two-year institutions and the historically Black colleges. The task of insuring equal opportunity fell to the more traditional, four-year, predominantly white colleges and universities as well. The year 1966 is said to have marked the beginning of a drive by many such institutions to bring previously excluded groups into the mainstream of higher education.[6] In part, this resulted from the impact of the new federal legislation itself, the Higher Education Act of 1965, which required that institutions participating in the Educational Opportunity Grants program make "vigorous efforts" to identify and recruit students of exceptional financial need.

Yet in March of 1968, a survey of major colleges and universities indicated that less than half had formal programs for "high risk" students.[7] Then in April of the same year came the death of Martin Luther King. In the wave of remorse as well as Black militancy following the tragic assassination, institutions across the country pledged themselves to new efforts in expanding opportunities for Blacks and other minorities. Many institutions established specific targets such as doubling minority enrollments. Memorial scholarships and special funds were established; counseling projects and new curricula in Afro-American studies were launched.

There were also pressures on higher education to go beyond such special programs. Many called for a fundamental reorientation of college admission procedures and the adoption of open enrollment policies. Some state universities and most two-year colleges already provided open access to high school graduates. But now the challenge was being addressed to previously selective institutions. The City University of New York, for example, adopted a controversial open enrollment plan in 1970 under which the senior and more prestigious schools of the university were committed to accepting and educating high school graduates disadvantaged both academically and socio-economically.

Such demands and changes divided the academic community. There emerged a fundamental contention between meritocratic and egalitarian values. The pressures on institutions to become more representative of the society around them tended to compete with pressures inherent in the academic enterprise to sustain "quality," the latter judged at least in part by the academic qualifications of incoming students.

Higher education was struggling with the perceived moral imperative of the times—to make good on the lofty American promise that an individual's chances for advancement through education should not be a function of his economic or social origins.

Today an intellectual debate has developed over the importance of education in reducing social and economic inequalities, and a wave of revisionism challenges the premises of liberal social reform policies adopted in the 1960s. Faith in education as the "great equalizer" is being called into question. The revisionists conclude that if we wish to reduce inequality in the society, we must focus on "equality of results" directly rather than "equality of opportunity."[8]

What impact the new intellectual analysis will have on future social and educational policies of the country is difficult to gauge. But the vision of equal educational opportunity, a legacy of the 60s, clearly remained a driving force well into the 70s. In a sense, Congress formally embodied this legacy in the Higher Education Amendments of 1968 which contained a provision, Section 508, calling for a study to recommend the means of "making available a post-secondary education to all young Americans who qualify and seek it." In 1968 Congress was looking ahead to unfinished business.

Financial Woes of Colleges and the Rising Price of a College Education

It was the best of times; it was the worst of times. On the one hand, the colleges and universities in the late 1960s had never known such prosperity. Income and expenditures of higher education doubled from 1957 to 1963 and again from 1963 to 1968, rising at a considerably faster rate than the surge of enrollments. Faculty salaries rose more rapidly than general wage and salary levels.

Capital investment expanded severalfold, providing the visible evidence of growth—new buildings and equipment and new campuses. Contract research mushroomed. Ph.D. production tripled in one decade. Practically all "trend curves" were up in what had become a major growth industry of the nation.

Crisis

On the other hand, college and university administrators, trustees, alumni spokesmen, association representatives, foundation officials and others concerned with the financial health of higher education warned of a mounting crisis. The most widely circulated study documenting the sudden financial stress concluded that a "new depression" was settling down on American colleges and universities.[9]

However it was termed, the financial status of higher education clearly shifted in the later 1960s. The boom began to level off when major income sources started to yield lower annual increases in the face of continuing upward cost pressures and a steeper rate of inflation in the general economy. Rising aspirations and heavy fixed commitments met head on with new fiscal realities.

Some of the evidence of harder times was clearcut and dramatic: Occasionally a college would actually have to close its doors, and a number of major institutions including Columbia and New York University began running sizeable budget deficits. But the more general experience of colleges and universities was the relatively quiet process of adjusting to a new financial frame of reference. The *New Depression* study characterized the change: "After a decade of building, expanding, and undertaking new responsibilities, the trend on campuses today is all in the other direction. The talk, the planning, and the decisions now center on reallocating, on adding only by substitution, on cutting, trimming, and even struggling to hang on. . . ."[10]

Nearly all institutions were feeling the effects to one degree or another—if nothing else, as a result of the general economic slowdown late in the decade. But some types of institutions faced particular circumstances.

The *leading universities* in graduate education and research, both public and private, were hit hard by a declining rate of increase in federal research support after 1965, and later a sharp curtailment of federal assistance to graduate students. Foundations, as a source of research and other support for these universities, also weakened.

The *private institutions* in general were squeezed by uncertain trends in alumni and other private donations, the failure of endowment income to keep pace with rising expenditure rates, mounting student aid budgets to finance the new commitment to equal opportunity, and, most of all, the growing pressure of competition from low-tuition and increasingly ubiquitous public institutions. Market forces were beginning to make many private liberal arts colleges uncomfortable about the future. They feared "pricing themselves out of the market" by further tuition increases but were increasingly at a loss to tap other income sources. As enrollment growth slowed in the late 60s and early 70s (the post-War baby boom had largely been absorbed), the competition for students intensified. And the tuition gap between public and private institutions was not getting any smaller.

Very *small institutions* as a group tended toward relatively greater financial insecurity. Their situation was usually less complicated than that of larger institutions, but often more severe. They typically had no endowment to speak of, did not draw heavily or at all on government research funds, and traditionally benefited little from the largesse of foundations or corporations.

Finally, *state-supported universities and colleges* were beginning to feel the effects of a declining rate of increase in appropriations and generally less favorable treatment by state legislatures.

Response

The new financial stringency forced many institutions to adopt cost controls and sometimes austere economy measures. On the revenue side, institutions searched for new sources of income and sought to generate a higher yield from established sources by stepping up drives for corporate and alumni gifts, adopting more enlightened policies for investing endowment funds, and the like.

Perhaps the most universal response, however, was to look to the federal treasury for help. The only apparent hope of major new operating support for higher education seemed to reside in Washington. Some came to this conclusion reluctantly. But lingering doubts about accepting federal money for fear of government control—once a strong deterrent among many smaller, church-related institutions—had all but disappeared. "On the question of federal aid, everybody seems to be running to the same side of the boat," as one college president put it.[11] "The only place the money can come from is the federal government—that's inevitable," said the President of Harvard.[12]

The Squeeze on Parents and Students

Parallel to the financial problems of institutions was a growing reaction among those who had to pay a part of the college bill, namely parents and students. In addition to hearing from college presidents, Congressmen would hear a great deal from their home constituents, particularly middle-income parents, about the rising price of sending a child to college.

Outside of profit-making postsecondary schools, tuition and fees charged to students generally cover much less than total instructional costs, particularly in tax-supported institutions, but also in private colleges and universities. Moreover, prices charged to students have declined over the years relative to rising levels of income in the country. But such facts offer little consolation to the average family trying to finance a college education for one or more children. Student charges increased rapidly during the 1960s. Most families with college-bound members, just like the colleges themselves, felt they were being squeezed tighter and tighter. Heavier inflation and economic recession at the end of the 60s intensified the feeling.

At this juncture, the major existing federal program designed for lower-middle and middle-income students was running into problems. The Guaranteed Loan Program had been established in 1965 to help these students obtain credit for college by insuring private loans against default. The annual volume of loans mounted quickly but could not keep pace with demand. The success of the program varied across regions, states and localities, and the availability of the loans at any given time was subject to trends in the money market. Banks in some areas were unwilling to participate. In periods of tight money, the loans were harder to come by and participating banks often rationed the supply by restricting new loans to established customers and upperclassmen rather than freshmen. As a result, many students who wished to borrow and had counted on the program were turned away.

Middle-income parents had been writing their representatives in Washington for many years to ask for relief in meeting college costs. Now the volume of such appeals increased and many took the form of complaints about the Guaranteed Loan Program. Congress was under pressure to do something to relieve both hard-pressed colleges and hard-pressed families footing the tuition bills.

Campus Unrest and Political Backlash

"A spectre is haunting America—the spectre of students," Clark Kerr wrote in 1967. "This is a phenomenon unique to the 1960s."[13]

Finances were perplexing but they tended to be overshadowed, certainly in the eye of the general public, by more dramatic developments in college life. From Berkeley in 1964 to Columbia in 1968, to Cornell and San Francisco State in 1969, to the Cambodia demonstrations in May of 1970 and the tragedies of Kent State and Jackson State, student rebellion jolted the country. The general ferment on the campuses, demands for "student power," sit-ins and other peaceful protest, mass demonstrations—and sometimes destruction of property, injury and death—fixated the news media and frightened many Americans.

Periodic unruliness of students was was not unknown in the history of American colleges and universities, but in the 1960s the traditional exuberance and defiant energy of youth were joined with new political and cultural dynamics. Unprecedented numbers of disaffected students, and "nonstudents," challenged the established order from the staging ground of college and university campuses. Gallup polls showed "youth protests" were perceived among the major problems facing the nation.

In fact, relatively few campuses were directly affected by the turmoil. It is estimated that in 1968-1969, near the height of the period, about 22 percent of colleges and universities experienced some type of protest.[14] But the dominant tone of the 1960s college generation was activist. It was, in any event, a long way from what had come to be called the "silent generation" of the 1950s.

The sources and forms of student discontent in the 60s were many and complex. Alienation and commitment, idealism and nihilism, violence and nonviolence, moderation and extremism, dialogue and confrontation all combined in a disparate movement. Fueling the movement as a whole, however, was a new sense of generational solidarity, a growing and self-conscious youth culture standing in many ways counter to the style and values of the larger society. Important in itself was the simple fact that more young people than ever before were located on college campuses, sharing both proximity and similar status.

Much of the student protest had its genesis in the civil rights issue and the quest for Black identity and pride. Then came the escalation of the war in Southeast Asia, viewed by growing numbers of students as both a misadventure and a moral disaster for the nation as well as a personal threat because of the draft.

Campus unrest became a divisive and highly political issue in the late 60s. The cry for "law and order" applied to the campuses as well as the cities. One result of the backlash against campus unrest was an outpouring of federal and state crackdown legislation.

In the Congress, the issue came to the fore beginning in the spring of 1968 after violence erupted at Columbia University and spread to many other institutions. There followed a string of legislative provisions to cut off federal assistance to disruptive students. It was a period of escalating rhetoric reaction and counterreaction. More campuses were hit by strikes, demonstrations and, occasionally, police-student clashes in the fall of 1968. Sentiment increased for tougher, more sweeping remedies.

Some voices were calling for a balanced view of the new turmoil on the campuses. The National Commission on the Causes and Prevention of Violence warned that punitive measures by the government would play into the hands of the militant minority by "radicalizing" otherwise moderate students. A group of 22 House Republicans made a private tour of more than 50 college campuses, then issued a public report to the President that urged positive measures, such as draft reform and lowering the voting age to 18, rather than "repressive" laws to deal with the complex problem of campus disorders. For its part, the Nixon Administration took a moderate stand on campus unrest legislation. Administration officials berated college administrators for "procrastination" in dealing with disorders and directed angry blasts at student militants, but the Administration maintained a policy of nonintervention with respect to campus law enforcement and internal university affairs.[15]

The campus upheaval itself reached a crest in the strike activity touched off by the invasion of Cambodia in the spring of 1970. The Kent State and Jackson State killings, followed by the bombing at the University of Wisconsin, provoked horror and seemed to produce a degree of reassessment and a tempering of revolutionary fervor among many students. The student movement was not over, but its intensity, after the high-pitched emotions and events of the previous several years, was perhaps bound to subside. The academic year 1970-1971 was a somewhat quieter year on the campuses.

The Scranton Commission on Campus Unrest asserted the need for such a leveling-off period when it called on "Americans of all convictions [to] draw back from the brink. . .We must regain compassion for one another and our mutual respect. . .Reconciliation must begin."[16]

The political backlash against campus unrest began to recede as the campuses cooled. It remained an issue in the 1970 midterm elections (with no visible payoff, however, for the President and office seekers who attempted to exploit it). But by 1971 the passion was gone. The issue had been played out in the Congress. A new concern, school busing, was destined to replace campus unrest as the major "backlash" issue of the day.

The campus unrest issue had the effect, as we shall see, of prolonging the entire process of producing new higher education legislation. But more importantly, campus unrest contributed to a changing climate of opinion about higher education in general that would condition legislative action in the early 1970s.

A New Burden of Proof

Father Hesburgh, President of Notre Dame and a prominent leader in higher education, warned his academic colleagues in 1971:

After a century when the society at large could not do enough for universities and colleges, when these institutions represented the epitome of just about everyone's hopes, a degree being the closest earthly replica of the badge of salvation, suddenly the great American public, our patron and faithful supporter, is rather completely disillusioned about the whole enterprise.[17]

One commentator declared the "end of an affair" between America and its colleges.[18]

The late 1960s brought to a close the days when higher education could merely assert its policies and its needs to a generally willing public, when the purposes and directions of higher education were largely self-justifying and readily assumed to be in the national interest. Perhaps the major catalyst of the change was the late 60s backlash against student rebellion and the counter-culture centered on the campuses. Loud dissent and long hair ruffled the image of higher education. But other disillusionments and other critiques were also setting in.

Inefficiency and Resistance to Change

Under financial stress, institutions of higher education were just beginning to tighten up on costs and administrative management. The taxpayers and the politicians were demanding it, for the notion was taking hold of a lush academic establishment gobbling up resources with little mind for economy or productivity, of university elites feathering their own nests at the public's expense. Under growing criticism for self-protective managerial practices, the colleges and universities were a vulnerable target of the widening taxpayer revolt. The intensity of Governor Ronald Reagan's running battle with the University of California was not matched elsewhere, but his call for the taxpayer's "money's worth" from public higher education found echoes across the country.

More broadly, there was a growing concern about wasteful competition and duplication of programs, facilities and functions *among* institutions of higher education. In state after state a movement was building for more rational utilization of postsecondary educational resources. By 1971, agencies existed in 47 states with varying degrees of responsibility for governance, planning and coordination of public higher education and, in some cases, the private sector as well. Higher education had "simply become too expensive and too significant for state government to allow it to function in the laissez-faire manner of the past."[19]

Another dimension of criticism stemmed from the paradox of academia's readiness to prescribe bold reshaping of the society at large while resisting equally significant change within the confines of the campus. Traditionally colleges and universities had been portrayed and had considered themselves to be at the cutting edge of social change; yet the academic enterprise itself seemed relatively set in its own ways. Mounting criticism during the late 60s focused on the "hidebound bureaucracy" of higher education, its stodginess about customary forms and conventions, its growing uniformity of structure and style.

The Questioning of Benefits to Society

Moreover, a new skepticism was emerging that questioned traditional assumptions about the inherent benefits of higher learning to society. Public financing of higher education had long been justified on the grounds that society was the principal beneficiary through research and expansion of knowledge, production of educated manpower for the economy, enhancement of the culture and the "quality of life." Such faith, seemingly unbounded in the post-Sputnik period, weakened in the late 60s. The public had new doubts, for example, about the course of science and technology and where it was leading the country. It no longer seemed so clear that higher learning and research would produce the answers to national problems.

On a theoretical plane, many economists were beginning to challenge the benefits-to-society claim of higher education. At the extreme, the conservative economist Milton Friedman vigorously maintained that such alleged benefits were always "vague and general," could not be measured and therefore should not be assumed to exist.[20] Few economists who analyzed the issue went as far as Friedman, but most tended to discount what they considered overblown assertions of social gains—external benefits—from higher learning.

The Questioning of Benefits to the Individual

Changes in the job market for college-trained people further jolted assumptions about the worth of higher education. A number of economic studies over the years, particularly those during the late 1950s and early 1960s focusing on the concept of investment in "human capital," reinforced the popular view that higher learning yielded handsome economic returns to the individual. In very large measure, an expanding economy delivered on this promise during the 1960s. But then a convergence of factors, economic recession above all, changed the picture. Unemployment and underemployment of the highly educated became a problem in unprecedented degree. Most dramatic was the sudden oversupply of Ph.D.'s. After several decades of shortage, which had been widely projected to continue, Ph.D.'s in physics, chemistry, history and other fields found themselves out of work or having to take jobs for which they were over-qualified. A large surplus of elementary and secondary school teachers also developed despite repeated projections of scarcity.

Largely unanticipated, such changes hit hard. To what extent they reflected short-term economic fluctuations as opposed to more long-run trends was not immediately clear, and the situation varied widely by field. But a basic transition seemed to be in the making. For many years the economy could not recruit enough highly educated personnel; demand was bouyant. Now supply and demand were coming into a rough balance, with continuing undersupply in some areas, such as the health professions, but distinct overproduction in others. While higher education was likely to remain a sound investment for many, the proposition now seemed less certain.

Thus higher education found itself on more difficult terrain. The erosion of faith in its performance and emerging doubts about its benefits to society and to the individual placed higher education in a less favored status in the competition for public resources. It would be easy to exaggerate this "crisis of confidence." But one thing seemed clear: Higher education's requests for assistance would be accepted less uncritically than in the past.

The argument of growth was gone; enrollment pressures were coming to an end. The principal rationale for the Higher Education Facilities Act of 1963 was that college enrollments were projected to double in the decade; the same could not be said of the 1970s. And the argument of society's need for more and more college-trained people became less persuasive. A new burden of proof fell on the higher education establishment.

The "Student-Consumer"

If institutions faced a deepening challenge, the other side of the coin was a new emphasis on the primacy of the student in the educational process—a reaffirmation that the student, the consumer of higher education, should be its principal concern.

A common denominator of much of the disaffection from higher learning was that the system had been slighting its primary job, instruction, particularly at the undergraduate level, and neglecting the needs of its primary constituents, the students themselves. To the extent that the student rebellion of the late 60s looked inward and registered a coherent protest about the university itself, this was perhaps the fundamental complaint—that students were becoming marginal rather than central to the business of higher education. And this complaint struck a note of conscience with many educators and policy-makers. There was a growing concern that perhaps students *had* in some ways become of secondary importance in the headlong expansion and professionalization of the academic system.

Former Commissioner of Education Harold Howe captured the essence of this concern when he asked the question, "Do our institutions serve the needs of students, or is it the other way around?"[21]

Several factors helped generate this trend of recognizing and reasserting the central importance of the student-consumer.

1. The 1960s were characterized by a mounting reaction to bigness and bureaucracy in many sectors of American life. People demanded that growth not come at the expense of the individual's identity and freedom, that institutions be "humanized" and adapted to individual needs.
2. A general movement for consumer rights was burgeoning across the country.
3. The new youth culture, while producing a backlash in public attitudes, also brought a greater sensitivity to the rights and responsibilities of

young people. In 1971, Congress approved the eighteen-year-old vote, and state after state in the early 1970s moved to lower the age of legal adulthood from twenty-one to eighteen. Campus *in loco parentis* rules governing student behavior fell by the wayside.

4. Finally, higher education was becoming a buyer's market as the enrollment boom faded. Students could no longer be taken for granted. More and more colleges found themselves having to compete for students possibly as never before to avoid retrenchment and in some cases even to survive.

Pressure for Reform and a Broader View of Education Beyond High School

Everything discussed so far in this chapter militated in favor of reform, experimentation and greater flexibility in the traditionally change-resistant structure of higher education. The drive for equal opportunity meant that institutions had to adapt themselves to new and different groups of students. Financial stringency meant that they had to look for new and less expensive ways of doing things (though tight budgets also tend to discourage some types of reform because an extra margin of resources is not available to try them out). Campus protest, questioning and self-doubt within the academic community, reappraisal and challenges from without, the new student-consumer theme all produced a new climate for change.

Educational reform has been a perennial concern in American colleges and universities but the energy for implementing reform has ebbed and flowed. A high-water mark seemed to be approaching in the late 60s as the demands and pressures for reform mounted. Columbia University President William J. McGill put it this way:

Reform in large institutions is possible only when people are running scared. Believe me, we in higher education are very nervous, and thus the next decade is likely to produce reorganization, curriculum reform, redefinition of professional life, and a variety of other innovations unlike anything seen in the last fifty years. Our survival depends on it.[22]

A number of institutions in the late 60s expanded opportunities for independent and off-campus study, modified or dropped standard course requirements, introduced new grading options, and adopted a variety of other experiments with less structured learning formats. Students were given the opportunity to evaluate faculty teaching on many campuses, and often a voice in designing curricula.

But more important than specific innovations, what began to stir was a shift in values, attitudes and perceptions of higher education—more flexible ideas about the nature and timing of what comes after high school, a general loosening of traditional models, a broader view of alternatives. The new currents of thinking ran along the following lines.

—Higher education should become lifelong learning, an activity that takes place not necessarily at a fixed and early interval in preparation for the rest of life but at different times and in different patterns appropriate to each individual. Higher education should be a continuing process, not rigidly confined in space and time.

—The educational "lockstep" pressures most high school graduates to go right on to college if they wish to continue their education at all. Yet many young people would be better off doing something else first and resuming their education at a later point when they might be more highly motivated and have a clearer sense of direction. A wider range of options should be encouraged so that going to college is not the only acceptable thing to do at age eighteen.

—The collegiate, liberal arts tradition has been overemphasized. Occupational, career-related programs should command greater recognition and resources.

—The dichotomy between work and formal study should be less sharp, combinations and alternating periods of employment or social service and classroom training should be more widely encouraged. Freer entry and re-entry, easier movement in and out of the educational system, should be facilitated.

—Part-time students, frequently relegated to second class status in higher education, should have opportunities equal to those of full-time students.

—Education takes place in many settings. The campus is not the sole repository of teaching and learning.

Today the reform thrust may have lost something of its edge; there seems to be a certain amount of pulling back from unstructured programs and approaches of a few years ago. But the experimentation and the reconceptualizing of higher education toward the end of the 60s formed an important part of the backdrop for the debate on new legislation.

* * * * * * * * * *

We have described in Part I the environment for federal policy making in higher education at the beginning of the 1970s:

—*A long history of federal involvement with higher education and certain fairly durable but not static assumptions about the appropriate nature of the relationship.* A basic policy consensus established implicit boundaries for new legislative activity.

—*An immediate past history of specific legislative enactments extending and diversifying federal programs in this field.* A body of statutes currently in effect provided the point of departure for any new legislation.

—*Complex conditions of ferment and reappraisal in higher education.* The environment of federal legislative action was influenced by trends and events on the campuses and changing perceptions of post-high school education.

Such were the parameters, the context in which new policy would be shaped. And it is the environment of policy making that sets the broad bounds for possible action and outcomes. But what is possible is not inevitable. Policy decisions are conditioned by an external environment but they are also conditioned by characteristics of the process itself—an "internal environment." The debate on the merits of the issues, the structure, idiosyncrasies and "rules of the game" of the system as well as the predispositions of policy-makers, the force and clash of personalities, and the element of chance— all play a part in determining results.

Notes

1. Woodrow Wilson, *Congressional Government*, World Publishing Company, Cleveland, 1961, p. 208.

2. U.S. Office of Education, *Digest of Educational Statistics*, 1971 Edition, Government Printing Office, Washington, D.C., 1971.

3. Carnegie Commission on Higher Education, *New Students and New Places: Policies for the Future Growth and Development of American Higher Education*, McGraw-Hill, New York, 1971, p. 17.

4. James L. Miller, Jr., "Coordination versus Centralized Control," in *The Expanded Campus,* Dyckman W. Vermilye, ed., Jossey-Bass, San Francisco, 1972, p. 244.

5. Lyndon B. Johnson, "Remarks in Providence at the 200th Anniversary Convocation of Brown University," September 28, 1964, II, *Johnson Papers, 1963-64,* Item 601, p. 1140.

6. Frank Newman, *et al, Report on Higher Education,* U.S. Department of Health, Education and Welfare, Government Printing Office, Washington, D.C., 1971, p. 44.

7. Survey by Southern Education Report, cited in "Higher Education's Strange Paradox," an address by Harold Howe, II, U.S. Commissioner of Education, to the American Association of University Professors, April 26, 1968.

8. Christopher Jencks, *et al, Inequality: A Reassessment of the Effects of Family and Schooling in America*, Basic Books, New York, 1972.

9. Earl F. Cheit, *The New Depression in Higher Education*, A General Report for the Carnegie Commission on Higher Education and the Ford Foundation, McGraw-Hill, New York, 1970.

10. Ibid., p. 3.

11. Quoted in Editorial Projects for Education, *A Special Report*, "The plain fact is. . .our colleges and universities 'are facing what might become a crisis,' " 1968.

12. Quoted in *Time*, June 23, 1967, p. 78.

13. Clark Kerr, "From Apathy to Confrontation," (unpublished paper) from a speech delivered in San Juan, Puerto Rico, 1967.

14. Carnegie Commission on Higher Education, *Dissent and Disruption*, McGraw-Hill, New York, 1971, pp. 28-29.

15. *Congressional Quarterly Almanac*, 1969, p. 725.

16. *The Report of the President's Commission on Campus Unrest*, September, 1970.

17. Theodore M. Hesburgh, "Resurrection for Higher Education," address at the 54th Annual Meeting of the American Council on Education, Washington, D.C., October 7, 1971.

18. Tom Wicker, "America and Its Colleges: End of an Affair," *Change,* September, 1971, pp. 22-25.

19. Lewis B. Mayhew, "Faith and Despair," in *Stress and Campus Response*, G. Kerry Smith, ed., Jossey-Bass, San Francisco, 1968, p. 271.

20. Milton Friedman, "The Higher Schooling in America," *The Public Interest*, Number 11, Spring, 1968, p. 110.

21. Quoted by Jack N. Arbolino in *New Teaching New Learning*, G. Kerry Smith, ed., Jossey-Bass, London, 1971, p. 67.

22. Ibid., p. 66.

Part II
The Education Amendments of 1972

If anything can happen, it will happen to S.659.

Congressional Staff Aide

3

Issues and Options

On May 25, 1972, CBS television broadcast an hour-long special entitled "Higher Education: Who Needs It?" One month later the Education Amendments of 1972 were signed into law.

Why, in mid-1972, did Congress pass bold legislation to aid students and colleges in new ways? Part of the explanation lies in the simple mechanics of policy making. The basic statutes authorizing federal education programs generally run for a fixed number of years and thus must be reviewed periodically. In 1971-1972 it was higher education's turn. But this fact does not suggest why there was major strife over the legislation, nor the shape of the final outcome, its magnitude and complexity.

During most of the 1960s, the federal role in supporting higher education developed in a fairly steady progression. The issues that for so long stalled school bills in Congress—civil rights, church-state, and "federal control"—seemed to impinge less on measures to aid higher education. After the debacle of the Kennedy education program in 1961-1962, higher education legislation had smooth sailing for the rest of the decade, and the scope of federal programs expanded, moving well beyond research support, albeit in an untidy, incremental fashion rather than according to a coherent design.

But following the breakthroughs of the early and mid-1960s, and the reaffirmation and consensus that seemed to be reflected in the uneventful higher education legislation of 1968, a new debate mounted—not over the principle of federal support but rather over its purpose and form.

The Making of a Policy Debate

One college spokesman wrote in 1969:

Higher education is now standing at a crossroads, and the direction it takes will be determined by the policies the Federal government adopts in deciding how to allocate its resources to higher education.[1]

A great many policy issues would be swept into the Education Amendments of 1972. Bills and amendments proliferated to bring about a legislative result touching nearly every dimension of the postsecondary system. But the overriding question was the relative emphasis to be accorded alternative basic strategies for channeling federal support to higher education. This was not a salient public issue. Yet within the higher education policy arena—those in the academic world, foundations, state agencies, and on the Washington scene who were concerned about the impact of the federal government on higher education—it was an issue of considerable significance. As the debate proceeded over several years, opinion tended to polarize around competing philosophies in a highly charged legislative struggle.

Several developments helped to launch an intensified debate over federal higher education policy.

Problems of Federal Funding

First, not all was well in the growing partnership between the federal government and higher education. Some educators were increasingly concerned about unintended consequences of the federal relationship.

With federal programs affecting higher education divided among a great many federal agencies, each with its own objectives and needs, institutions were being pulled in different directions. In the case of research and development, the federal government engaged the services and facilities of an institution of higher education (or an individual department, faculty member, or faculty team) much as it would those of any other producer. "At first the atmosphere within the university was one of heady excitement over the possibilities of this kind of partnership, as the wind tunnel or cyclotron was constructed on campus," wrote one university president. "Gradually, however, it became apparent that the effect of these practices was not altogether salutary. . . ."[2] Lunging after every federal opportunity, it was discovered, could deflect the institution from its main tasks and put a drain on institutional resources because of matching requirements and cost-sharing arrangements.

The federal project grant system, moreover, tended to undermine university governance and a sense of community in university affairs to the extent that it diverted the basic loyalty and attention of faculty from the institution to the federal agencies that supported them. And the uncertainty of federal funding from year to year complicated budgetary planning and sometimes left the institution saddled with long-term commitments in areas where federal participation unexpectedly declined or ended.

Other concerns stemmed from the pattern of federal funding. The distribution of federal support was highly uneven geographically (generally favoring the Northeast and far West), among types of institutions (favoring a relative few major universities), and by field (heavily favoring the natural sciences and engineering over the arts, humanities, and social sciences). Federal support was also heavily concentrated on graduate education; the undergraduate sector was relatively neglected. Legislation of the mid-1960s helped in some measure to right these imbalances. The Higher Education Facilities Act and the Higher Education Act provided new support to a broader base of institutions. The National Foundation for the Arts and Humanities, established in 1965, inaugurated a modest program of aid for these neglected areas. But wide discrepancies persisted.

One group of college and university leaders warned that federal policies were causing:

. . . distortion of academic development, disruption of institutional integrity and the imposition of burdensome, sometimes inconsistent, administrative regulations. Want of concern for the impact of federal funding on individual colleges and universities as institutions has left some unaided, others selectively assisted, and a few heavily committed to federal programs. Some institutions receiving no aid face extinction; those receiving selective support suffer internal distortions, while those heavily dependent on federal aid have become prisoners of unstable financing.[3]

The Expectation of a Larger Federal Role

Whatever the perceived liabilities, hardly anyone in higher education was calling for dismantling the federal programs or halting further growth in federal support. There was an increasingly widespread assumption, in fact, that the federal contribution to financing higher education would rise substantially—that it was a matter of necessity.

Alan Pifer, President of the Carnegie Foundation, estimated that the percentage met by the federal government might go as high as 50 percent by 1975, more than double what it was in 1968.

My prediction is based simply on the obvious inelasticity of other (state, local, private) sources in relation to the expansion task ahead. . . [W]e are forced. . .to a very simple conclusion. If this nation's needs for higher education are to be met in years to come, the federal government will have to accept the principal part of the consequent financial burden.[4]

He speculated further that over the very long range, perhaps by the year 2000, the financing of higher education, like the support of agriculture, might "come to be regarded as almost exclusively a federal responsibility," though Pifer conceded that this was a "heretical" thought, for it called into question the historical assumption of the primacy of state support.

But as financial anxieties welled up in the higher education community during the late 1960s, more and more academic leaders were inclined to agree with Pifer's acceptance of a greatly enlarged federal role, if not his precise prediction. Pifer and other spokesmen were painfully aware of federal budget constraints imposed by the Vietnam War, but they shared a sense of urgency about the financing of higher education. Before long, it seemed, the federal government would have to come to grips with its critical responsibility in this area.

Pleas for a Coherent Federal Policy

If a larger federal commitment was inevitable, it seemed essential to begin developing what had never existed before—an explicit, comprehensive federal strategy for higher education. It was argued that the country could no longer afford an unplanned, haphazard federal approach to such a vast and important enterprise.

Pifer, for example, called for a "high level, dispassionate, non-political debate on the future of higher education. The inauguration of such a debate is surely the first priority for both Washington and the colleges and universities. . . [W]e must now use every means at our disposal deliberately to develop a coherent, articulated set of national policies" for higher education.[5]

Advocates of a more integrated federal approach were not, of course, pushing for a ministry of education or an otherwise nationally controlled system. No one wanted to jeopardize institutional autonomy or undermine higher education's unique pluralism and decentralization. What was being advocated was coordination of federal actions as they impinged on higher education—an overall plan or set of goals geared explicitly to the nation's needs and problems in higher education, rather than the exigencies of the federal government itself.

President Johnson seemed to be responding to this concern when he said in his education message of 1968 that it was time to "shape a long-term strategy of federal aid to higher education, a comprehensive set of goals and a precise plan of action."[6] And he directed the Secretary of HEW to begin the task.

New Analytical Thinking

While the leadership of higher education became increasingly concerned about finances and the federal role, the same matters were drawing the attention of a growing number of policy analysts, primarily economists, whose orientation was to examine these questions in terms of pricing, scarce resource allocation and the distribution of costs and benefits under alternative public expenditure patterns. The late 1960s brought a surge of new scholarly and analytical interest in the economics of higher learning. This development was part of a broad trend both in and out of government to try to bring systematic tools of analysis to bear on public policy issues.

Within government, the movement is said to have originated in the Defense Department early in the decade under Secretary Robert McNamara and his

Assistant Secretary, Charles J. Hitch. They implemented a "planning-programming-budgeting" process designed to unify and systematize decision making in the department and assure maximum "cost effectiveness" in carrying out defense objectives. Efforts to replicate the "PPB" system in departments and agencies outside defense met with mixed results; domestic social policy, it was found, typically did not lend itself to the same kind of quantitative analytical techniques applied to "hardware" decisions in the Defense Department (and there is difference of opinion about the ultimate efficacy of what was attempted in the defense area). But the concept of establishing a strong analytical foundation for basic policy and resource allocation decisions of the government took hold within the federal establishment. "Program planning and evaluation" units were set up at departmental and agency levels throughout the government.

Outside government, there was a parallel growth of policy-related research in universities and "think tanks" like Brookings, the Urban Institute, and the Rand Corporation. "Policy studies" came into vogue in some academic circles. Economists and other social scientists turned their attention to public policy issues, particularly after the government stepped up its involvement with domestic social concerns in the mid-60s. Higher education finance was one area—like housing, urban renewal, elementary and secondary schooling, transportation, and health—that attracted the interests of policy analysts from the academic ranks.

One result of this new analytical focus was a growing body of literature on the subject of higher education finance. For example, the *Public Interest*, a prestigious intellectual journal, devoted most of its Spring 1968 issue to a "Symposium on Financing Higher Education," focusing particularly on federal policy choices. The journal called attention to "a major and frequently intense debate about such policy choices. . . Few echoes of this debate reach the general public." Yet what is at stake "may be nothing less than a reshaping of the American social order."[7]

Basic Alternatives

Most schemes for new federal aid to higher education in the late 1960s and early 1970s tended to emphasize one of two support strategies: channeling aid through *institutions* or channeling aid directly to *students*. There were, however, two other broad options that merit brief mention first: to channel funds through the *states* in the form of block grants and indirectly to channel aid through *parents* by way of special income tax exemptions, deductions or credits for their children's college expenses.

Aid to the States

The concept of "revenue sharing," turning a portion of federal resources over to state governments for their use, was in the air, and some proponents of the concept hoped it would supplant many categorical federal aid programs. Such existing programs, it was suggested, could be "folded into" revenue sharing. The Nixon Administration, for example, proposed a special revenue sharing plan in the elementary and secondary field that would lump together certain federal school aid programs into block grants to the states. But few advocated this approach in higher education. Simply underwriting and reinforcing patterns of support at the state level, unrelated to any national objective, did not seem to be an appropriate or adequate response to the federal responsibility in higher education.

The Tax Relief Idea

For many years hundreds of bills had been introduced in the Congress to extend college tax relief to middle-income families and, depending on the specific proposal, upper-income families as well. The idea drew wide political support, though for somewhat incompatible reasons. It had of course substantial appeal as a way to help hard-pressed parents faced with sharply escalating college costs. Yet at the same time it was advocated as a scheme to bolster hard-pressed private institutions on the assumption that the colleges could ultimately capture most of the savings to parents and students by raising tuition.

Proponents also argued that tax relief was the one way to get large-scale federal funds for higher education without the danger of federal control. The money would flow to the colleges free of strings and bureaucratic red tape. And, it was argued, tuition tax credits got around the church-state controversy; religiously affiliated institutions would be benefited but without stirring constitutional questions.

Opposition to the idea came on several fronts. The most consistent argument against it was that it would discriminate against those not in a position to benefit significantly from tax relief because they have little or no tax liability—poor families in particular, but also veterans and self-supporting students. Nearly all the major higher education associations strongly opposed tuition tax credits as inequitable, unsound from the standpoint of tax policy, and likely to draw resources away from other federal programs of assistance to higher education. Representatives of public higher education were particularly vehement in condemning a program of subsidies that would tend to give preferential treatment to parents of students in high-cost institutions. They argued that public institutions would have to abandon their commitment to low tuition in order to gain under the plan.

Further opposition came from those who were concerned about the potential drain on the U.S. treasury. Representative Wilbur Mills, chairman of the powerful House Ways and Means Committee, made clear he would not countenance such legislation:

If we decide that certain programs, however worthy their purpose, cannot be financed at this time by increased spending, because other needs have priority, we should not then turn around and sanction some form of indirect subsidy—in the form of special tax relief—for these programs.[8]

The executive branch was also unsympathetic; Treasury Department spokesmen had regularly spoken out against such "backdoor financing."

Periodically during the 1960s, however, strong pressures for college tax credits developed in the Senate. Such pressures, in fact, helped produce the Guaranteed Loan Program for middle-income students in 1965; it was designed by the Johnson Administration and incorporated in the Higher Education Act as a way to help defuse the tax credit movement, led by Senator Abraham Ribicoff of Connecticut. In 1967, the Senate actually passed a Ribicoff college tax credit bill as an amendment to a separate tax measure, but later deleted it. Editorializing against the Ribicoff bill, the *New York Times* summarized the arguments in opposition:

On all counts—fair taxation, equitable financial assistance to students and far-sighted federal support of higher education—the tax credit proposal should be defeated.[9]

It *was* defeated in 1967. Another Ribicoff college tax credit bill passed the Senate again in 1971, only to be knocked out this time in conference with the House. Tax relief for college expenses seemed to be an idea whose time would not come.[a]

The Mainstream of Debate

Leaving aside aid through the states and the much-discussed but ill-fated tax relief approach, the principal debate centered on proposals for direct aid to students and aid to institutions—and the general balance between the two.

Several forms of federal student assistance—grants, work-study, direct and insured loans—were already well established. The question was whether and how to enlarge the federal student aid commitment. Likewise, various types of grants to institutions were already a part of the prevailing pattern of

---

[a]Advocates of tuition tax relief, particularly representatives of small private colleges, also pushed the closely linked idea of tax credits for private donations to institutions of higher education. They wanted to broaden the tax break for charitable contributions to colleges by permitting a direct offset against the tax itself rather than the tax base, i.e., a tax credit rather than the existing tax deduction. Though a number of bills to accomplish this were introduced in Congress, the idea made little headway. In fact, with the strong pressure on Congress for tax reform in the late 1960s, higher education found itself having to fight to preserve the *existing* tax incentives for voluntary donations to colleges and universities.

"categorical" federal support targeted on specific national objectives. But "institutional aid" was becoming a term of art in higher education that meant something different from institutional funding that was built into existing federal programs. Increasingly this term was coming to mean undesignated, "free" money available to a more or less comprehensive range of colleges and universities[b] to be used by the institutions at their own discretion, not necessarily in any one expenditure category or for any predetermined purpose. The question was whether and how the federal government should undertake such a new commitment.

Federal institutional aid had for some time been available to particular types of institutions with responsibilities in specific areas that were deemed important by the federal government. The Bankhead-Jones Act of 1935 provided small yearly payments to land-grant colleges specializing in agriculture and the mechanical arts (the "land-grant teaching fund"); Title IV of the National Defense Education Act incorporated an allowance to universities for each graduate student holding a Title IV college teacher fellowship; the National Science Foundation extended several types of grants to institutions for development in the sciences. However, the concept of broad-based, unrestricted institutional grants to generally strengthen the higher education system was not yet a part of the federal policy consensus.

Few people perceived the student aid versus institutional aid issue as an either-or proposition. Most called for a mix of strategies. It was a matter of relative emphasis—which general direction federal policy should take, which basic priority should be reflected in future federal programs affecting higher education.

One conceivable option was to maintain the existing configuration of federal aid, with its patchwork of student assistance, institutional support of a limited nature, and varied categorical programs. But widely shared concerns about the inherent difficulties of current support patterns for higher education and the growing expectation of a larger federal role weighed heavily against this. Few if any voices advocated simply the status quo.

Who Pays, Who Controls

The emerging policy debate was more than an abstract, technical argument about the mechanics of federal support. It was an intense debate because it touched on deeper issues—how the burden of paying for higher education should be shared, how influence should be distributed within higher education, and how to make the system more responsive.

On the "who pays" question, no one could project with certainty the

---

[b]Almost all proposals for institutional aid limited eligibility to accredited, nonprofit institutions.

effects of different federal strategies, nor was it clear that the federal government would necessarily have a decisive impact in this respect, particularly in light of the dominant state role in determining patterns of higher education finance. Yet concern about the potential long-term consequences of the federal role in pricing higher education—and thus the relative share of total costs borne by students—tended to underlie much of the debate. There were fears, for example, that a dominant student aid approach would ultimately have the effect of shifting the principal burden to the student. In this line of reasoning, a substantial influx of federal student aid would encourage institutions to increase their tuitions more readily, producing an "escalation which would require ever-increasing student financial aid funds to enable students to meet the ever-increasing costs of going to college."[10] Students who could qualify for the available aid would be taken care of; others would have to resort to loans or other means to cope with the inflationary spiral. Institutional aid, on the other hand, was presented as a strategy for enabling institutions to hold the line on student charges. Underwrite the institutions themselves with federal funds, it was argued, and relieve the burden of costs on all students.

Thus, when federal aid was being debated, it was at times really an argument about how the bill for higher education should be divided between the public (government) and the principal users (students).

The choice of federal strategies also touched on power relationships. The way money is allocated affects the way power is allocated. If more public resources are channeled directly to students, their choices and preferences would come to have more influence in educational decision making. One opponent of the student aid approach warned that students having the "power of the purse" would "be in the driver's seat."[11] A strategy of general support for institutions, by contrast, would tend to strengthen the hand of college and university trustees, presidents, and others having general authority over institutions. The return of federally collected revenues to the states would increase the importance of higher education policy-makers at the state level.

Also underlying the policy debate were conflicting notions about how the federal government could most effectively encourage diversity and quality in higher education. An argument for student aid was that putting greater purchasing power in the hands of students would make institutions more responsive to market pressures, therefore more diverse, flexible and change-oriented. Advocates of institutional aid, on the other hand, maintained that the diversity of the entire system would be jeopardized without basic support to insure the survival of all its elements, and that individual institutions would be less capable of change and innovation without such support.

Sources of Policy Ideas

To identify the seminal sources of major legislation is perhaps a futile task. There is a jumbled transition at best between policy thinking and policy outcomes; the process tends to amalgamate values and viewpoints in nonlinear fashion. And most "new" policy ideas that gain currency in the political arena have antecedents that go far back, predating those individuals or groups currently identified with them. But short of tracing the precise lineage of policy ideas, we suggest here what was available to policy-makers—the "schools of thought" and sources of policy thinking, the solutions that were being talked about and who was talking about them.

The Higher Education Associations

As organized representation of higher learning proliferated during the 1960s, there was some concern that "Washington is becoming filled with the babble of many voices speaking for higher education."[12] With new national associations popping up to represent different segments of the system and more individual institutions establishing their own Washington outposts, "what higher education thinks" on a particular issue seemed more difficult to determine than ever. Yet toward the end of the decade there was one cause that increasingly united the disparate elements of higher education's leadership in the nation's capital: institutional aid. At least on this issue, a new solidarity was developing.

This was particularly evident among six groups that had come to be identified as the "major" national higher education associations, a coalition consisting of: the American Council on Education, the "umbrella" organization with the most extensive and diverse institutional membership; the National Association of State Universities and Land-Grant Colleges and the American Association of State Colleges and Universities, which together covered the four-year public institutions; the Association of American Universities, the exclusive club of less than fifty prestigious public and private universities strong in graduate education and research; the Association of American Colleges, representing four-year liberal arts colleges, particularly the small privates; and the American Association of Junior Colleges. Together these associations could claim to represent virtually every accredited, nonprofit postsecondary institution in the country, and each was on record endorsing across-the-board institutional support.

The American Council reflected this consensus when it declared in its 1969 statement, *Federal Programs for Higher Education: Needed Next Steps*, that "the principal unfinished business of the federal government in the field of higher education is the necessity to provide support for general institutional purposes." The Council called for a more basic role for the federal government than in the past:

A century ago responsibility for higher education might well have been regarded as a state or local concern. As we approach the end of the twentieth century higher education has become a national asset and a national responsibility. Our college-trained population has become so mobile that no individual state or region can be assured that its investment in advanced education will provide commensurate returns.[13]

The statement went on to marshal the major arguments for an institutional grants program:

It can provide a broad base of support for institutions of established quality to strive toward greater quality. It can provide a broad base of support for other approved institutions to strive toward the quality that inadequate previous resources have denied them. It can help institutions, public and private alike, to slow down the trend toward increased student fees—a trend that is in direct contradiction to all our efforts to provide access to higher education for all our young people.[14]

Some of the associations had come a long way in arriving at a position that favored massive new federal support. A 1952 commission of the Association of American Universities "reached the unanimous conclusion that we as a nation should call a halt at this time to the introduction of new programs of direct federal aid to colleges and universities. We also believe it undesirable for the government to expand the scope of its scholarship aid to individual students."[15] Only in 1968 did the Association reverse this position to endorse both the existing mixture of various types of federal aid plus the concept of broad institutional grants.

In the case of the Association of American Colleges, deep concerns about federal control and the potential divisiveness of the church-state issue had long dominated attitudes toward the expanding federal role in higher education. New federal programs were received with misgivings. An especially conservative element of the AAC membership had vigorously supported tax credit legislation in hopes of derailing other forms of federal aid. But toward the end of the 1960s this cautious tradition gave way. Experience and financial necessity overcame suspicions of federal support. The indirect avenue of tax relief was apparently a dead end. And on the constitutional issue, the Higher Education Facilities Act of 1963 and the Higher Education Act of 1965, extending a variety of aids to church-related institutions, had been enacted and implemented without major controversy. The Association adopted a more positive stance in federal affairs and in 1968 endorsed general-purpose federal institutional aid.

Times had changed and the major associations were closing ranks on what seemed to be an overriding mutual interest: a broad, sustained commitment from the federal government to strengthen the higher education system as a whole. The one stumbling block to a completely united front was the problem of agreement on precisely how institutional support should be distributed. It was generally acknowledged that a discretionary grants system administered by a federal agency would be unworkable; Great Britain's favorable experience with a "University Grants Committee" could not be carried over to the massive American system of higher education. Some type of automatic formula would be essential. But views differed on the specific elements of a formula. Should it be based on enrollments (the simple "capitation" approach), degree production, research commitment? Adjusted according to level (lower division, upper division, early graduate, advanced graduate) and type of instruction? Should quality be a factor or should the formula be strictly egalitarian among institutions? While the associations sought to avoid open disagreement on such details, emphasizing instead their strong consensus on the general principle of institutional aid, there was no doubt that the several constituencies of higher education would have different preferences.

Two of the associations were already committed to supporting a limited institutional aid proposal, known as the Miller Bill, that was under active consideration by the House Committee on Science and Astronautics in the late 1960s. This was a science-based measure that would have provided unrestricted grants to all types of institutions but according to a formula which gave special weight to institutional effort in the sciences. The land-grant and state college associations initially developed the bill and arranged its sponsorship by Representative George P. Miller of California. With no immediate prospects of moving on institutional aid in the education committees of Congress, the two associations decided to press ahead with a friendly House Science Committee. If the principle of institutional aid could be established in the sciences, it might serve as an entering wedge, and the formula could be broadened later to include other fields. After extensive hearings, the House Science and Astronautics Committee reported out the Miller Bill in 1969, but that was as far as it went.

The other associations were generally noncommittal about specific institutional aid formulas except to the extent that they expressed views on the Miller Bill. The American Association of Junior Colleges testified against the measure on grounds that the formula would provide the biggest grants to large graduate universities and relatively little support to undergraduate four-year and two-year institutions, thereby perpetuating the past imbalance of federal funding. The Association favored federal institutional grants but not the Miller Bill. While ready to join with other groups in supporting a suitable formula for a broad-based program, the AAJC was at the same time beginning to push legislation of its own providing special institutional support to community colleges.

The Association of American Universities endorsed the measure but did so with reservations, namely that the bill treated only the natural and social sciences and failed to recognize the cost differentials between instruction at the masters and Ph.D. levels. Responsible for producing over 60 percent of Ph.D.'s awarded annually, the AAU institutions felt that the high cost of advanced graduate programs should be reflected in any institutional support formula.

Whether a diverse higher education community could come together on a specific proposal when the time was right remained to be seen. Most association and academic leaders were optimistic. "The important thing is that we've all agreed on the principle. . .[T]he minor difficulties can easily be worked out," said Fred H. Harrington, president of the University of Wisconsin.[16] And as time went on, some of the associations indicated increasing flexibility. "We will support any bill with a reasonable formula for institutional aid, relying on further legislation to correct inequities as experience reveals them," the land-grant and state college groups said in 1971.[17]

For the major associations institutional aid loomed larger and larger as the vital issue of federal policy in the late 1960s and early 1970s. On the question of student aid, their general posture was that the current federal student assistance programs were adequate to the task and only needed to be funded more fully; no major new thrusts were needed. None of the associations, of course, proposed that institutional support supplant existing federal programs, student aid or otherwise. Institutional aid was envisioned as a necessary complement to what had been already established—the "largest single missing piece" needed to complete the "mosaic" of federal aid to higher education.[18]

The land-grant and state college organizations, however, were at best ambivalent toward student aid, claiming that the "most effective and most urgently needed form of aid to individuals in obtaining a college education is a program of support for educational institutions to enable them to keep charges to students low." Student aid programs "result in pyramiding budgetary costs and administrative complexities without getting at the problem," the associations argued. They supported the federal student grant, loan and work programs only because of "the necessity of dealing with situations as they exist while working toward more fundamental solutions."[19]

By contrast, AAC's attitude was more positive. Many private colleges looked on direct student assistance, taking into account differing tuition levels, as a means of enabling them to compete with low-cost public institutions.

Dozens of smaller and specialized organizations in Washington were actively concerned with particular federal programs and particular aspects of new federal legislation. Constituencies like the Catholic colleges and universities, predominantly Black institutions, Lutheran colleges, law schools, and graduate schools all had their own representation on the Washington scene. There were also the associations representing profit-making institutions, traditionally set apart from "higher education" yet with an important stake in the development of federal policy toward postsecondary education, particularly the broadening of eligibility for federal student aid to include their students.

But the major associations constituted the most visible and audible presence for higher education in Washington. On the central issues of federal policy toward higher education, many of the special mission and small clientele groups took their cues from the more comprehensive associations, or simply let these associations speak on their behalf.

The Views of Economists

In the "full-cost pricing" model of higher education finance, government would stay out of the picture entirely (except perhaps to insure adequate student loan financing) on the theory that education primarily benefits the individual and should therefore be bought and sold in the marketplace like any other good at prices reflecting more or less true costs. Public subsidies are inappropriate because they distort market choices based on costs and benefits that presumably are perceived accurately by the individual.

Though rarely advocated in this extreme as a real-world alternative, the doctrine of full-cost pricing serves as a reference point for economic analysis of higher education. Nearly every economist writing on the subject of higher education finance in the late 1960s urged a freer play of market forces and challenged prevailing public subsidy patterns on grounds of equity and efficiency. Most were in agreement that some degree of public investment in higher education was justified. But the economists argued that traditional public support for higher education tended to be both regressive, in effect transferring resources in the wrong direction on the economic scale, and inefficient, wasting resources on those who do not need subsidies and undermining fair competition among institutions.

The economists maintained that low-tuition policies, made possible by heavy state subsidization of public institutions, have the effect of scattering benefits rather than pinpointing them on those students and families least able to pay, and of putting private higher education at a severe competitive disadvantage, possibly endangering the future of many private institutions. One economist wrote:

Today's heavy reliance on state subsidies for public institutions and tuition charges for private institutions aggravates rather than alleviates the problem of attaining equality of opportunity. . . It is particularly discouraging that sufficient resources are being devoted to higher education to provide equal opportunity for the proportion of the age group now in college, but the confused pricing structure of our dual system makes inefficient use of these resources. Many students from affluent families are highly subsidized, while many students with substantial financial need are either penalized or eliminated.[20]

The general prescription offered by economists was to establish greater student sovereignty in the allocation of resources within higher education by having states reduce their general subsidies to institutions, raise general student charges, and expand direct aid to students with financial need. Spokesmen for public higher education condemned such schemes as politically unrealistic. The economists, they charged, were providing a respectable rationale for state legislatures to hike tuition; yet the legislatures were unlikely to take the complementary step of proportionately increasing student assistance, and the result would be to further reduce access for needy students.

In terms of federal options, the economic analysts likewise strongly favored a student-oriented approach, rather than general support for institutions. Proposals to "simply appropriate money and spread it around by means of a formula are an expensive and ineffective way" to deal with the financial problems of higher education.[21]

One of the few economists who argued strongly *for* extending the principal of low-fee public higher education was Howard Bowen, President of the University of Iowa and frequent spokesman for the land-grant association. "There must be a point of entry and a track through the system that presents a minimum of financial barriers," Bowen held.[22] Bowen further maintained that students and parents were already paying the principal costs of higher education—three fourths of the national total, he estimated, if one takes into account the substantial foregone earnings of the student while in school. In addition to a combination of need-based grants and long-term loans for students (with less emphasis on the latter than most other economists favored), Bowen proposed federal institutional aid to undergird the entire system and to help the colleges and universities keep their charges down.

The Zacharias Plan

An unconventional loan concept that appealed to many economists was the idea of adjusting repayment to the student borrower's future earnings rather than setting a fixed-payment obligation. Instead of a standard rate of interest, the student would agree to pay back a small set percentage of annual income over a long period, perhaps (under a national scheme) as a surcharge on his income tax. The rationale was that young people would be more willing to borrow for their education if they could pool or "mutualize" the risk in this manner, knowing that they would never face a loan debt out of proportion to their income. Those who enter relatively low-paying professions, or for whatever reason do not become affluent, would repay less than the amount borrowed to attend college; those with larger earnings, paying back at the same percentage rate of annual income, would in the end repay more than the amount borrowed.

Versions of this idea had been recommended over the years by the economist Milton Friedman and others, but in 1967 a presidential advisory panel for the first time drew national attention to it in a report calling for the establishment of an "Educational Opportunity Bank" as an agency of the federal government authorized to lend money to postsecondary students on a "contingent repayment" basis. Headed by Jerrold R. Zacharias, an MIT physicist, the panel said its plan might not be considered a loan program at all but rather a "device for enabling students to sell participation shares in their future incomes."[23]

A key objective of the Educational Opportunity Bank proposal was to increase both loan capacity and the willingness of students to borrow so that colleges and universities could raise tuition and fees to "something closer" to actual instructional costs. The panel argued that the plan would enhance the viability of the private sector of higher learning by reducing the price differential with public higher education, and that the entire system would benefit from healthier competition and greater responsiveness to market pressures. Moreover, the panel argued, students of all economic backgrounds would have the wherewithal to choose more freely among a wider range of education and training options, and they would be encouraged to take greater responsibility for their own education and thus take it more seriously.

The Zacharias report was released by the White House for public discussion without any official endorsement. Not surprisingly, it stirred an immediate controversy, with representatives of public higher education denouncing the report as a "Pandora's Box of ill-considered, obsolete, and contradictory ideas" that would destroy the tradition of society sharing the cost of higher education.[24] The land-grant and state college groups labeled the "so-called" opportunity bank the "Student Life Indenture Plan." Sentiment among private colleges was divided, some representatives favoring the plan at least in concept but generally cautious about its practicality.

The Zacharias proposal attracted enough interest to generate resolutions in both houses of Congress calling for feasibility studies. Senator Winston Prouty of Vermont was particularly intrigued, calling the Bank idea a "kind of Social Security in reverse—that is, the benefits would come first, then the repayment."[25] But the resounding opposition from most of the higher education establishment, questions about the plan's technical soundness, and the uncertain budgetary implications of launching and sustaining the bank seemed to limit any realistic prospects for legislation to follow through on the proposal. The idea continued to pick up scattered interest in the academic community; and two private universities, Yale and Duke, began limited income-contingent loan programs of their own in the early 1970s. Implementing the concept on a national basis, however, would remain highly controversial.

The Carnegie Commission

In 1967 the Carnegie Foundation created a prestigious fifteen-member Commission on Higher Education to study and make recommendations on issues facing higher education as the nation approached the year 2000. The Foundation made clear that the new commission "was not being asked to speak *for* higher education but rather *about* higher education and its needs" in relation to national concerns.[26] Clark Kerr, former President of the University of California, was named Chairman. Members included several eminent college and university presidents, a former governor, a noted sociologist, and three business leaders.

Over the next six years the Carnegie Commission produced several bookshelves full of studies and reports cutting a wide swath through the field of postsecondary education. Perhaps the most important dimension of the Commission's work concerned the evolving role of the federal government in higher education. From the early stages it was decided that the Commission should address issues of public policy, particularly with new federal legislation on the horizon. The Commission would try to have an impact, not through day-to-day lobbying or commenting on specific legislative proposals, but by widely publicizing its findings and recommendations and circulating them among government officials in the form of brief reports.

The first report of the Commission, *Quality and Equality: New Levels of Federal Responsibility for Higher Education*, came out in late 1968 and proved to be a durable basic statement of the Commission's views on federal policy. Starting with a diversity of opinion—two or three members were advocates of an educational opportunity bank as the principal solution, another block leaned toward formula-based institutional aid—the Commission managed to hammer out a consensus.

The major plank in the Commission's proposed program was a student aid approach that combined need-based educational opportunity grants, supplementary aid to match nonfederal student grants, work-study, loans, and special graduate student assistance. The report was unclear on some of the details of this package and how it would relate to existing federal student aid programs. The Commission had in mind some new concepts about how federal student aid should be administered. It talked about maximizing the students' freedom of choice by putting most of the funds in a "national reservoir" and aiding individual students wherever they decide to attend, rather than allocating the funds by institution or region or field. It talked about an assurance of aid for all students with demonstrated need. The publicity surrounding *Quality and Equality* suggested a "civilian GI Bill" was being proposed—a federal entitlement for needy students. On the other hand, the report implied simply a vast expansion of the established Educational Opportunity Grants and College Work-Study programs, which operated through state allotments and institutional allocations, with the institution making the final decisions on which students are aided.

But the specifics were less important than the Commission's basic decision to stress student aid. Here is where the Commission urged the greatest expansion of federal efforts.

In its expansive view of the federal role, Carnegie placed the principal emphasis on aid to the student, but it also proposed a very substantial new program of direct assistance to institutions—though not of the type the higher education associations were advocating. While not explicitly rejecting an across-the-board formula approach, the Commission opted instead for "cost-of-instruction supplements" to colleges and universities based on the numbers of enrolled students holding federal grants.

This approach, already established as a feature of federal graduate fellowship programs, was based on the rationale that the federal government should reimburse the institution for part of the additional costs it incurs in admitting federally-aided students. Tuition payments do not cover the full costs of education. Moreover, the Commission noted, many federally-aided students are educationally as well as economically disadvantaged and require special educational assistance, such as tutoring and counseling. The institutions could use the supplements at their own discretion for general operating purposes, though the Commission said it assumed that a portion of the funds would be allocated for special remedial and other programs meeting the needs of the educationally disadvantaged.

Finally, the Commission proposed an independent federal agency, organized along the lines of the National Science Foundation, to encourage experimental development in higher education.

In 1970 the Carnegie Commission issued a second report on federal policy, only slightly revising most of its earlier positions. On institutional aid, the Commission held to its original position despite strong pressures on some Commission members, particularly those who were also active in the higher education associations. The associations wanted unfettered, general support of institutions not hinged, as in the Carnegie proposal, to student aid. But the Commission was again unwilling to endorse general federal aid and stood by cost-of-education allowances as an alternative. A basic concern of Clark Kerr and other members of the Commission was that the initiation of across-the-board federal support could lead eventually to a unitary federal system of higher education, with the states relinquishing their traditional role in this field.

The Rivlin Report

Almost simultaneously with the release of the first Carnegie Commission report, but quite independently, an in-house government task force was completing work on a report that advanced basically the same priorities and recommended many of the same mechanisms of federal support as Carnegie.[c] The study originated in 1967 in the Department of Health, Education and Welfare and was formally carried out in response to President Johnson's 1968 directive to begin developing a federal strategy for higher education. Alice Rivlin, an economist and Assistant Secretary of HEW for Planning and Evaluation, chaired the Advisory Task Force consisting of top officials from most of the federal agencies concerned with education. *Toward a Long Range Plan for Federal Financial Support of Higher Education* was issued in January, 1969, just prior to the change of administrations.[27]

The Rivlin Report, as it came to be known, converged with the Carnegie Commission on the central objective of equal educational opportunity and the pursuit of this objective primarily through student assistance, calling for a student aid program that would "dramatically and clearly indicate that the

[c]There was a considerable degree of convergence between the two reports, but not as the result of coordination. Most commission reports tend to codify thinking and opinions that have already gained at least some currency; this seems to have been the case with the Carnegie and Rivlin groups.

federal government has established a policy of removing financial barriers to college attendance." The report argued:

While student aid alone will not correct the problem of inequality of opportunity, studies indicate that college-going among the poor is significantly influenced by the amount of student aid... An equal sum spent on institutional aid, by contrast, would have far less effect on equality of opportunity.

The report built a case against formula aid to institutions on several grounds. Not only was it a less effective strategy in equalizing opportunity, but unless given in disproportionate amounts to private institutions, the Rivlin report argued it would not alleviate the dual pricing problem that is eroding the private sector. Moreover, the only politically acceptable formula would probably be one that "does not lead to a relative decline in the importance of any class of institutions... Clearly a system which tries to maintain the relative position of different types of institutions will not be particularly adaptable to the changing needs of students and society in general."

The Rivlin group was also concerned about possible distortion of the development of the higher education system. Any given formula provides rewards "based upon a necessarily oversimplified measure of institutional outputs or inputs... [which] tends to encourage institutions to increase the rewarded measures... For example, subsidies based on degrees might encourage some institutions to crank out more degrees than they otherwise felt appropriate, while formulas based upon enrollments produce different pressures...."

Like Carnegie, the Rivlin committee came down in favor of cost-of-education allowances to the institutions. The Committee also recommended fuller funding of the Developing Institutions program to help Black colleges, special institutional aid for "centers of excellence" and new sustaining grants for institutions based on a percentage of their federal research awards. Both the Carnegie and Rivlin groups were concerned about the special problems of major universities hit by the leveling off of federal research expenditures.

In all, the Rivlin committee proposed a substantial amount of federal funding channeled to institutions but, again like Carnegie, steered away from a general aid formula. In fact, one of the initial reasons for launching the Rivlin study in HEW was a desire to counterbalance the mounting pressures for such institutional support. "A lot of people felt that many colleges would soon have to close their doors," one member of the Rivlin task force recalls. "Some sort of institutional aid seemed almost inevitable at the time and our hope was to try and steer it in the right direction."

The Newman Report

The 1971 report of the Newman Task Force must also be considered among key influences on policy thinking. Headed by Frank Newman of Stanford University, this group did not concern itself expressly with the federal role in higher education.

It presented more a critique of the higher education system than an action plan for the government. Yet inferences could be drawn from its widely publicized report.[28] Because it questioned the view that more money would solve higher education's problems, for example, the Newman Report was perceived as a counter to pleas for general federal aid. The Newman Report implied strong support, alternatively, for federal strategies emphasizing change and innovation in higher education.

* * * * * * * * * *

Other sources of policy ideas could be mentioned. No one had a monopoly on policy thinking; recommendations concerning the federal role in higher education were rife. Yet these were the principal issues and options that were in the air. They would be filtered, fashioned and dealt with by political institutions in a process that normally begins with the framing of an administration program.

Notes

1. Allan W. Ostar, "Higher Education and National Policy," in *Agony and Promise*, G. Kerry Smith, ed., Jossey-Bass, San Francisco, 1969, p. 28.

2. Keith Spalding, "The Relevance of Federal Programs to the Purpose of the Institution," *The Educational Record*, Spring, 1966, p. 141.

3. The Wescoe Committee, *Report of the Advisory Committee on Higher Education to the Secretary of HEW*, Chaired by Clark Wescoe, Chancellor, University of Kansas, (photocopy), 1968, p. ii.

4. Alan Pifer, "Toward a Coherent Set of National Policies for Higher Education," Speech to Annual Meeting of the Association of American Colleges, January 16, 1968.

5. Ibid.

6. Quoted in *Toward a Long-Range Plan for Federal Financial Support of Higher Education, A Report to the President*, Department of Health, Education and Welfare, January, 1969, p. 2.

7. "A Symposium on Financing Higher Education: The Policy Dilemmas," *The Public Interest*, Number 11, Spring, 1968, p. 99.

8. Quoted in Ronald A. Wolk, *Alternative Methods for Federal Funding of Higher Education*, Carnegie Commission on Higher Education, Berkeley, California, 1968, p. 5.

9. *New York Times*, May 6, 1967, p. 30.

10. Ostar, p. 31.

11. Russell I. Thackrey, "A View from Public Higher Education," *Proceedings: Symposium on Financing Higher Education*, Southern Regional Education Board, June, 1969, p. 54.

12. Ostar, p. 29.

13. American Council on Education, *Federal Programs for Higher Education: Needed Next Steps*, Washington, D.C., 1969, p. 17.

14. Ibid., p. 19.

15. The Commission on Financing Higher Education—1952, excerpted in *Institutional Aid: Federal Support to Colleges and Universities*, The Carnegie Commission on Higher Education, 1972, p. 101.

16. "Educators Seek General U.S. Aid," *New York Times*, November 13, 1968.

17. The National Association of State Universities and Land-Grant Colleges and the American Association of State Colleges and Universities, *Recommendations for National Action Affecting Higher Education: A Joint Statement*, Washington, D.C., January, 1971, p. 4.

18. John F. Morse, "The Federal Role in Education: One View," *Proceedings: Symposium on Financing Higher Education*, Southern Regional Education Board, June, 1969, p. 53.

19. The National Association of State Universities and Land-Grant Colleges and the American Association of State Colleges and Universities, *Recommendations for National Action Affecting Higher Education: A Joint Statement*, January, 1968, pp. 18, 20.

20. Allan M. Cartter, "Student Financial Aid," in *Universal Higher Education: Costs and Benefits*, American Council on Education, Washington, D.C., 1971, pp. 121-122.

21. Michael Clurman, "Does Higher Education Need More Money?", Joint Economic Committee, *The Economics and Financing of Higher Education in the United States*, p. 634.

22. Howard R. Bowen, "Tuitions and Student Loans in the Finance of Higher Education," Joint Economic Committee, p. 626.

23. *Educational Opportunity Bank*, A Report of the Panel on Educational Innovation, Washington, D.C., August, 1967. The panel was under the auspices of the President's Science Advisory Committee.

24. Quoted in *Higher Education and National Affairs*, Newsletter of the American Council on Education, Volume XVI, Number 31, September 15, 1967, pp. 1-4.

25. Ibid., p. 1.

26. Carnegie Commission on Higher Education, *Quality and Equality: New Levels of Federal Responsibility for Higher Education*, December, 1968, Foreword.

27. *Toward a Long-Range Plan*. Subsequent quotes are from the report.

28. Frank Newman, *et al, Report on Higher Education*, Department of Health, Education and Welfare, Government Printing Office, Washington, D.C., 1971. This was the initial report of the Newman Task Force. A series of later reports by the Task Force outlined specific policy recommendations.

4 An Administration Program

As the Nixon Administration took office and the 91st Congress convened in January, 1969, it was unclear where the principal policy leadership in education and other domestic areas would come from. Through two Democratic administrations, Congress had grown accustomed to working with an activist presidency controlled by the same party. Congress had bargained and jousted with the executive as always, and had delayed, amended or otherwise worked its will on Administration proposals. But there was little question that most of the major legislative impulses of the period came from the executive branch; Congress generally looked "downtown" for policy initiation.

Under a Republican Administration, particularly a newly elected President who was expected to be generally negative if not hostile toward social programs, legislative-executive relations would not be the same, though no one could be certain what the new pattern would be. Greater partisanship seemed inevitable. (It was the first time in over a hundred years that an incoming President faced a Congress in which both houses were controlled by the opposition party.) It also seemed quite possible that Congress would become more self-starting, more self-reliant in the development of new legislation—either by necessity (if the executive failed to initiate) or choice (if the Administration's position offered no common ground). It would be a time of testing between the two branches.

The 1968 elections had rendered few changes in the general make-up of Congress—the Democrats lost a total of two seats but still held commanding majorities in both houses—or the committees handling education. The House Committee on Education and Labor remained a generally liberal, though frequently divided committee, an arena of volatile coalitions and sometimes bitter wrangling. Representative Edith Green (D-Oregon) continued to chair the subcommittee with jurisdiction over higher education, one area within the full committee where accommodation had been achieved fairly readily through most of the 1960s. It remained to be seen whether this pattern could be sustained in the next legislative round for higher education.

In the Senate, Claiborne Pell (D-Rhode Island) became Chairman of the Subcommittee on Education, the single panel of the Labor and Public Welfare Committee that considers education bills. He succeeded Wayne Morse (D-Oregon), who was defeated in his reelection bid for a fifth Senate term. No basic philosophical shift was likely, however; Morse and Pell shared a liberal, expansionist outlook on the federal role in education. And nothing suggested

that Pell would alter the bipartisan, low-key tradition that had long characterized the Senate Education Subcommittee—though perhaps as a new chairman,
the Senator would be especially eager to make his mark and establish a legislative record.

Yet in 1969 there was no compelling reason for Congress to reconsider or
press ahead with new higher education legislation. The 90th Congress had just
extended the basic authorizing statutes for three years, so there was no impend-
ing deadline. A few bills were introduced for discussion purposes, one based
largely on the recent recommendations of the Carnegie Commission. The House
Science and Astronautics Committee pursued its proposed version of institutional aid, the Miller Bill. But Congress was concerned about higher education
in 1969 almost exclusively in relation to campus unrest. The clamor for punitive action to curb student rioters was running high, particularly in the House,
and a great deal of Congressional energy was expended on this highly political
issue.[a] Otherwise, it was an off year in terms of legislative activity affecting
higher education. The only substantive bill passed in 1969 was a measure designed
to shore up the Guaranteed Student Loan Program under tight money conditions by providing a special allowance to participating lenders.

Neither was the Administration under immediate pressure to act on higher
education, which was just one of many policy areas where the new Administration was feeling its way. On the campus unrest issue, Nixon officials engaged
in some tough rhetoric while opposing Congressional attempts to legislate a
solution. When rising interest rates seemed to threaten a crisis in the Guaranteed
Loan Program as the 1969-1970 school year approached, the Administration
responded by proposing the special allowance to lenders, which Congress enacted.
But an overall Administration policy on higher education did not materialize
in 1969. Major problems—the war, the economy—obviously preoccupied the
White House. Even among HEW programs education commanded secondary
attention, behind such emerging priorities as welfare reform.

The education lobby groups meanwhile were preoccupied with battles
over appropriations and proposed student unrest legislation in Congress. In
November of 1968, just after the elections, the major higher education associations had called a press conference to announce they would urge the new
Administration and the 91st Congress to adopt a general institutional aid program.[1] The months following offered the associations little opportunity to
press their case. Instead, representatives of higher education found themselves
having to cope with the Congressional uproar over campus violence, fending
off measures they considered a potential threat to individual rights and academic autonomy. They were also trying to protect current higher education
programs from proposed budget cuts.

---

[a] See Chapter 6.

A Hidden Legislative Process

Though higher education policy held a relatively low priority in the early stages of the Nixon Administration, it was under study here and there in the executive branch, and toward the end of 1969 internal pressure started to build for the formulation of an Administration program. There came a recognition that Congress before too long, probably in early 1970, would begin in earnest to consider revising and extending the higher education legislation beyond the mid-1971 expiration date (later pushed back by one year), and the Administration had better put its oar in the water soon if it wanted to have any influence on what Congress did. Instinctively, the Congressional education committees would be expecting something to come from the Administration and would be prepared to give it a hearing, but they would not wait indefinitely.

A new legislative cycle was underway, and the first act was played out within the Nixon Administration, culminating in a set of proposals that the President sent to Congress in March, 1970. This was a largely self-contained exercise that took place almost entirely out of congressional and public view, an extreme example of what has been called the "secret legislative processes of the Executive Branch."[2] Much of the early groundwork for the Administration's program was laid by HEW planning staff; decisions on the final package were made by an interagency group operating in fairly strict confidence at the White House level.

False Starts

Before the White House group began pulling things together, several tentative probes and initiatives were being pursued simultaneously at different locations in the bureaucracy, with no effort to connect or coordinate what various people were doing. It was a fluid situation; internal relations within HEW and between HEW and the Executive Office of the President took time to sort out under a new administration. On higher education, no one group clearly had the action. And because higher education policy was not a "front burner" issue, the situation was allowed to drift in the early stages.

The line agency concerned with education would, of course, have its own plans and "models" about what should be done in higher education. A series of task forces was established in the Office of Education (OE) in early 1969 to start generating proposals for the new Administration; one of these was on higher education. But it did not take long for tensions to develop between OE and the new regime in HEW. Top levels of the Department under Secretary Robert Finch tended to distrust what was coming up from the OE bureaucracy. The departmental leadership reflected the impulse of a new administration to look for fresh ideas and reexamine settled ways of doing things. OE tended to be perceived as an obstacle—too strongly tied to the education "trade associations," lacking a reform orientation, insufficiently sensitive to budget constraints, and staffed with Democrats from the New Frontier-Great Society years.

A principal responsibility of the OE task force on higher education was to figure out what to do with Section 508 of the Higher Education Amendments of 1968 which required the executive to produce a study and recommendations on how to equalize postsecondary educational opportunity. Part of the job was farmed out to a private consulting group, which turned in a report over the summer of 1969 that Department officials decided was unacceptable. According to a former HEW analyst, the report presented a "full menu" of the needs of higher education but set no priorities. The Office of the Secretary "canned" the consultants' report. (Later, having nothing else to show to comply with Section 508, the Administration informed Congress that the President's forthcoming message on higher education would have to serve in lieu of a formal report.)

Meanwhile, another locus of higher education policy development had emerged in the Office of the Assistant Secretary for Legislation in HEW. In earlier years this office had combined its traditional role of day-to-day Congressional liaison with the legislative planning function. It was not until the mid-1960s that a separate post, Assistant Secretary for Planning and Evaluation, was established in the Department. Now the Office of Legislation set about to generate legislative ideas for higher education, drawing on OE views and also meeting with higher education representatives on the outside. Its initiative was more externally oriented than other higher education planning efforts underway in the Administration. But internally there was a lack of communication and a degree of friction with the recently institutionalized planning staff at the Secretary's level. In time the latter group prevailed, having the stronger mandate for policy development from Secretary Finch.

The HEW Planning Office and the Reassessment of Student Aid

Finch recruited a California political associate and lawyer, Lewis H. Butler, to be his Assistant Secretary for Planning and Evaluation, and on higher education policy, Butler picked up where the outgoing Assistant Secretary, Alice Rivlin, left off. The two were on the same general wavelength in terms of a federal strategy that emphasized student aid and consumer choice. The Rivlin Report itself, although produced at the tail end of the previous Administration, continued to serve as a key reference for policy planning.

Having opted for student aid as the preferred strategy, Butler and the planning staff were then concerned about rationalizing the federal effort that was already being made in student assistance. To begin with, they assumed there was not going to be much new federal money available for higher education any time soon. The President was talking fiscal responsibility, and the message had gone out to the agencies to keep their spending requests and expectations under control. No major budget initiative in higher education seemed likely. The relevant question, therefore, seemed to be how to maximize the equity and efficiency of the current investment. Building on the critique implicit in the Rivlin Report, the analysts focused on weaknesses of the existing student aid programs and began thinking in terms of a substantial overhaul.

A principal concern was that federal commitments in the student loan area unnecessarily diverted resources that could be used more effectively in a program targeted on the neediest students. Under the NDEA loan program, the government was providing nearly $200 million annually in direct capital contributions to loan funds administered by colleges and universities. Why not get this program off the federal budget and rely instead on private capital, with the government providing insurance to lenders against student loan defaults? The Guaranteed Loan Program already provided the mechanism. For several years, the cost conscious Bureau of the Budget had favored this shift as a way to cut the budget, though NDEA loans had become a congressional favorite, and so far Congress had refused to abandon the direct loan program.

The government was also providing substantial interest subsidies under both the direct and guaranteed programs, benefiting large numbers of middle- to high-income students. NDEA loans provided for repayment at a fixed rate of 3 percent beginning one year after the student had completed school. Many but not all of the loans went to poor students. Under the Guaranteed Loan Program, the government paid the interest during the school years, and up to one year after leaving school, for any student whose adjusted family income was below $15,000, a level that reached well into the middle class. The borrower then began repayment at 7 percent, the maximum set by Congress in 1968. Analysis showed that the interest subsidy costs for guaranteed loans were "taking off into the stratosphere." This was an uncontrollable budget item, a government obligation not subject to discretionary appropriations but geared automatically to the volume of approved subsidized loans.

When Congress passed the Emergency Insured Loan Amendments of 1969, another subsidy element was added to the guaranteed program, a special federal payment to banks and other lending agencies of up to 3 percent over the 7 percent ceiling on interest charged to the student. The 7 percent maximum had quickly become outdated as interest rates rose in the first half of 1969. Lenders were becoming increasingly reluctant to make loans at this rate, and it was estimated that many thousands of students would be unable to borrow for the fall semester. Staff papers had been drafted in the planning office arguing for elimination of the interest ceiling on insured loans so that the program would not be adversely affected by fluctuations in the money market. Assistant Secretary

Butler adopted this position, and he in turn persuaded Secretary Finch. But in the final crunch, the Treasury Department carried the day within the Administration. Charls E. Walker, Undersecretary of the Treasury and an architect of the original Insured Loan Program in 1965 when he was representing the American Bankers Assoication, put together the special allowance proposal that became the Administration's response to the loan crisis in the summer of 1969.

The HEW planners continued nonetheless to study more permanent solutions to the loan problem that would allow reduction of the subsidy element and put less strain on the federal budget. One idea they were looking at was the establishment of a "secondary market" for Guaranteed Student Loans. The government would charter a corporation, something akin to the Federal National Mortgage Association in the housing field, which would raise capital by selling government guaranteed obligations and then purchase student loan "paper" from lenders. In addition, it could "warehouse" loans, that is, buy notes on condition that the seller would repurchase them later. The objective would be to increase the liquidity and thus the attractiveness of student loans to banks and other lending agencies, generating more funds for the student loan market.

The planners were also concerned about inequities in the distribution of federal student aid funds administered by institutions of higher education. To obtain assistance under the Educational Opportunity Grant (EOG), College Work-Study, or NDEA loan programs, a student first had to gain admission to a qualified institution and then apply through the financial aid office at that institution. How much federal money an institution could make available to its students depended on state allocation formulas and the action of Office of Education panels reviewing institutional applications. How much aid an individual student received and the mix of aid—grant, loan or work—depended in turn on the institution's allotment of funds and, finally, a determination of the student's need by the college student aid officer.

The conviction grew among the HEW planners that the delivery system for federal student aid was haphazard and inconsistent. The system seemed to fail, in the first instance, to provide students with adequate advance knowledge of the amount of aid they could count on; too many contingencies were involved. Above all, the system seemed to violate an important principle: that students with the same financial need should be treated equally. Some needy students attending high-cost institutions received substantial assistance while others of equal financial plight received very little or none.

Programs of the 1960s that carried the lofty promise of equalizing educational opportunity were inadequately designed, it seemed, to achieve their avowed objective; they were not delivering on the commitment. An HEW official recalls:

The basic concern was that the existing programs failed to reach a lot of poor people, particularly those in community colleges and small institutions such as the Black colleges in the South that don't have the wherewithal to influence national policy to their advantage or are simply not aware of the existence of programs in which they could participate. We began to realize that the existing student aid programs were dealing with only the tip of the iceberg. Dropouts who left school because of the lack of financial aid, students from families who don't encourage the pursuit of a college education, as well as students from non-participating institutions all were being overlooked.[3]

This diagnosis led to the concept of establishing a floor of federal assistance for all needy students. The existing programs would be restructured into a basic entitlement so that every student started out with a minimum level of resources to pursue a postsecondary education. The amount of aid a student received would depend on what the student and his family could be expected to contribute, determined on the basis of a standard formula geared principally to family income. State allocation formulas would be abolished; discretionary decisions by college student aid officers (the "Santa Claus syndrome" in the words of one planner) would be minimized.

Such an approach to reforming student assistance fit perfectly with the "income strategy" that was taking hold within the new Administration. The reassessment of student aid by the HEW planners came in the wake of the Family Assistance Plan set forth by the President in August 1969—the Administration's celebrated and controversial guaranteed income proposal designed to simplify and reform the welfare system. The basic idea was to strip away bureaucracy and put needed cash, rather than well-intentioned but ineffectual social services, directly in the hands of poverty-stricken individuals so that they could make their own choices in the marketplace. The concept of a student aid entitlement was akin to the same philosophy. It turned out to be an acceptable and attractive idea within the Administration in part because the development of the welfare reform proposal had already broken the ice.

Presidential Counselor Moynihan

The key advocate of an "income strategy" and principal author of the Family Assistance Plan was Daniel P. Moynihan. A social scientist from Harvard who had served in both the Kennedy and Johnson Administrations, Moynihan joined the Nixon White House Staff in 1969 to advise on domestic policies. He brought ideas and intellectual clout, and he had the ear of the President.

During most of his two-year stint at the White House, Moynihan was chiefly concerned with the welfare reform issue, but he also took an active hand in education policy. Moynihan provided the closest counterpart the Nixon White House had to a Douglass Cater, Lyndon Johnson's respected education adviser.

In early 1969, when the escalation of campus protests was sitrring a backlash on Capitol Hill, Moynihan was instrumental in formulating the Administration's stand against punitive legislation. He felt strongly that government had no business trying to mandate order on the campuses or otherwise attempting to regulate the internal affairs of academic institutions—and, furthermore, that such attempts would never work, that they would be counterproductive. Moynihan influenced the President to voice a "hands off policy" in March, 1969, and, except for the Vice President, the spirit of this policy was observed fairly consistently by cabinet members and other Administration officials, at least until the Cambodia invasion and the 1970 election campaign.[4]

Moynihan's noninterventionist view with respect to campus unrest also characterized his thinking about the proper nature of federal support for higher education. The system of research funding and categorical aid that had grown piecemeal since World War II, he believed, tended to distract and sometimes seriously distort the academic enterprise. Through its disjointed demands and largesse, the federal government was indirectly wielding too much influence over postsecondary institutions. In Moynihan's view, a new pattern needed to be established, a new type of support without interference.[5]

The presidential counselor fixed on an idea that had been advanced by the Carnegie Commission in December, 1968, the proposal of a national foundation for higher education. Moynihan was a close associate of Clark Kerr and had been affiliated briefly with the Carnegie Commission before joining the President's staff. The autonomous, freewheeling character of the proposed foundation, as well as its orientation toward reform and experimental development, dovetailed with Moynihan's thinking. He liked the concept: a new independent agency with its own board of directors drawn from higher education to channel federal money in accord with higher education's own perceived needs and priorities. And the proposal seemed to carry the advantage of legitimacy and credibility having come from the prestigious Carnegie group.

Moynihan also saw such a foundation as a potential vehicle for addressing another problem that concerned him—what he considered to be a leveling trend within higher education. New Ph.D. programs, for example, were still proliferating across the country while the universities with long-established commitments to advanced studies and research were badly squeezed financially. The very best institutions, the "centers of excellence" in the system, were in danger of losing that excellence if their resources continued to dwindle. A new foundation for higher education, Moynihan thought, could direct selective aid to such institutions to insure maintenance of their quality.

The Hester Task Force

While Moynihan and his staff were pulling together thoughts on the foundation proposal and other possible Nixon initiatives in education, another White House staff contingent had set in motion a completely separate and potentially competing exercise in higher education policy development. Arthur Burns, also a senior advisor to the President (and a keen rival of Moynihan within the White House circle), had created a series of outside presidential task forces to consider domestic issues. One was on higher education and Burns asked James Hester, President of New York University, to organize and head it up. Hester proceeded quickly to produce a report, but the effort came to naught in terms of any impact on the shaping of an Administration program in higher education. It was partly a victim of timing. By January 1970 when the report was submitted, Burns was preparing to leave the President's staff to become Chairman of the Federal Reserve Board. With Burns gone, there was no one in the White House to follow through on the Hester task force. Those in the White House and in HEW who did review the report dismissed it as special pleading by higher education interests. "Strictly an institutional aid lobby" was one HEW aide's reaction, though the report did place first priority on directly assisting economically disadvantaged students.[6] The White House sat on the report for several months before releasing it with as little fanfare as possible.

The White House Working Group

The ultimate stage of formulating the Administration's higher education program was an exercise in internal coalition-building. It involved considerable bargaining among elements within the Administration including HEW, White House staff and the Office of Management and Budget (OMB).[b] Diffuse policy thinking and a variety of viewpoints had to be blended into a set of recommendations that the President could forward to Congress. The mechanism for bringing this about was a top-level Working Group on Higher Education organized in late 1969 by Edward Morgan, a lawyer and assistant to the President for domestic affairs, and Richard Nathan, the human resources division chief in OMB. Morgan chaired the group. The other key members were Moynihan, Nathan, Butler of HEW (Secretary Finch had delegated full responsibility in this area to Butler), and James Allen, Commissioner of Education. The Office of Science and Technology and the Labor Department were also represented.

The Working Group first launched into the question of student financial aid. Butler sold the group on the reform concepts that had been germinating in HEW. Simplifying the means of federal support to higher education and placing greater reliance on market forces by channeling a larger share of subsidies through students strongly appealed to most of the members. So did the objective of distributing existing aid more equitably and establishing a floor of resources for all students. Consensus came easily on these basic principles. It was then a matter of hammering out the details of the new student

---

[b]Formerly the Bureau of the Budget. The Nixon Administration reorganized it into the Office of Management and Budget later in 1970.

aid approach—the reassembled package of grants, work-study and loans—and how it would be administered.

Members of the Working Group sensed the growing concern about a financial crisis besetting institutions of higher education. This concern and pressures for a federal response were mounting rapidly by the winter of 1969-1970 when the Working Group met. And some support for institutional aid was expressed by Office of Education delegates. But this sentiment was far overpowered by Moynihan, Butler, Morgan and others who were skeptical of indiscriminately supporting all postsecondary institutions, and their view was reinforced by the OMB representatives who argued against institutional aid on budgetary grounds. If additional federal resources could be devoted to higher education, the group's clear preference was to put the bulk into direct student assistance.

Once the student aid proposals had been nailed down, the centerpiece of the Administration's program was in place, and the Working Group could turn its attention to other pending questions. Moynihan had yet to broach his idea for a higher education foundation. There were also several loose ends that the Working Group needed to consider. The special plight of Black colleges was a concern, and the Office of Education had some proposals in this area. OMB wanted somehow to dispose of a series of small categorical programs, particularly several that had been authorized in 1968 but never funded like Networks for Knowledge, Education for the Public Service, and Law School Clinical Experience. Some Working Group members were especially interested in strategies for stimulating reform of higher education.

When Moynihan finally set forward his proposal of a national foundation, it seemed to provide an umbrella to accommodate all of these ideas and more.[c] Moynihan had merged his own notion of sustaining excellence at the top of the academic system with the Carnegie conception of an independent federal entity supporting new programs and innovative experiments in higher education. Lee Dubridge, the White House science adviser and former top university president, also pressed the excellence objective. Now the Working Group injected additional purposes into the foundation scheme. The foundation would absorb the narrow program categories that OMB had wanted to mop up. It would also provide the mechanism for channeling assistance to Black institutions, and might even serve as something the Administration could point to in lieu of general institutional aid. On top of all this, the foundation would become the new focal point for designing more coherent relations between the federal government and higher education.

The foundation proposal gathered momentum as various priorities were

---

[c]See Chester E. Finn, Jr. "The National Foundation for Higher Education: Death of an Idea," *Change*, v. 4, March, 1972, for a thorough and insightful account of how the foundation proposal evolved in the Working Group. Also relevant is Paul S. Shapiro, "On the Proposed National Foundation for Higher Education," Center for Educational Policy Research, Harvard University, May 18, 1971.

read into it. Moreover, it was now February, 1970, and there was pressure on the Working Group to get its recommendations before the President. To nearly everyone the foundation seemed a generally worthy venture, and it offered a convenient framework for wrapping things up in the Working Group.

The only dissent was from HEW and the Office of Education. The prospective foundation would clearly pull much of the responsibility for higher education policy entirely out of the Department. The Bureau of Higher Education in OE would retain the student aid programs, but almost everything else would be consolidated under the autonomous foundation. The new agency, fashioned after the National Science Foundation, would have completely independent stature with its own board of directors. The Department balked at the proposed shift. HEW representatives were also critical of the ambiguous nature of the foundation proposal as it had evolved in the Working Group and of Moynihan's particular conception of selective support for "centers of excellence." The latter smacked of elitism. One HEW official characterized the foundation as "Moynihan's idea for keeping the great institutions alive in bad times. . .something like the monasteries during the Dark Ages which should be preserved as vessels for culture and enlightenment."

The President's Views

There is little to suggest that President Nixon was deeply involved in any phase of shaping the Administration's higher education proposals. Indeed, this was a President who seemed relatively isolated on domestic issues, in contrast most obviously to President Johnson, who immersed himself in the substance of education and other social legislation. President Nixon reportedly spent considerable time with his Cabinet and staff working over his welfare reform and revenue sharing proposals—the Administration's top domestic priorities in the early going—but otherwise seemed largely removed from domestic policy development.

There were, however, a few key decisions on the Nixon higher education program that did filter up to the President for his personal consideration. For example, the President in effect gave the final go-ahead for the foundation proposal. Moynihan sold the President on the idea and HEW's objections were laid aside. At several decision points President Nixon also ratified the basic choice of a progressive student aid strategy; he came down in favor of targeting funds on the lowest-income students.

Yet it is difficult to gauge the extent to which the Administration's emerging higher education program reflected the President's own personal leanings. Certainly this was not a program that he personally inspired or initiated. It resulted from policy development internal to the Administration occasioned by a coming legislative deadline; the program worked its way upward to the

President's level. No Presidential directive or prior statement had touched off the planning. In such circumstances of minimal interest and involvement of the President, the way issues and alternatives are packaged and presented to him perhaps has an especially important influence on outcomes. It seems likely that certain themes struck responsive chords with the President—individual opportunity (the President, after all, had himself struggled in his youth and had worked his way through law school), self-help (loans and work were an important part of the student aid package), reform of outmoded educational structures and techniques, streamlining federal support and eliminating unnecessary or misdirected programs. The substance, and understandably the details, of what was being proposed may have been less important as far as the President was concerned.

It has been suggested that President Nixon at this early stage was "especially aware of the responsibility of his Administration to propose solutions to public problems arguably more effective than those of his predecessors."[7] One might speculate, alternatively, that because the President had no attachment whatever to programs and legislation inherited from previous administrations, he may have been particularly receptive to revisionist approaches offered by his advisers, as in the proposed higher education program.

This was not a President who was strongly identified with support of education. During the 1968 campaign he had only briefly touched on the subject, and in earlier years, as a Congressman and as presiding officer of the Senate during his Vice Presidency, he had voted against federal aid-to-education. In contrast to Kennedy and Johnson, Nixon was not expected to be an "education president." His own pre-inauguration task force on education had advised:

Speaking candidly, we do not believe that President-Elect Nixon. . .would at present by most Americans be considered to have the kind of special concern for education the times require. . . . [E]stablishing his image as an education-minded President must be one of Mr. Nixon's highest priorities for his initial weeks in office. His concern for education must become vivid and real. . . .[8]

During his first year in office, President Nixon had done nothing in line with this advice. He had not yet advanced any new programs or ideas in education. And his veto of the fiscal year 1970 Labor-HEW appropriation bill, which contained substantial increases for education programs, tended to confirm suspicions that he was basically unfriendly to education.

But in early 1970, the White House was putting the finishing touches on a proposed higher education program, as well as a set of recommendations related to elementary and secondary schooling, which at least the President's advisers and presumably the President himself perceived as genuinely positive initiatives, heavily oriented toward reform but clearly affirming the importance of education to the nation and the importance of a federal role in support of education. While some critics would see in the proposals a retreat from federal responsibilities, the White House was advancing what it considered a rationalized federal approach that would more effectively deliver on lofty commitments of the past and direct funds to where the problems really are in education.

The higher education program, in fact, almost seemed an anomaly coming from a conservative Republican Administration. The program was cast in the mold of 1960s liberalism in the sense that it put first priority on aiding the poor. And while it was not a massive federal spending proposal, it did call for expenditures several hundred million dollars over existing levels of support—an overall commitment that probably exceeded what Administration planners and particularly the OMB budget watchers had anticipated when they started out. Enthusiasm for the program, and willingness to commit funds to it, seem to have grown as the ideas took shape.

Since leaving the White House, Daniel Moynihan has chided liberals and academics for not perceiving a distinction between President Nixon's "symbolic politics," directed at the middle American constituency that elected him, and what his Administration was actually proposing in the way of social legislation:

In a steady succession of legislative messages he proposed to spend more money for the direct provision of the needs of low-income groups than any president in history. Early on an almost schizophrenic style took hold of his Administration. Symbolic rewards were devised for "middle America," while legislative proposals were drafted for the "other America."[9]

Somewhat different perceptions, it should be noted, have been offered by other former Nixon Administration officials who suggest that the basic disinterest and lack of ideology on the part of the President and his closest aides allowed subordinates to push through worthwhile programs during the Administration's first two years.[d]

Two Messages to Congress

Whatever the origins or nature of his own commitment, the fact is that the President sent two education messages to Congress in March of 1970. The first, entitled "Education Reform," challenged the educational community and the nation to join in a "searching reexamination of our entire approach to learning. . .We must stop congratulating ourselves for spending nearly as

---

[d]Lewis Butler, for example, has stated, "The President didn't care very much about what our education and health policies were just as long as they were salable. This was also true for environmental programs." Quoted in Lou Cannon, "Former Administration Officials Portray President's Isolation," *The Washington Post*, July 9, 1973, p. A-3.

much money on education as does the entire rest of the world. . .when we are not getting as much as we should out of the dollars we spend."[10] The message proposed the establishment of a National Institute of Education in HEW to sharpen priorities and expand support for educational research, development and evaluation. The National Institute of Education was another idea nurtured by Moynihan which the President then advanced.[e]

There followed the message on "Higher Education," the first presidential message ever devoted exclusively to this subject. "No qualified student who wants to go to college should be barred by lack of money."[11] So read the President's opening declaration. This now became the official refrain of Administration policy toward higher education, to be recited often by Administration spokesmen. In its pursuit, the message and the accompanying bill outlined a plan intended to guarantee that every full-time undergraduate student would have at least $1400 a year to pursue a college education.

This "financing floor" would be a combination of what the student and his family could be expected to contribute plus federal aid in the form of grants, work and subsidized loans. Since $1400 was the amount that the Administration estimated a family of roughly $10,000 annual income (more or less depending on the size of the family) could afford, students from families above that income level would receive no federal aid. A low-income student would be eligible for the amount of assistance required to bring his available resources up to $1400. If he came from a family with income of $3,000 or less, he would probably receive the entire $1400 through federal programs and no contribution would be expected from the family. Above $3,000, some contributions would be expected, rising to the $1400 level as income approached $10,000, with eligibility for aid declining in direct proportion. Also, the grant component (actually a mixture of grant and work-study) would vary according to income level, expanding as income declined. But even the lowest-income students would receive a substantial part of their assistance in the form of a subsidized loan. Precise eligibility rules—the schedule for calculating the expected family contribution and determining the make-up of the aid package—would be set by the Secretary of HEW under the proposed plan.

For students above the limit of eligibility as well as low-income students who needed more than $1400 to go to the institution of their choice, the Administration called for reliance on federally guaranteed but nonsubsidized loans. The interest ceiling and the special allowance to banks would be eliminated; banks would lend to students at the market rate, or perhaps one or two points below because of the government guarantee. The interest subsidy during

---

[e]For an account of the origins and development of the Nixon Administration's proposal for a National Institute of Education, see Chester E. Finn, Jr., "The National Institute of Education," *The Yale Review*, Winter, 1975, pp. 227-243.

the school years would also be eliminated, though students would have the option of deferring the interest and paying the accrued amount later.

Subsidized loans received by low-income students as part of the $1400 floor would be on traditional NDEA terms: 3 percent interest beginning only after the student is out of college. However, both types of loans, subsidized and nonsubsidized, would be financed through the private market. There would be no further federal capital contributions to the NDEA loan program.

To increase the availability of guaranteed loans, the President proposed the creation of a National Student Loan Association to serve as a secondary market and warehousing facility. The government-sponsored private corporation would seek to draw additional capital into the student loan field from new sources like insurance companies, pension funds and college endowments, and it would encourage banks to do more student lending by replenishing their supply of lendable funds.

This, then, was the Administration's plan for making student aid more equitable and advancing the cause of equal opportunity: on the one hand, directing available subsidies to the neediest under a system that purportedly would treat students equally according to their ability to pay and would give students advance knowledge of how much federal aid they can plan on; on the other hand, wider and easier access to guaranteed, nonsubsidized loans for all students regardless of income level.

A second feature of the Administration's program was support for career education—a small amount of special federal aid to strengthen noncollegiate alternatives, particularly in two-year community colleges and technical institutes. Secretary Finch had been touting this idea in HEW and in speeches around the country, and its inclusion reflected his personal interest.

Finally, the President called for the establishment of a National Foundation for Higher Education to encourage "excellence, innovation and reform," to strengthen institutions or programs that "play a uniquely valuable role in American higher education or that are faced with special difficulties," and to serve as "an organization concerned, on the highest level, with the development of national policy in higher education."[12] All the unfunded programs from the Higher Education Amendments of 1968 would be consolidated under the Foundation, as would the unfunded International Education Act of 1966 and three ongoing programs—community services (Title I of the Higher Education Act), college teacher fellowships (Title IV NDEA), and foreign language and area studies (Title VI NDEA). The new agency would be authorized to fund projects in any of the areas where categorical support was to be phased out.

The bill that was forwarded along with the Administration's message also proposed repeal of the college construction grant and loan programs. Only a few existing higher education programs, such as assistance to developing institutions, were to be continued.

The Reaction

Congressional reaction to the first message on education reform was mixed. Democrats hit the President's broad suggestion that commitment of substantial new federal funds to compensatory education and other school programs should await the results of research showing what works best. But the specific proposal of a new agency, the National Institute of Education, to revitalize and coordinate education research attracted some interest and eventually bipartisan sponsorship in both the House and Senate.

The fallout from the higher education message was another story. The Administration's bill was roundly denounced on almost all sides in Congress. The chief complaint, particularly from Democrats, was that it would cut out federal assistance to hard-pressed middle-income families. And there was objection to the heavy emphasis on loans for both middle and low-income groups; this would force too many students to "mortgage their futures" to finance an education.

The clash between the Administration and Congress on these issues was tinged with irony. The *Washington Post* reported an apparent role reversal:

Liberal Democrats attacked the Nixon Administration's higher education proposals at a House hearing yesterday, claiming they short-changed the middle class 'silent majority.' These Democrats usually concentrate on the needs of the Nation's poor.[13]

There was, moreover, an element of distrust on the part of many Democrats; they were suspicious that the Administration's concern for low-income students was largely rhetoric to conceal a program designed to hold down the long-run federal budgetary commitment to student aid.

There was further irony in the argument that developed over where basic student aid policy decisions should be made. Some Congressional critics charged the Administration plan would lodge too much power with the Secretary of HEW, leaving no flexibility for student aid administrators at the campus level. The Nixon Administration had loudly promised to "reverse the flow of power to Washington," and its revenue sharing proposals were consistent with this theme. But in the area of student assistance the approach seemed to be turned on its head.

Other questioning of the Administration's student aid plan came down to whether the plan was, in fact, adequately designed to achieve its objective of equalizing opportunity. For one thing, the program would be restricted to full-time undergraduates in nonprofit institutions; it did not cover part-time students or students in proprietary institutions. Yet these restrictions, which seem to have been prompted by the Administration's concern to keep projected budget costs down, ran counter to the spirit of the President's message in which he called for an inclusive definition of postsecondary education. Meanwhile, congressional opinion increasingly favored a broadening of eligibility for all federal student aid to include both part-time and proprietary school students.

Critics were also concerned that the Administration plan might skew the enrollment of low-income students toward two-year public schools, thus reinforcing stratification of higher education, with poor students concentrated in the low-cost public sector and wealthier students attending more expensive state universities and private institutions. The $1400 package would be approximately enough to finance attendance at a local community college. Many low-income students would therefore find it easier to gain access to postsecondary education, but students from poor families who wished to attend high-cost institutions might be adversely affected. In essence, the Administration's plan would spread a somewhat larger amount of total federal aid among a much larger universe of low-income students than under previous programs.

Most of the higher education associations and the AFL-CIO joined the chorus of opposition to the Administration's student aid proposals. They charged the Administration with abandoning the middle class as well as excessive reliance on loans. The overall Administration approach, particularly the loan scheme, which provided for long-term repayment, touched off fears among some college and university representatives that the Administration was bent on full-cost pricing of higher education.

Perhaps the major disappointment for the associations was the failure of the Administration to propose institutional aid. They also objected to ending the principal programs of the Higher Education Facilities Act.

The Foundation proposal got a chilly reception, partly because its mission seemed vague: Was it primarily to bail out financially troubled national universities? Why help only them? What will promoting "excellence," "innovation," and "reform" mean in practice? And how would the Foundation relate to the National Institute of Education? The functions of the two proposed agencies seemed partially to overlap. While one would finance and conduct research and the other would make project grants, both would be concerned with the discovery of experimental approaches to learning; and while the Foundation would focus exclusively on higher education, the Institute could range over all levels of education, not just elementary and secondary. Yet the relationship between the two agencies, and why one could be placed in HEW and the other on its own outside HEW, were not spelled out to the satisfaction of congressional critics.

The major charge against the Foundation was that it was being used by the Administration as a garbage can for old programs. Any potential enthusiasm among the associations or on Capitol Hill for the concept of a higher education foundation was dampened by the accompanying proposal to abandon several existing types of support. The clienteles of these programs as well as their congressional sponsors and guardians naturally took a dim view of their demise and inclusion in the laundry list of possible objectives for the Foundation. And the garbage-can approach contributed further to a sense of ambiguity about the Foundation's role: Was it to have ongoing program responsibilities, or would it have complete flexibility to support promising endeavors through individual grants? The Foundation seemed to be a miscellaneous affair.

Also, the vague suggestion by Administration spokesmen that the Foundation was somehow a substitute for general institutional aid—or that the Foundation, once established, would be the appropriate agency to study the pros and cons of such support—was, if anything, a source of irritation to the higher education groups. They felt, rightly so, that they were being put off. The Administion simply did not believe in general aid to institutions.

The career education proposal won support from the American Association of Junior Colleges, but amidst the general clamor against the rest of the Administration's bill, it attracted relatively little notice. Too, the career education proposal suffered from ambiguous drafting; it was not completely clear how the program would operate.

The Reasons

Several factors were working against a favorable reception for the Administration's program in higher education. First, parts of it had in fact been put together in some haste and were more abstract and conceptual than pragmatic. Aspects of the student aid plan were complicated and difficult to explain. Secretary Finch and others who presented the program to Congress did not have an easy time trying to illuminate the details of just what the Administration intended in some areas.

Second, the program had been developed in-house, with minimum sensitivity to political realities. It was produced in "cavalier fashion," one HEW official concedes. "The Administration just did it. There was no consultation with members of Congress or anyone on the outside." Another Administration aide recalls:

There was very little political calculation that went into our policy making. . . . Thus there were tactical mistakes in the bill—for example, putting some of the categorical things into the Foundation. We should have been able to anticipate that kind of red flag. . . .

The program emanated from parts of the executive branch that tend to be insulated from the normal type of interest group and congressional pressures that play on the Office of Education. The latter had relatively little part in the process. And at the HEW level, poor relations between the legislative office and the planning office minimized the contributions of the former, which normally provides political and congressional readings as input to policy planning.

Third, once the Administration's program had been presented, there was a problem of negative feedback from the Administration's own ranks, especially veteran staff in the Office of Education who disagreed privately with aspects of the program. Through their regular lines of communication with Congress, they helped to undercut the Administration's position.

Another conflicting voice within the ranks came from Spiro Agnew. At about the time the Administration was advancing its recommendations to aid disadvantaged college students, the Vice President was making inflammatory statements about the evils of open admissions and special treatment for minorities in higher education. He warned that the "cluttering of our universities. . . is a major cause of campus. . .unrest."[14] The Administration seemed to be talking out of both sides of its mouth on the issue of equal opportunity for higher education.

Another reason that the Nixon higher education program was not warmly received was simply that others had different mind-sets on the subject. The associations in particular were fixated on maintaining existing federal programs and inaugurating federal institutional aid. They were not apt to embrace the kind of new directions being offered by the Administration.

Revisions Under Secretary Richardson

Congress did not act on higher education legislation in 1970, and the Administration resubmitted its proposals in early 1971.

In the interim the locus of education policy leadership within the Administration shifted entirely to HEW. The formulation of the President's 1970 messages had been a joint endeavor, shared basically between the White House and HEW. But Moynihan departed in late 1970, and there was no one left in the White House to sustain his creative interest in education policy.[f] Meanwhile Elliot Richardson replaced a battle-weary Robert Finch as Secretary of HEW and Sidney Marland succeeded James Allen as Commissioner of Education, Allen having been unceremoniously forced out by the White House for his public criticism of the Cambodian invasion.

A man for all seasons, Richardson directed his sophisticated and probing intelligence to the problems of a sprawling, "unmanageable" department. Unlike Finch, he took personal command of policy development within HEW. Richardson was interested in everything and thrived on hard analysis and good debate,

---

[f]Moynihan's departure coincided with the apparent general shift of power within the White House during 1970-1971, favoring a more tightly held staff operation of John Ehrlichman and H.R. Haldeman. The atmosphere became less receptive to creative policy thinking. One former Administration official has stated bluntly, "Only Moynihan was interested in ideas. When he left, it became a philistine environment. . . . Ideas just kind of stopped at the White House staff." Quoted in Cannon.

according to admiring associates. He wanted to hear ideas and alternatives from both staff and line agency personnel and to make basic decisions himself after weighing all available viewpoints. He had a special interest in education policy because of his earlier role in creating the National Defense Education Act while Assistant Secretary of HEW in the Eisenhower Administration.

A New Dialogue

Richardson's style also called for openness and easier interchange with Congress and with outside groups. "As I understand it," he is said to have remarked to staff, "the President's higher education message in 1970 was prepared with more secrecy than the SALT talks. That is not the way to do it." His dictum was to consult with everybody.

Heretofore there had been minimal communication between the Administration and the higher education associations. The associations' main contact with the Administration was through Peter Muirhead, an "old pro" in the Office of Education who was intimately associated with the development of federal higher education programs since the late 1950s. Muirhead was one key official of the agency who became a vigorous advocate of the Administration's new program in higher education and yet maintained a rapport with the higher education lobby. "For a long time," an HEW aide says, "Peter Muirhead was the one thin line of credibility between the Administration and the associations."

Under Richardson and Commissioner Marland, a wider dialogue began to develop. New avenues of communication opened up, especially toward the end of 1970 when HEW officials started meeting on a regular monthly basis with a delegation of prominent college and university presidents. The discussions were sparked by a speech Moynihan delivered at the American Council on Education's annual meeting in which he charged the higher education establishment with a lack of effective leadership and failure to present its case to the executive branch. Responding to the challenge, leaders of the American Council immediately offered to meet with Administration officials. The effort to repair communication ensued.

The meetings had no set agenda and resulted in no specific commitments by the Administration; their purpose was simply to air major issues. Richardson attended regularly, recognizing the symbolic importance, if nothing else, of consulting with leaders of the higher education community.

Richardson and Marland also sought more systematic contacts with Congressional committee leaders on both sides of the aisle. They hoped to alter the Administration's image of impermeability stemming from the development and presentation of the first Nixon message on higher education.

Refinement and Minor Concessions

The more solicitous attitude toward Congress and the somewhat improved relations with the associations, however, did not mean the Administration would necessarily change course on higher education. In fact, the basic positions advanced in 1970 were sustained when the President delivered his second higher education message to Congress on February 22, 1971. The policy lines had already been set; changes made in the second round under Richardson were primarily in the nature of refinement, with a few conciliatory gestures toward the higher education groups and congressional opinion.

Richardson supported the proposed reorientation of federal student aid, targeting funds by income level. Some conservative voices within the Administration called for abandoning the grant-work-loan approach and shifting to a loans-only policy as a way to save on the budget, but the earlier position held. The only significant modification in the student aid package was an expanded loan provision to help low-income students seeking to attend more expensive institutions. This was one adjustment the Administration made in response to outside views. The Administration remained firm, however, in not expanding eligibility for subsidized aid to middle-income students.

Also in response to association and congressional concerns, the Administration backed off its 1970 proposal to terminate the authorization for college construction grants and direct loans, although it still had no intention of seeking actual appropriations for these programs.

The proposed career education/community college program was scuttled in 1971. Former Secretary Finch's rhetoric and genuine concern in this area had not been matched with sound, well-formulated proposals. The Office of Education, which was assigned the task, seemed to lack the required interest and capability. The Office of Management and Budget, always eager to lop off budgetary commitments, considered the 1970 proposals sloppy and insisted they be dropped.

Another Run at the Foundation

The principal creative contribution of Secretary Richardson and his staff in putting together the 1971 higher education message (in contrast to 1970, it was drafted entirely in HEW and only slightly edited by the White House) was a substantial recasting of the Foundation proposal. Moynihan's inspiration the first time around, the Foundation was recaptured and reconceived by HEW in 1971. The National Science Foundation model was dropped. Instead of a free-standing agency, the Foundation was now to be a part of HEW, with a Board and Director reporting through the Commissioner of Education to the Secretary. And all of the extraneous purposes that had been attached to it were stripped away. The ongoing higher education programs that were to have been absorbed by the new agency would remain in the Office of Education; the "centers of excellence" theme was set aside; and the problems of predominantly Black institutions were addressed separately in the President's message, primarily through increased funding of the Developing Institutions program. The Foundation's central mission would be to foster experimentation and reform throughout postsecondary education. It would seek new patterns of attendance to break the education "lockstep" and new approaches to diversify institutional offerings.

The revised mandate of the Foundation, and much of the language and tone of the President's message citing the need for change in higher education, were drawn directly from the Newman report. The Newman task force was not part of a planned strategy of policy development within the Administration, having originated in a somewhat offhand manner under Secretary Finch. But timing and circumstances gave it a significance and impact exceeding that of many government commissions of a more traditional character. Finch and Lew Butler had asked a fellow Californian, Frank Newman of Stanford, to organize a small task force—not necessarily of top names in higher education but people both in and out of government who had ideas—and to come back with a report. The group worked with no fanfare or formal status and only a small private foundation grant, but it had an open field to say what it wanted. When its report, a wide-ranging critique of the structure of higher learning in the United States, was ready in the late summer of 1970, Finch was gone and the new Secretary had no particular stake in what the task force had produced. Yet Richardson read the report carefully and was both intrigued by the unconventional, candid style and impressed by the case for fundamental reform of higher education.

The linkage between the Newman report and the Foundation concept was a natural. Richardson was advised that the Foundation proposal as originally conceived was going nowhere in Congress and would be shot down again if it were resubmitted in the same form. The Secretary gave his go-ahead for the reformulation, with clearcut emphasis on the theme of innovation and reform.

Thus the Foundation, already a part of the Administration's program, became the vehicle for the ideas of the Newman report, which Richardson found exciting. In a sense, Richardson had gained a little running room. Squeezed on one side by the White House, which at this stage had no interest in any new initiatives in education (or most other domestic areas), and on the other by institutional aid advocates in the higher education community, he was in a bind.[g] Now he had something positive to champion. The Newman report was formally released in March, 1971, with a laudatory foreword by the Secretary. It received wide and favorable press coverage, though it was immediately attacked by the major higher education associations as a "distorted and misleading" description of the state of higher learning.[15]

To give the Foundation proposal more prominence, the Administration used a new strategy in introducing its 1971 higher education program. Instead of a single omnibus measure, the Administration offered two bills—the first dealing with student aid reform and reauthorization of certain existing higher

---

[g]Despite Richardson's confident relationship with President Nixon during this period, he had increasing difficulty getting past the "White House Guard" on many issues.

education programs, and the second advancing the National Foundation for Higher Education.

Congressional reaction to the President's 1971 message and the two Administration bills, however, was barely an improvement over the previous year. The Foundation generated somewhat more interest but hardly wild enthusiasm. It still seemed ill-defined to some Members of Congress. The Administration had contracted with the Rand Corporation for an intensive planning study as back-up for the National Institute of Education proposal but had undertaken no such effort in relation to the Foundation proposal. For the latter Congress had only to go on the relevant passages in the President's message and the bill itself. Some questioned this seeming imbalance of preparation.[h]

In the academic community the Foundation proposal picked up support here and there but few strong advocateṣ. There was still an element of distrust about the Administration's intentions. To a few college leaders, the Foundation seemed to raise the spectre of federal control of higher education (ironically since Moynihan's original concept was to provide a support mechanism that would avert this danger). To many it seemed perhaps a good idea but not something to get terribly excited about. The general "nonresponse" of higher educators baffled and annoyed the Foundation's advocates within the Administration. They expected a more positive reaction particularly because the Administration had backed off its previous gambit of dumping old programs into the Foundation. In any event, they felt the President was offering a sincere idea that at least deserved the higher education community's thoughtful consideration, which they felt it was not getting.

The litany of criticism leveled at the rest of the Administration program was much the same as in 1970: neglect of the needs of middle-income students; termination of the direct federal loan program under NDEA, which had a proven record of aiding students from all income classes; too much reliance on loans (especially private market loans) in the overall student aid approach; ending certain existing programs; and no proposed program designed to relieve the financial distress of higher education institutions.

For "One Dupont Circle"—home of most of the higher education associations and shorthand for the higher education lobby—the continued lack of a recommendation for institutional aid was again a major disappointment. Officially, the issue was "under study" in HEW. But at most levels of the Department, not to mention the White House and OMB, there was still—in early 1971— very little disposition to accommodate the constituency pressures for this form of aid.[i] Secretary Richardson himself was not persuaded. He had listened patiently

---

[h]The feeling in HEW was that the Newman Report and other current studies on higher education reform provided adequate background for planning purposes in the case of the foundation.

[i]At a later date the Administration reconsidered and modified its opposition to institutional aid. See Chapter 6.

as the delegation of higher education leaders repeatedly pressed their case for across-the-board assistance in their monthly meetings with the Secretary. But Richardson remained skeptical, and his reservations were undoubtedly reinforced by the Newman report, which challenged the "conventional wisdom" that simply more money was the answer to higher education's problems.

* * * * * * * * * *

With most of the Administration's legislative initiatives in higher education spurned, ignored or taken only half seriously for the second year in a row, and a deadline for legislative action drawing nearer, it seemed that Congress would be left largely to its own devices.

This was something of a switch. It would, for sure, be a far cry from 1965 when the Elementary and Secondary and Higher Education Acts breezed through Congress, the delicate consensus building among constituent groups having already been accomplished by the executive branch. The congressional committee leaders in that year were glad to have the White House orchestrate compromise on the touchy issues that had repeatedly destroyed education bills.[j] This time around, Congress would have no such reprieve. The context, of course, had changed drastically. The executive was controlled by the opposite party and an adversary relationship had clearly taken hold in the area of education policy. The Nixon Administration had built a consensus internally but not externally on its higher education program. It had staked out a position for Congress to consider, it had raised questions and planted a few ideas, but hardly succeeded in setting the legislative agenda. This time Congress would have to sort out the issues (indeed, decide what the issues were) and generate a bill.

Notes

1. David E. Rosenbaum, "Educators Seek General U.S. Aid," *New York Times*, November 13, 1968, p. 30.

2. James L. Sundquist, *Politics and Policy: The Eisenhower, Kennedy and Johnson Years*, The Brookings Institution, Washington, D.C., 1968, p. 492.

3. From a background interview conducted by the authors. Subsequent quotations drawn from such interviews and from the authors' own experience are not referenced through the remainder of the book.

4. Chester E. Finn, Jr., "The National Foundation for Higher Education: Death of an Idea," *Change*, Volume 4, March, 1972, p. 23.

[j]See Eugene Eidenberg and Roy D. Morey, *An Act of Congress*, W.W. Norton, New York, 1969.

5. The discussion of Moynihan's views on the federal role in higher education relies on Finn, "Death of an Idea," as well as interviews conducted by the authors.

6. *Priorities in Higher Education, The Report of the President's Task Force on Higher Education*, August, 1970.

7. Daniel P. Moynihan, *The Politics of a Guaranteed Income: The Nixon Administration and the Family Assistance Plan*, Random House, New York, 1973, p. 155.

8. *Report of President-Elect Nixon's Task Force on Education*, 1969. The Report was never officially released by the White House, but copies circulated, and it was printed in the *Congressional Record* on March 12, 1969. Alan Pifer, President of the Carnegie Corporation, chaired the Task Force.

9. Moynihan, p. 156.

10. *Weekly Compilation of Presidential Documents*, March 9, 1970, p. 304.

11. Ibid., March 23, 1970, p. 381.

12. Ibid., p. 382.

13. Eric Wentworth, "Nixon Education Proposals Scored," *The Washington Post*, April 16, 1970, p. A-2.

14. Quoted in Robert W. Hartman and Alice M. Rivlin, "Higher Education: An Analysis of the Nixon Proposals," The Brookings Institution, April 23, 1970.

15. "Critique of the Newman Report," Washington Higher Education Secretariat, One Dupont Circle, Washington, D.C., April 8, 1971.

5

The Senate: Gentlemanly Agreement

The process of generating a higher education bill in Congress in the absence of a unifying Administration initiative presents a study in contrasts, for the House and Senate, constitutionally coequal, are very different in customs, procedures, style and tone. The two chambers charted separate courses and landed quite some distance apart. That two deliberative bodies, in fact, approached the same task in such contrasting fashion and produced such disparate results is a curiosity in itself. Only more remarkable is that they were able to blend their massive, complex and conflicting versions of a higher education bill into a measure that became law.

The Senate story comes first because the Senate was the first to vote a bill. Many observers had expected the reverse: that the House would act initially, the Senate following (possibly deferring to see what came over from the other chamber). The Member of Congress most widely identified with education, after all, was Edith Green. She was knowledgeable, experienced, and vocal on the subject, and her specialty was higher education on which she typically displayed an impressive, unmatched command of the legislation. A former educator herself, frequent speaker at education association meetings, and recipient of numerous honorary degrees from colleges and universities, she was respected and championed in most quarters of the academic community.

Claiborne Pell, on the other hand, was relatively unknown among educators and did not enjoy a reputation as a major power in the Senate. Yet his quiet, inconspicuous manner could be deceptive as he was at the same time capable of tenacity and single-mindedness once he had set about to accomplish a legislative end. So while press coverage and the attention of the educational world tended to focus on the efforts of the veteran legislator from Oregon and the lively politics of the House Committee, the second-term Senator from Rhode Island meanwhile unobtrusively steered to Senate passage "the most sweeping aid-to-education bill ever considered by Congress," leaving the House in the position of having to catch up.[1]

The Senate Subcommittee on Education

"Power is nowhere concentrated; it is rather deliberately and of set policy scattered amongst many small chiefs," Woodrow Wilson wrote of Congress.[2] Today, as in Wilson's time, congressional committees serve as "little legislatures."

83

Here is where most of the crucial decisions on most bills before Congress are actually made. The committees of Congress are "where the work is done."

Perhaps one should say the *subcommittees* of Congress. Reliance on sub-committees dates from the mid-nineteenth century and has grown most rapidly since the Legislative Reorganization Act of 1946. One of the purposes of that measure was to stem the fragmentation of the committee structure. The feeling then was that there were too many committees to deal sensibly with legislation, so the number was reduced from 33 to 15 in the Senate and from 48 to 19 in the House. But the trend toward specialization continued unabated. In the aftermath of the 1946 reorganization, subcommittees flourished, increasing from a total for the two houses of 180 in 1945 to more than 258 in 1968.[3] The proliferation of issues facing Congress at midcentury doomed hopes of greatly simplifying the structure. Congress has adapted to a complex world by dividing and subdividing its work among many small decision-making units.

The use and role of subcommittees vary depending on tradition, the leadership style of the full committee chairman, and the scope and character of the committee's task. Power has been tightly held by the full chairman in some committees; Senate Finance and House Rules (and until the 94th Congress, House Ways and Means) have no subcommittees and conduct all business in full session. In others the parceling out of the committee's jurisdiction and the sharing of power have been institutionalized. The Senate Labor and Public Welfare and House Education and Labor Committees fall into this category. Here judgments made in subcommittee are usually sustained by the full committee and subsequently on the floor. Deference to the subcommittee and its chairman tends to be the norm, particularly in the Senate, though actual experience rests on such factors as the working relationship of the full committee and subcommittee chairmen, the standing of the subcommittee leader among his colleagues, and the nature of the legislation at hand. The less controversial the subcommittee's jurisdiction, the more likely it is to enjoy autonomy, and the more likely its recommendations are to carry through the full committee.

The Senate Subcommittee on Education in the late 1960s is an example. This panel had seen its share of controversy, but the era of partisan, ideological divisions over the principle of federal aid to education was in the past, and, in fact, these divisions never wracked the Senate as they did the House. The Senate Subcommittee was a fairly harmonious, bipartisan sanctuary where broadly shared values about the importance of education tended to overshadow real or potential differences on the specifics of legislation. Ease of accommodation had become a tradition in the Subcommittee, and its chairman was allowed substantially free reign within the full committee.

While strongly favoring federal support of education, recent chairmen of the full Labor and Public Welfare Committee were inclined to leave the education panel largely to itself, their principal legislative interests residing elsewhere. Senator Lister Hill (D-Alabama), who led the Committee for more than a decade, was chiefly identified with health legislation and himself headed the Health Subcommittee; he fully entrusted the education portfolio to Wayne Morse. Hill's successor in 1969, Ralph Yarborough (D-Texas), likewise left education legislation to the respective subcommittee, now headed by Senator Pell. The same pattern continued under Harrison Williams (D-New Jersey), who took over the Committee after Yarborough's defeat in 1970 and whose major concerns were in the labor and health fields.

The Chairman

The prerogative and the burden of bringing out education bills, taking them through committee and to the floor of the Senate thus rested largely with the chairman of the Subcommittee. One Senator held considerable power in shaping the Senate approach to education policy.

But the hallmark of the Subcommittee's leadership was fairness. Senator Morse had established the custom. As much as the relatively noncontroversial character of the Subcommittee's work, it was Morse's habit of according respect and equal participation to minority and majority alike that sustained general harmony on the panel. The late Senator's public reputation—combative, unyielding, caustic—hardly characterized his mild manner within the special province of the Senate Education Subcommittee. Here he was admired and warmly regarded for his fair dealing. Morse had been through the many years when aid-to-education bills died. He was oriented toward compromise and sought to fashion measures that could survive. There developed a laissez-faire spirit of letting every member have a part of the action, of blending different viewpoints and priorities into bipartisan bills. Claiborne Pell was to carry forward in much the same style.

The tone of the Senate panel contrasted sharply with the turbulence of its House counterpart. Whatever disagreements they may have had, the Senate education policy-makers were usually able to find common ground and avoid the kind of political slugfests often witnessed among their House colleagues on the Education and Labor Committee.

Senator Pell took over the education panel in 1969 based on seniority in the full Committee. He had not previously served on the Subcommittee, but he had a long-standing commitment to legislation aimed at broadening educational opportunity. The Senator was especially interested in making some measure of postsecondary education or training "a matter of right." As far back as 1969, he had introduced a bill to give every student in the country a flat $1000 grant through the first two years of college.

As chairman of the relevant subcommittee, he would have the chance to develop and press his ideas further. He was committed, if not to the specific proposal embodied in his earlier bill, to the general notion of a federal entitlement for the individual student. In the Senator's view, the patchwork of existing federal higher education programs fell short and would continue to fall short of guaranteeing opportunity; something more direct, basic and simple was required. He would not seek to dismantle existing programs, but he did want to move beyond the status quo.

Pell's expansive, liberal values were in line with those of his predecessor. Both Pell and Morse were liberal Democrats who consistently favored extending the federal commitment to meet social welfare objectives. Senator Morse himself was intrigued by the concept of entitling every student to a grant, and he was not necessarily satisfied with the outcome of the Higher Education Amendments of 1968, which had only slightly expanded and modified federal policy toward higher education. Before his defeat and departure at the end of the 90th Congress, he was looking toward 1971 as the time for a landmark bill in higher education.

So, too, Pell's instinct was to envision significant legislation on the horizon, perhaps the more so because his role as chairman represented a new opportunity for leadership. After eight years in the Senate, Pell had landed his first major subcommittee. He had previously headed the relatively inconsequential Railroad Retirement Subcommittee.[a] Now he was moving into an area of broad public interest, an area in which he had deeply felt ideals if not extensive prior experience or technical expertise.

Pell's record and role in the Senate reflected a low profile. He never had a taste for aggressive self-promotion, the staple of politics. By the norms of the Senate, indeed, he was self-effacing. Moreover, he had a penchant for esoteric and relatively obscure issues like metric conversion and banning nuclear weapons on the seabeds.

"Pell isn't at all a typical politician," observed a Rhode Island journalist. "Basically he thinks like a diplomat."[4] This was a matter of temperament, and perhaps a reflection of the Senator's elevated social background and seven years in the Foreign Service. He went about his Senate work with diligence and energy but was little given to attracting public attention. "I go up and down the halls trying to explain my ideas to others," the Senator said. "I've done most of my work quietly . . . I don't think my record is known."[5]

In his 1966 reelection campaign, Pell could point to a few fairly respectable achievements, if no real milestones, for a first-term Senator. He had been a major sponsor of the High Speed Rail Transportation Act of 1965 to bring improved passenger service to the Northeast corridor, and he had helped enact legislation to encourage education and research in the marine sciences. The Senator could also claim a role in creating the National Foundation for the Arts and Humanities.

---

[a]Senator Pell had also previously chaired a special subcommittee on the arts and humanities. In 1969, in addition to the education panel, he came into the chairmanship of the subcommittee on Oceans and Environment of the Foreign Relations Committee.

Pell had little difficulty winning his 1966 race, but 1972 might be a different story. He needed to counter his opponents' claim that all he was interested in was "trains and seaweed."[6] It would not hurt to have a major legislative accomplishment under his belt as Chairman of the Subcommittee on Education.

The Members

The lineup on Pell's Subcommittee in 1971, during the formulation of the Senate higher education bill, was as follows:

Subcommittee on Education

Democrats	Republicans
Claiborne Pell (R.I.), Chairman	Winston Prouty (Vt.)
Jennings Randolph (W. Va.)	Jacob Javits (N.Y.)
Harrison Williams (N.J.)	Peter Dominick (Colo.)
Edward M. Kennedy (Mass.)	Richard S. Schweiker (Pa.)
Walter Mondale (Minn.)	J. Glenn Beall, Jr. (Md.)
Thomas J. Eagleton (Mo.)	
Alan Cranston (Calif.)	

On the majority side, Pell had a powerful group of colleagues backing him up: Randolph, a member of the Senate's inner club who by seniority could have headed the full Labor and Public Welfare Committee but chose instead to continue as chairman of Public Works; Williams, the Chairman of Labor and Public Welfare; Kennedy and Mondale, both potential presidential candidates; Eagleton and Cranston, junior but aggressive and respected members of the Senate.

All were liberal Democrats, and all were committed to a broad federal role in the support of education. The senior members had each played a part in shaping the aid-to-education legislation of the previous decade, and they wanted to preserve and build on this legacy. Some had specific ideas (and bills) on what should be done next in higher education, but there were no entrenched positions. All certainly shared Pell's fundamental concern that the job of equalizing educational opportunity was far from complete. There was a general concern as well about the plight of private colleges and the need to preserve a diverse higher education system.

Philosophically, no great gulf separated Republicans and Democrats on the panel. Prouty, Javits and Dominick were longstanding Subcommittee members with a record of constructive contribution. Javits, liberal Republican, was ranking minority member on the full Labor and Public Welfare Committee and often a pivotal, mediating influence within the Committee. Prouty and Dominick were considerably more conservative on issues of social welfare and federal involvement, yet had something of a soft spot for education programs. Schweiker, a liberal, and Beall, a low-key conservative, were relative newcomers to the Subcommittee. As a group, the Republicans might be somewhat less receptive to new programs and new spending; on the other hand, Javits could be as expansive and creative as the Democrats in spinning off legislative proposals. No one on the minority side felt obliged to "carry water" for the Administration if he disagreed with the Administration's recommendations, and none was apt simply to obstruct.

Openness and flexibility could be expected on both sides. The senior members of the Subcommittee were used to dealing with one another; they had teamed up many times in the past to expedite bills and forge compromises. Here in microcosm was the solid, club-like character of the Senate.

Senate members by and large are not looking for issues. They have enough to worry about. It is not unusual for a member to serve on fifteen or more subcommittees of four or five different committees. Most find it physically impossible to stay fully abreast on all fronts. The late Senator Dirksen candidly admitted: "I would not dare say to the people of Illinois that I knew all about all things that go on. . .To do so I would really need roller skates to get from one subcommittee to another."[7] On a given morning, a Senator may have three or four subcommittee hearings or executive sessions going on at the same time.

In an area like education, where philosophical differences are muted to begin with, the members are not likely to get bogged down unnecessarily. The tendency is to let the subcommittee chairman and his staff carry the ball for the most part through the hearings and early stages of a bill's development; then, as the "mark-up" stage approaches, to strive for bipartisanship in putting the pieces together—all in fairly relaxed fashion.

No member, certainly, would try to upstage Senator Pell; it was his Subcommittee, and the chairman's prerogatives are respected. At the same time, each member knew that his interests would be considered and protected by the chairman.

The Role of Staff

Staff influence is a dimension of power in the Senate that is subtle and complex. One political scientist has written:

Like the President of the United States on an appropriately smaller scale, a Senator is an institution. He is what he is plus what he can add to himself by the considerable array of brains and skills the law allows him to buy. . .[F]irst-rate professionals do more than carry out assignments. In the offices of individual Senators they learn to think like the boss; they determine to some degree who sees him and what importunities reach him. In the committee rooms they identify the problems and provide the facts and questions. The product of the Senate is to some unmeasured and perhaps immeasurable degree their product. Their influence probably would be very easy to overstate, but it does exist.[8]

In both the House and Senate, professional staff members, in varying degrees and in different ways, clearly share in the exercise of power. Yet the constraints on staff influence are equally impressive. Whether in the personal office of a Member or on a committee, a staffer always knows that he serves at the will and in the interest of his principal; that is the most important reality of congressional staff work. The staff member's status as hired help is never forgotten.

It is frequently observed that the Senate is more staff-oriented than the House; that members of the Senate, because they have so many more concerns and are spread so thin, are especially dependent on staff assistance. While both houses depend on—indeed could not function without—professional staff, there is clearly a difference in the nature of staff operations in the two bodies. Members of the House tend to have a tighter grip on the specifics of legislation. They are often more experienced and expert in their legislative assignments because they serve on fewer committees than do Senators and, on the average, have served longer on those committees. House staff, as a result, have less latitude and tend to be more cautious. Generally, their principals are keeping closer tabs on the movement of bills.

By contrast, a Senator's attitude is often: "Don't bother me with the details of legislation on any one committee unless absolutely necessary." A Senate staffer usually has a considerably longer leash. He operates in the knowledge of his Senator's general political posture and views on the issues, receives periodic cues and feedback from the Senator, and over time may internalize many of the Senator's habits of mind. But Senate staff, more often than their House counterparts, must act on the basis of a broad mandate rather than explicit instructions from their principals. While House members are frequently drawn into the "nitty-gritty" of issues, the Senator has fewer problems presented to him; his staff is conditioned to handle as many as possible of the concrete and specific questions that arise.

In their committee work, as a means of economizing time, it is not unusual for Senators to deal with broad concepts rather than exact legislative phrasing. The latter is filled in and worked out by the staff after the Senators have made the basic decisions and provided the necessary guidance. A good part of what would be accomplished during mark-up sessions by members of a House panel is often handled at the staff level in the Senate.

Such a pattern was well established in the Senate Subcommittee on Education and was perhaps particularly suited to the style of its new chairman, Senator Pell. Pell considered himself an "idea man"—envisioning and formulating new directions for legislation—rather than a legislative craftsman.[9] Thus Pell might tend to be especially dependent on staff. But his mode of operation was not necessarily out of the ordinary in the Senate. The propensity to think broadly and conceptually, leaving the precision work to lesser beings, is inherent in the nature and self-image of the Senate as an institution.

The pattern does leave considerable room for staff creativity, and in the case of the Senate Education Subcommittee something of an identifiable tradition and style of legislative draftsmanship had developed under Senator Morse and would continue under Senator Pell.[b] The staff sought to build a consistent logic into the legislation, to craft education bills that both held together philosophically and advanced certain long-term objectives. The latter included expansion of the total federal commitment to the support of education and the assertion of maximum congressional control over education policy while minimizing administrative discretion lodged with the executive branch. The evolution of the statutes was seen as analogous to a chess match, with the interrelationship of the pieces and long-run strategic factors always being considered.

But it is difficult to say where the guidance and thinking of the Senators leave off and staff creativity and advocacy begin. Again, the importance of staff in shaping legislative outcomes should not be overstated. In both House and Senate, staff are always accountable. Senate staff may be somewhat more freewheeling than their opposite numbers in the House, but they too can be pulled up short if they go out of bounds. Everything decided at the staff level is subject, or at least potentially subject, to final ratification by the members.

Bills and Hearings

The Senate higher education legislation was written and passed over the spring and summer of 1971, but the preliminaries took place during the prior Congress of 1969-1970.

Senator Pell immediately reintroduced his previous scholarships bill. He wanted to extend the principle of universality beyond the secondary level of education, and he believed in a straightforward approach. But Pell recognized that his scheme probably would not fly. To endow every student in the country with $1000 annually for two years would run into many billions of federal dollars. The price tag was unrealistic.

Over the winter of 1969, the Senator began to muse about alternatives. He was on vacation in the Alps, and as he was skiing down a mountain, the

---

[b]The Senate Subcommittee on Education was unusual in having its own legislative draftsman rather than relying on the Office of Legislative Counsel, which serves the committees and individual members. Wayne Morse's chief subcommittee staff aide, Charles Lee, decided that creative drafting could be done only by a draftsman immersed in the subject. He recruited Richard Smith, an Office of Education attorney, to draft the Subcommittee's bills. When Morse was defeated in 1968, Lee left the staff, but Smith remained as Associate Counsel. Stephen Wexler, a labor attorney from Rhode Island who had been serving on Senator Pell's staff, became Counsel to the Subcommittee.

solution occurred to him: introduce a need factor by entitling the student to a set amount of funds *minus* the amount of federal income tax paid by the parents. The mechanism had the virtue of simplicity; it would be easy to administer, and a student could readily compute in advance how much he might receive. And it would direct the funds to the neediest students because, Pell reasoned, income taxes paid were roughly related to a family's financial well-being. Pell sketched his ideas on a placemat that he carried home with him to Washington and gave to his subcommittee staff.

S. 1969

The staff proceeded to draw up a bill, fleshing out the concepts Pell had jotted down. The new income tax-related program would be titled "Basic Educational Opportunity Grants" and would be available for all four undergraduate years, with an annual maximum grant per student of $1200. The existing Educational Opportunity Grants program administered through the colleges would continue but would be designated Supplemental Educational Opportunity Grants. The bill would also provide cost-of-instruction allowances to the institution for each of their students receiving federal grant assistance.

In introducing his new bill, S. 1969, the Senator called attention to the growing debate on how to finance postsecondary education and indicated he had serious misgivings about some of the approaches being recommended. Tax credits, a massive loan program for all students, general aid to institutions—all these solutions seemed inadequate to the task of equalizing educational opportunity. But he was favorably impressed by the recent Carnegie Commission and Rivlin reports.[10] The bill's emphasis on direct student aid was consistent with the central theme of both Carnegie and Rivlin, though the income tax mechanism for determining eligibility was Pell's idea.

The proposed cost-of-instruction allowance to institutions was also in line with these reports, which had advanced the concept of channeling aid to colleges and universities in such a way as to give them an incentive to admit and educate financially disadvantaged students. Pell, however, had his own formula for determining the amount of the cost-of-instruction allowance: It could not exceed $1,000, less the tuition charged by the institution. Pell wanted to encourage institutions to accept disadvantaged students, but he did not want to subsidize high-priced schools or encourage low-priced schools to raise their tuition.

The Mondale Bill

Other members of the Education Subcommittee also dropped bills in the hopper early in the 91st Congress. Senator Mondale had just joined the panel and was eager to put forward proposals that would reflect the latest and best thinking on federal higher education policy. Like Pell, he gravitated toward the Carnegie and Rivlin recommendations. The Senator and his staff consulted the Rivlin report especially and sought help in drafting a bill from Alice Rivlin and others who worked on that study.

Though their bills differed on specifics, Pell and Mondale had independently come to essentially the same position on the importance of direct student aid. Making grants available "on a national basis, regardless of where a student lives or where he wants to attend college," Senator Mondale said in outlining his bill, "is the single most effective way to remove the financial obstacle to college attendance by needy and lower-middle-income students."[11]

There was an additional element in Mondale's philosophy, however. He wanted to insure not just access to the postsecondary system but a full range of choice among types of institutions. Private higher education must not, Mondale felt strongly, become the exclusive preserve of the rich. This concern was reflected especially in a later version of his bill in which the formula for the direct grant program was geared to the cost of attendance at the institution of the student's choice. A sliding scale of percentages would determine how much of the student's actual cost of attendance would be covered by the government. This approach differed sharply from Senator Pell's. The Subcommittee chairman's proposal was to establish a floor, a foundation for all needy students; it would not treat students differently because they attended differently priced institutions.

The Kennedy Bill

Senator Kennedy advanced the "Higher Education Bill of Rights." This proposal was almost identical to a measure first introduced in the House by Representatives Ogden Reid (R-New York) and John Brademas (D-Indiana) and closely patterned after the major recommendations of the Carnegie Commission report, *Quality and Equality*. The heart of the bill was a vastly expanded and revised Educational Opportunity Grants program plus cost-of-instruction allowances to institutions. Senators Javits and Prouty from the minority side joined Kennedy in sponsoring the legislation, though all three indicated they were doing so primarily to stimulate discussion and were not necessarily wedded to the specifics.

The Williams Community College Bill

Another bill, the "Comprehensive Community College Act of 1969," came from Senator Williams of New Jersey and a bipartisan host of cosponsors. It was a popular measure, designed to give greater federal recognition and support to the development of community-based, two-year institutions. The American Association of Junior Colleges provided the initial impetus and primary support. While part of the loosely united front of higher education associations favoring general aid to all institutions, AAJC also felt the time was ripe, with public enthusiasm for the community college concept running high, to try to redress the imbalance of federal support by going for an institutional aid program for its own institutions. Senator Williams was a logical choice to lead the cause because his state of New Jersey was underdeveloped in the community college field and was beginning to move rapidly to catch up. It also gave Senator Williams, primarily identified with labor, a chance to sponsor a major education bill.

Bills from the Minority Side

When President Nixon finally advanced a set of higher education proposals in March, 1970, still another bill was placed in consideration. The Republican Senators were not enthusiastic about the Administration's ideas. As much as the Democrats, the minority members of the Subcommittee harbored reservations about the student aid program. "I would say they are sort of embarrassed by it," one staff aide allowed.[12] But members of the President's party accept with grace the obligation to sponsor the President's proposals. Thus Senator Javits introduced and explained to his Senate colleagues the Administration's bill. A brief and typically cordial exchange followed between Senators Javits and Pell.

Mr. PELL. Mr. President, I am delighted to have the bill introduced, and I am so glad that the senior Senator from New York, who takes such a leading role in the whole field of education, is doing so. . .

I am glad to see the Administration proposal. I would hope that we could give some serious thought to my idea . . . of granting . . . students aid that they would receive as a matter of right. . . .

Mr. JAVITS. Mr. President, I am very grateful for the statement of the distinguished Senator from Rhode Island. I assure him that his views will not be overlooked. I know the President will be grateful to the Senator for the fine spirit of cooperation he has shown in this and any other matter related to education.

The Senator from Rhode Island has given support which is not only bipartisan, but also unpartisan, in its approach to the whole problem of education. . . .[13]

Mutual courtesy and deference flow easily among Senators, especially in an area where bipartisanship is customary. The Administration bill would not be dismissed out of hand; it would get a hearing. At the same time Pell made clear that he was intent on his own income tax approach, and Senator Javits, unwedded to the Administration's proposals though serving as their formal sponsor, assured the Chairman his proposal would be seriously considered by the minority.

Senator Javits also had several proposals of his own, some amending current programs, others calling for new initiatives in higher education. One Javits bill envisioned a new federal-state partnership in student aid. Over twenty states including New York had recently started need-based scholarship programs, and Javits wanted to offer a federal incentive to these states to increase their level of effort and to other states to establish new programs. The bill also called for "educational opportunity centers" in low-income areas across the country to facilitate the recruitment of disadvantaged students into higher education. This proposal was patterned after a program already under way in New York State and followed from one of the recommendations of the Carnegie Commission.

One other bill from the minority side was a proposal for general grants to institutions of higher education based on the number of baccalaureate degrees awarded, with 15 percent of the appropriation set aside for two-year colleges and distributed on the basis of enrollments. This was the only Senate bill providing the type of broad-based formula support that the coalition of higher education associations generally favored. Introduced by Senator Dominick, the measure was identical to a bill originated on the House side by Representative Albert Quie (R-Minn.). From at least one perspective, the bill seemed quite consistent with traditional Republican philosophy—dispensing federal funds with no strings attached, an alternative to narrow program categories with onerous matching and other requirements. The Republican Administration, however, was not calling for (indeed, had strong reservations about) any such general aid to institutions.

There was no dearth of relevant bills pending before the Pell Subcommittee when the Chairman opened hearings on higher education in early 1970. Yet the 1970 hearings were general and groping, and only occasionally focused on specific legislative alternatives. Continuing off and on through the late summer, they meandered over a range of concerns—the financial status of higher education, the extent and causes of student unrest, the special problems of Black colleges, college library needs, language and area studies, and the difficulties of the Guaranteed Loan Program. Pell often presided alone at these preliminary hearings, other members attending when a home state witness was scheduled to appear or when the testimony held special interest. Two days were devoted exclusively to community colleges, enabling Senator Williams to get into the record a large volume of testimony supporting his bill.

Pell had hoped that legislative action on higher education could be concluded in 1970, but this prospect waned as the months passed. He was disappointed: "The climate was not right; nothing jelled; there was no consensus for action either among the witnesses or the Subcommittee members."[14] More than anything else, the continued political backlash against campus unrest made 1970 an inauspicious year for Congress to move ahead in higher education.

The 1970 hearings did make several points clear. First, the Administration's higher education program—except for selected features like the secondary market to shore up the Guaranteed Loan Program and possibly some version of the National Foundation to stimulate reform in higher education—was destined for oblivion in the Senate. The hearings were laced with questioning and criticism of the Administration's proposals, from the Senators as well as the witnesses.

Second, the Chairman left no doubt of his single-mindedness as he hammered away on the theme of college as a matter of right. He kept returning to what he considered the fundamental challenge of public policy in higher education: to establish a floor that would assure every student a chance to attend college, not necessarily MIT or Princeton but at least a low-cost community or state college.

Finally, there was evident in the hearings a developing antagonism between Senator Pell and some representatives of the higher education community. The Senator felt his quite earnest proposals were being overlooked by the higher education lobby. He queried witness after witness: What did they think of his bill, S. 1969? The response was usually halting and hedged; most of the witnesses had not read the bill and, in a few cases, had scarcely heard of it. "The Senator resented not being taken seriously," according to his staff. On some occasions, his irritation was unconcealed. He lectured one ill-informed witness:

I would be wrong if, as chairman of the Education Subcommittee, I did not, in all fairness, consider all the different ideas and proposals that come to us. I have expressed great disappointment that the higher education community hasn't taken the trouble to reflect on and study our ideas which we think will help solve the problem. . . .

If we have the courtesy and interest to familiarize ourselves with your thoughts and views, I think you, as specialists in this field, should have opinions, pro or con, on our views up here on the Hill, because we have an active problem-solving responsibility.[15]

And he put the higher education community on notice not to be surprised by the eventual outcome:

I intend to press this approach of mine as far as I can in these hearings, and I would like to see an approach of this sort incorporated into whatever bill we report. . . .

So, while it has been taken quite flippantly so far, it would seem to me that it might conceivably get into the final version of the bill.[16]

Of the major higher education associations, only two presented testimony—the American Association of Junior Colleges (in support of the Williams bill) and the National Association of State Universities and Land-Grant Colleges. The Land-Grant Association told Senator Pell its principal interest was a simple extension of all the existing statutes: "We feel that the big thing is to extend and continue the legislation that is on the books."[17] The Land-Grant representatives reflected the lukewarm attitude of most of the associations toward new directions or innovations, apart from general institutional aid. And for the latter the associations were placing their hopes in Representative Green and the House Committee.

Birth of S. 659

Early in the 92nd Congress, Pell announced his intention to "act swiftly" on higher education. Enough of the tentative probing of the previous Congress. The student unrest issue no longer cast such a long shadow, and the legislative expiration date for higher education programs was drawing closer. It was time to get on with the enactment of a bill.

On February 8, 1971, Pell introduced a measure he hoped would become the vehicle for committee action. S.659, "The Education Amendments of 1971," combined an extension of all existing higher education programs with his proposal from the prior Congress of basic grants to students plus cost-of-education allowances to institutions. It also incorporated several new elements:

—*Establishment of a warehousing account in the Treasury Department for the purpose of helping lenders expand the supply of Guaranteed Student Loans.* Senator Pell saw this limited device as an alternative to the Administration's bolder recommendation of a National Student Loan Association that could actually buy and sell student loan paper. Pell opposed setting up such a new agency, fearing it would constitute a long-range commitment to loans as the prime federal approach to financing higher education.

—*Unification at the state level of all responsibility for the administration of federal higher education programs requiring the use of a state agency.* Each state would have to designate a single commission—"broadly representative" of the public and of the higher education community—to administer such federal funds as college construction aid, undergraduate equipment support, and community services. In addition, federal funds would be extended to the state commissions to carry out comprehensive statewide planning of post-secondary education. Tucked away inconspicuously as a new section 1202 of the Higher Education Act, these provisions of the Pell bill had potentially far-reaching implications for the state role as well as federal-state relations in higher education. The proposals originated in discussions between Pell's staff and the organization of State Higher Education Executive Officers. The latter group, committed to a broader state role in postsecondary planning, welcomed federal recognition and support for this objective. Pell and his staff embraced the logic of using federal funds as a lever to encourage a more rational approach to the utilization of postsecondary educational resources in the states.

—*Creation of a new Education Division in HEW with three parts: the Office of Education, a new National Foundation for Postsecondary Education, and a new National Institute of Education.* The Foundation and the Institute, both Nixon Administration proposals, were incorporated in the bill for several reasons. First, while Pell and his staff were not totally sold on the proposals, the ideas behind them seemed to be fairly reasonable: an agency to generate innovation and reform in postsecondary schooling, something the Carnegie Commission and others were recommending and something that seemed genuinely needed; and a unit designed to upgrade education research, a proposal that responded to a general state of malaise about the quality, effectiveness, and relevance of what was going on in this field. But more important, their inclusion was a gesture toward the Administration, and this made sense from Pell's point of view not so much because he hoped or needed to win Administration backing, but because he wanted minority support on the Subcommittee. Down the road it would be easier for the Republican Senators to support the Pell bill if at least a few things were adopted from the Administration's program. Finally, incorporating the Foundation and the Institute provided a rationale for creating the Education Division in HEW, which Pell envisioned as a preliminary step toward a long-range goal he personally believed in—an entirely separate Department of Education with Cabinet status.

Also thrown into the measure were a number of amendments to existing higher education programs, an extension of several vocational education programs for which authority was running out, and various administrative oversight provisions.

An omnibus bill was in the making. The saga of S. 659 had begun.

Common Ground

All ten Democrats on the full Labor and Public Welfare Committee cosponsored Pell's new package. This was mainly a courtesy to the Chairman, but it also reflected fairly general agreement on the principles Pell felt so strongly about. Only Mondale had a potentially competing proposal; he reintroduced his own comprehensive bill in March of 1971. Senator Kennedy chose not to revive his earlier "Higher Education Bill of Rights," deferring to Pell whose bill embodied basically the same concepts.

Senator Williams, now Chairman of the full Committee, was preoccupied with other issues and was prepared to give Senator Pell an open field on the higher education bill, with only one stipulation: that something be done for community colleges. The Senators reached an early understanding that the Williams Community College Bill would be meshed into the Pell omnibus bill at the appropriate time.

Republican Views

The minority members of the Subcommittee felt obliged to await the Administration's revised proposals before making any moves of their own. The President's second message on higher education arrived in late February, this time with two accompanying bills. Senator Javits introduced the Foundation bill (and became the principal Senate supporter of this idea), and Senator Prouty, ranking minority member of the Education Subcommittee, offered the general bill calling for student aid reform.

Prouty noted improvements in the Administration's program over the previous year but emphasized that he was introducing the bill mainly "for the sake of discussion." Clearly the Republicans were still not satisfied with the Administration's approach in student aid—the minimal commitment to grants and heavy emphasis on loans, even for the poorest students. Yet Senator Prouty did share the Administration's concern about disparities in existing federal student aid due to state and institutional allocation procedures; he favored the objective of predictability and assurance of a basic amount of aid to each needy student. "It is this concept of establishing a minimum floor of assistance that appeals to me most," Prouty told his Senate colleagues. "For too long a discussion of higher education as a matter of right has been avoided."[18] The words seemed to echo Senator Pell.

There was a tacit convergence of philosophy between the conservative Vermont Senator and the liberal Democrat from Rhode Island. Their voting records were far apart on many issues, but on education they shared the same commitment. Prouty had served for more than a decade on the Education Subcommittee and had supported the major enactments of this period. He had also lined up in favor of increased appropriations for education programs, voting to override President Nixon on this issue. In the postsecondary field, the Senator liked to say that he favored a "GI Bill for everybody someday." Prouty was also interested in new approaches to student loan financing, including the income-contingent repayment idea publicized by the Zacharias Report.

Whatever bill was to come out of the Education Subcommittee, part of the script could be written in advance. A major new thrust in student aid was a foregone conclusion. Thinking on both sides of the aisle pointed this way.

Attitudes on Institutional Aid

Senator Dominick's 1970 bill providing general assistance based on baccalaureate degrees fell by the wayside. The Administration, of course, opposed it on budgetary and policy grounds. In addition, a number of objections had been raised against the formula, in particular, that it would encourage institutions to produce as many graduates as possible with no quality control. Dominick never pushed the bill and did not reintroduce it in 1971. Thus the only remaining type of institutional aid in bill form on the Senate side was the cost-of-education allowance, a feature of both S. 659 and the Mondale Bill.

Publicly, all the Senators expressed concern about the financial condition of colleges and universities. With mounting public discussion of a financial crisis in higher education, they could scarcely avoid the issue. But there was a genuine uncertainty about how to respond properly.

Most of the Senators instinctively questioned the idea of general federal support for all higher education on the basis of enrollments, degrees or other automatic factor. Privately, the attitude of some Senators was that if an institution was so weak it could not attract sufficient numbers of students to remain solvent, it probably should close down. To guarantee the survival of every college and university in the country, they felt, was not an appropriate federal role. Assistance to institutions should have a more substantial rationale. The cost-of-education allowance concept appeared to meet that requirement, for it linked institutional grants to a national objective on which the Senators all agreed: equal opportunity. Institutions would receive direct help only to the extent that they accommodated needy students on federal assistance.

At the staff level, skepticism toward general assistance ran deep and was reinforced by a constitutional argument. The view of the Subcommittee staff was that a per-student or other general aid program, providing funds to public and private nonprofit (including religiously controlled) institutions alike, would almost certainly run afoul of First Amendment strictures against church-state entanglement. On the other hand, it was felt that cost-of-education allowances could probably be justified constitutionally on the grounds that such payments constituted partial reimbursement for a "federal burden" imposed on the colleges and universities. According to this rationale, since tuition and fees do not cover full instructional costs at either public or private institutions, an institution in effect would be incurring additional costs when it accepted each additional needy student enabled to attend by federal assistance; and in doing so, the institution would be helping to meet the national objective of equalizing opportunity. Though no one could predict how the courts might rule, the staff believed that a more defensible constitutional case could be mounted for cost-of-instruction allowances than for more general aid to institutions.

A Stumbling Block

While there was tacit agreement on the big issues, there was at the same time a delicate problem that might stand in the way of bipartisan legislation. Senator Pell still had his mind set on the original idea that had come to him on the ski slope—the income tax subtraction method as a simple rule of thumb for determining each student's need for a Basic Grant. But as some of the Senators, staff and outside observers thought about its implementation and impact, serious reservations began cropping up. In short, the weight of opinion was that income taxes do not provide a reliable reading of income level nor do they sensitively reflect a family's overall financial strength and ability to pay for college.

Senator Pell knew there were rough edges to his proposal. He acknowledged problems such as the family with income all or mostly from municipal bonds or other tax write-offs. But he felt that these cases would be exceptional, and that on balance the system would be reasonably fair. Above all, he felt, his approach had the merit of simplicity. The Senator wanted a direct, easily understood method by which the student could apply and qualify for federal assistance, one that would not force the student "to bare. . .his family's economic soul" through an involved means test.[19]

The issue was aired when the Subcommittee began a new set of hearings on higher education legislation in the early spring of 1971. Several witnesses, including HEW Secretary Richardson, enumerated defects in the proposed use of income taxes as a measure of need: the lack of consideration of unusual but necessary expenses of the family, unless such expenses can be classified as tax deductions; the neglect of a family's assets; the lack of sensitivity to the number of dependents in the family; and the many loopholes that permit some wealthy individuals to incur little or no tax liability. Concern was also expressed that the tax-related formula would encourage middle- and upper-income parents to declare their college-age children emancipated, thereby giving up a tax deduction but enabling the children to qualify for the maximum grant.

Not only witnesses but some of Pell's colleagues on the Subcommittee gently tried to dissuade the Chairman from his *idée fixe*. But Pell appeared to be unmoved; he was extremely reluctant to abandon the simple approach embodied in S. 659.

One other specific provision in the Pell bill that drew a critical reaction was the formula for cost-of-education allowances—$1000 minus the tuition charged by the institutions. Higher education spokesmen noted that it would provide no assistance at all for private colleges and universities because their charges almost invariably exceed $1000. On this point Pell indicated early in the hearings that he was flexible, acknowledging that the formula unfairly excluded private institutions. The Senator's intent had been to discourage institutions from raising tuition to capture the benefits of increased financial aid available to their students, but Pell agreed that this problem should be dealt with in another manner.

Negotiating a Bipartisan Bill

The Subcommittee hearings continued through early June, 1971, but in mid-May the members met briefly in closed session to take a look ahead and talk things over. Nothing was decided except: (1) More staff work was required. The staff was given marching orders to start putting together a document that would provide the basis for a bipartisan bill. (2) The bill should be student-oriented, putting the needs of students first and the needs of institutions second. On this there was firm agreement. On the problem of the Basic Grants eligibility formula, it was left to the staff to try to figure out a solution.

For the next month and a half, extensive deliberations took place at the staff level, principally involving key aides to Senators Pell, Prouty and Javits.[c] In round after round of bill drafting and negotiating, the staff representatives sought to hammer out a consensus. Aides to Senator Pell first tried tinkering with the income tax approach to meet some of the objections that had been raised. But eventually it became clear that the Republicans would not go on the bill unless another mechanism altogether was substituted, and this message was communicated to Senator Pell.

What finally emerged from the staff negotiations—and won Senator Pell's approval—was the following formula.

> *Basic Grant entitlement* would equal $1200 minus the expected contribution from the student's family.
>
> *Limitation*: no grant to exceed one-half the cost of attendance at the institution in which the student is enrolled.
>
> *"Expected Family Contribution" to be based on uniform regulations published by the Commissioner of Education* taking into account family income, number of dependents, asset holdings, and unusual but necessary expenses of the family.
>
> *Part-time as well as full-time students eligible,* part-time defined as at least half-time attendance.

Pell had been stubborn about retaining his original formula for the sake of its simplicity. He had resisted other approaches because he wanted to avoid a system involving complicated regulations and application procedures. Ultimately, however, he came to grips with the reality of having to bring along his Republican colleagues on the Subcommittee, and he compromised gracefully.

The basic formula negotiated by the staff was not new in concept. The Mondale bill and the Administration's program both called for a standardized determination of how much the family could be expected to contribute as the basis for arriving at the student's eligibility for federal assistance. Something along these lines was also being discussed among certain House members. Representative Quie was particularly interested. In fact, it was Quie's principal staff aide on the House Committee, Robert Andringa, who planted the idea for the formula with Republican aides in the Senate—a rare instance of interchange between Senate and House staff. Committee aides generally keep their distance from their counterparts on the opposite side of the Hill.

---

[c]The key staff aides engaged in these negotiations were Stephen J. Wexler and Richard D. Smith, Counsel and Associate Counsel, respectively, to the Subcommittee on Education; Roy H. Millenson, Minority Staff Director, Subcommittee on Education; and Stephen Hand, Legislative Assistant to Senator Prouty.

At about the same time Pell's staff came around to the same idea—the expected family contribution as the basis of eligibility. This seemed to be the answer; staff on both sides were agreed. It was then a matter of taking the formula to Senator Pell. When Pell gave his assent, the breakthrough had been achieved that was necessary to assure bipartisan solidarity and smooth sailing for the higher education bill in the Senate. The Chairman and the two senior Republicans on the Education Subcommittee were now teamed up on the most important provision of the bill.

Details of the formula fell in place easily once the basic approach had been settled. The student would qualify according to standards of eligibility uniformly prescribed by the Commissioner of Education. There would be one schedule for dependent students and a separate one for students determined to be emancipated or self-supporting. Neither Pell's staff nor the Republican staff aides were comfortable lodging so much discretionary authority with the Commissioner. On the other hand, it seemed impractical to write complete schedules of eligibility directly into the law. To provide a check on the Commissioner's authority, the staff agreed on a provision giving Congress a chance to review and disapprove the proposed schedules, in which case the Commissioner would have to draw up new ones.

The one-half cost limitation in the formula was added at the insistence of the Republicans, reflecting their traditional attitude that the government should not provide a "free ride" for any student. The restriction to one-half the student's cost of attendance also reflected Senator Prouty's view that the Basic Grant program should be "neutral" among different types of institutions. He felt that without such a limitation, low-cost public institutions might become unduly attractive relative to higher-priced private colleges because the student could get nearly his whole way paid at the public school with the Basic Grant.

The staff was juggling other parts of the bill as well through May and most of June. On institutional aid, having set aside the $1000-minus-tuition formula, the staff came up with several alternative approaches that would be set before the Subcommittee when it met again in closed session. In addition, a number of things were grafted on to the Pell bill:

—*A scaled down version of Senator Williams' community college bill.* The full committee chairman's prime legislative interest in higher education was hardly to be passed over, but the original $6 billion package, Pell's staff insisted, had to be reduced. Williams' staff and the junior college association agreed to a more realistic proposal. The funds would be open not only to two-year community colleges but four-year institutions as well, as long as they offered community college type programs—a change pressed by a number of big state university systems with two-year branch campuses and technical institutes. State planning requirements in the original Williams bill were retained and easily harmonized with Section 1202, the state planning provision already contained in S. 659.

—Several Javits-sponsored amendments, including his proposals for state scholarship incentives and educational opportunity centers.

—A legislative package sponsored by Senator Kennedy aimed at strengthening the elementary and secondary education of American Indians. The Subcommittee had held hearings on the subject earlier in the spring, and Pell agreed to incorporate the Kennedy bill into S. 659.

—A bill sponsored by Senator Schweiker to promote and advance ethnic heritage studies. Again the Chairman was willing to accommodate the special interest of a subcommittee colleague, even though in this case Pell was not particularly enthusiastic about the idea.

—A measure pushed by Senator Lee Metcalf, Democrat of Montana, to develop consumer education programs in schools and colleges. Metcalf sat on neither the education panel nor the full Labor and Public Welfare Committee, but Pell incorporated the Metcalf bill into S. 659 to avert a possible floor amendment later.

—Provisions establishing land-grant status, and thus special support, for the College of the Virgin Islands and the University of Guam. This was an uncontroversial idea that had been around for several years.

So it went in the late spring of 1971, the staff negotiating the make-up of the Basic Grants Program and melding bits and pieces of other legislation into a single bill.

Except for a perfunctory hearing before the Subcommittee in late May, the higher education associations were not involved at this stage. At best they monitored the Senate situation from a distance. Neither was the Administration aggressively involved, though the Senate staff did consult HEW and Office of Education legislative representatives as the bill took shape. This was not really a matter of negotiating with the Administration, since the Subcommittee had clearly rejected the Administration's proposals and was prepared to legislate on its own. But the staff hoped at least to neutralize potential Administration resistance.

So far as the Administration was concerned, the bill was becoming too big and too expensive. The Administration had no taste for the miscellaneous "goodies" that were being tacked on to the measure by various Senators; OMB officials were alarmed at the budgetary implications. Moreover, the Administration found objectionable certain provisions buried in the bill that would tighten up congressional oversight and control of the administration of education programs.

On the other hand, the centerpiece of the Senate bill—the Basic Grants program—carried a strong appeal for the Administration. A basic student aid "entitlement," after all, had been the centerpiece of the President's program as well, albeit a more conservative, less costly proposal. The President had called for a consolidated grant/work/loan package as a substitute for previous federal programs. The Senate bill envisioned an entirely new grant program as the foundation for all other student aid sources, including previous federal grant, work and loan programs, which would be continued. The Senate proposal was clearly more generous. Yet the principle was essentially the same: to establish a floor of assistance for all needy students. Therefore, once Senator Pell abandoned the income tax feature of his proposal, as Secretary Richardson and others had urged, the Administration could not very well fault the Senate program, even though it was bound to cost considerably more than the Administration wanted to spend. "The way the Basic Grant came out was philosophically so close to what the Administration had been thinking they were stuck with it. We schlepped a billion-dollar program onto them," a Senate aide observed. The Senate bill's overall emphasis on student aid rather than institutional aid—a consumer-oriented strategy of placing money in the hands of students to give them greater leverage in the higher education marketplace—coverged with the Administration's own philosophy.

Moreover, if there were going to be direct support for institutions, the Senate policy-makers and the Administration were agreed that it should follow federally-aided disadvantaged students in the form of cost-of-education allowances. Under heavy pressure to revise its earlier stand on the issue and recommend *some* type of institutional aid, this is where the Administration came out, again converging with the trend of thinking in the Senate.[d]

Thus there was a great deal—including the Administration's own proposals for a National Foundation for Higher Education and a National Institute of Education—that the Administration could only applaud in the bill that was taking form in Senator Pell's Subcommittee. There was much else that the Administration did not like. But with aides to Republican Senators Javits and Prouty doing their best to mediate, the Administration was coming around to a position of at least tacit support for the emerging Senate legislation. On higher education the Nixon Administration was gradually aligning itself with liberal Democrats and Republicans of the Senate—strange bedfellows but a potentially powerful coalition.

The Mark-up Sessions

Because the staff had done their homework and basic agreements had been reached in advance among key members, the formal mark-up phase proceeded smoothly and quickly. The Subcommittee went into closed session again in late June to make its final decisions on the bill.

Subcommittee

The only real issue centered on efforts by Senator Mondale to modify the Basic Grants formula to incorporate the sliding-scale mechanism from his own bill. Mondale wanted to adjust the formula so that students choosing to attend

---

[d]See Chapter 6 for the circumstances of the Administration's change of position on institutional aid.

higher-cost private institutions could receive larger awards. He felt the Basic Grant should insure a range of choice among institutions, not just a floor of aid. Senator Schweiker shared Mondale's concern and joined in the proposal. But the Subcommittee Chairman was dead set against it. Pell objected strongly to the notion of favoring students in expensive schools. He felt this would encourage increased tuition levels, which he opposed, and he felt it was elitist. "Not everybody has to go to Princeton," Senator Pell said repeatedly. Mondale and Schweiker argued that private higher education should not be stereotyped along the lines of the rich Ivy League school. But Senator Williams and other members sided with Pell and the Mondale scheme was set aside.

On institutional aid the Subcommittee adopted the last in a series of formulas offered up by the staff. The concept was simple—institutions would be rewarded with a cost-of-instruction payment for each enrolled recipient of a Basic Grant. The formula, however, was complicated. Built into it was a special weighting to favor small colleges, plus extra payments to institutions enrolling Basic Grant recipients in numbers above certain threshold levels. The program also contained a stiff requirement reflecting Senator Pell's strong concern that the impact of federal student aid must not be dissipated through tuition hikes. To receive its funds under the cost-of-instruction allowance program, an institution would have to refrain from raising its undergraduate tuition rate above what it charged in 1970-1971.

Unlike most other parts of the bill, the institutional aid formula had the sponsorship of no one in particular on the Subcommittee. It was a staff-devised solution. And it was adopted not so much because any Senator was firmly committed to the cause of institutional aid as because of the need to have an alternative to the broader, enrollment-based institutional aid that was being developed in the House under the leadership of Representative Green. The Senate Subcommittee was looking ahead to an eventual conference with the House.

The Senators left no doubt, however, that they placed the highest priority on student aid, a preference graphically expressed by a provision added during the Subcommittee mark-up that came to be known as the Prouty Amendment. Senator Prouty himself was not present during the mark-up sessions, having recently taken ill with the cancer that would claim his life only a few months later. But the Senator remained keenly interested in the bill and had several conversations with Senator Pell from his hospital room. Following one of these conversations, Pell offered an amendment on behalf of the ailing Senator that stated that no payments could be made to institutions under the cost-of-instruction formula in any year in which the Basic Grants program was not fully funded or if funding of the other student aid programs fell below 1972 levels. The limitation, readily accepted by the Subcommittee, was meant to insure that institutional support would not come at the expense of student assistance. The Senators and the staff reasoned that it would also have the effect of forcing the representatives of higher education institutions to lobby hard for generous funding of the student aid programs to trigger the institutional aid formula.

Thus the potential of the institutional aid program adopted by the Subcommittee was tightly circumscribed by two conditions: (1) no undergraduate tuition increases by the recipient institution beyond 1970-1971 levels; and (2) prior funding of student aid programs.

One other Subcommittee amendment, sponsored by Senator Beall of Maryland, was the so-called bail-out—an authorization for a small, temporary fund from which the Commissioner of Education could selectively aid colleges and universities determined to be in "serious financial distress." The program was supposed to rescue institutions at the financial brink, though it was generally acknowledged that identifying which institutions needed help most would pose administrative and political problems and thus implementation might well prove impractical. The bail-out provision reflected the Subcommittee's concern about the much-discussed financial crisis in higher education, but it was as much a symbolic gesture as anything else, and it clearly indicated that the Subcommittee was not prepared to legislate a permanent solution.

In fact, the Subcommittee had reached an important conclusion: that it simply did not have adequate data and evidence to evaluate the nature and causes of the financial strain in higher education or the most appropriate means to deal with it. Thus, along with the bail-out, a provision was written in directing the Commissioner to conduct a study analyzing the financial conditions of higher education institutions and the merits of alternative policy proposals, and to report back to Congress. The Senators were frustrated at not having sufficient basic information and analysis on the postsecondary system; this was a quest for the wherewithal to make more informed policy decisions in the future.

Full Committee

On June 30, the Subcommittee completed work on the bill and ordered it reported to the full Labor and Public Welfare Committee, which took it up in two brief sessions in mid-July.

The major amendment voted in Committee was an increase in the Basic Grant ceiling, which had been set at $1200 in the original Pell bill. Committee chairman Harrison Williams took the lead on this issue. He wanted to raise the maximum to cover more students in the middle-income range as well as provide larger grants for low-income students. Senator Mondale, having lost his bid in Subcommittee to liberalize the formula by incorporating a sliding scale based on costs of attendance, also pressed for a more generous maximum grant. Senator Williams proposed an increase to $1500. The Republicans, particularly Senator Dominick, were concerned about the budgetary impact of expanding the formula and countered with a more modest proposal that would limit the grant to $1200, $1300, and $1400 in successive undergraduate years. The result was a compromise: The ceiling would be *$1400* for all undergraduates. This happened to be the same figure that the Administration had used in its proposed student aid package. It also turned out to be an amount that would permit Basic Grant eligibility up to an income level of roughly $12,000 for an average size family, depending upon the specific criteria developed by the Office of Education. This seemed to the Committee a reasonable cut-off point, providing some aid to moderate-income families as well as the very poor.

The rest of the Basic Grants program was left essentially intact, as was most of the rest of the bill. The full Committee tampered very little with the Subcommittee's handiwork. There was some debate over authorization levels—Republicans protested they were too high in certain programs—but accommodation was readily achieved.

Only a few provisions were added in the Committee mark-up. One called for another study of postsecondary educational finance, to be focused on future federal and state roles, alternative forms of student aid, and the development of national uniform standards for determining per-student costs of providing postsecondary education in different types of institutions.[e] Among alternative forms of student aid to be studied, the Committee specified loan programs based on income-contingent lending, reflecting Senator Prouty's special interest in this concept. The notion of uniform cost standards grew out of Senator Pell's concern during the hearings that college representatives were not able to produce solid estimates of how much it actually costs institutions to educate students, and that no common form of fiscal measurement existed in higher education.

Before wrapping up the bill, the Committee made one last compromise. At the insistence of Senator Dominick, the Committee adopted provisions for creating a student loan marketing association instead of the Treasury Department warehousing account featured in Senator Pell's original version of S. 659. The SLMA, or "Sallie Mae" as it would come to be known, followed the Administration's prescription for expanding the potential of the Guaranteed Student Loan Program.

On July 15, the Labor and Public Welfare Committee unanimously ordered S. 659, the Education Amendments of 1971, reported to the Senate.

"Like a Sears Roebuck Catalog": The Committee Report

During the closing weeks of July, the staff put together the documentation that would accompany the bill when it went to the floor: a narrative statement explaining the legislation, cost estimates of the new authorizations, a section-by-section analysis of the bill, a complete account of how it would change existing laws, and supplemental views of the committee's minority members. All in all, nearly six hundred pages went into the Committee Report on S. 659.

---

[e]The two separate studies of postsecondary finance mandated in the Senate legislation were later combined in conference with the House. The National Commission on Financing Postsecondary Education resulted.

How had the Senate Committee bill become such a massive production?

Part of its sheer bulk was a matter of technical draftsmanship. In putting S. 659 together, Pell's staff had sought to "recodify" the basic higher education statutes. The Higher Education Facilities Act, the International Education Act, and portions of the NDEA were all transferred to the Higher Education Act of 1965, thus combining into one law the previously scattered legislative authority for higher education programs administered by the Office of Education. And within the new comprehensive statute all student aid programs were brought under Title IV. The process of recodification added to the length and seeming complexity of S. 659 and the accompanying Committee Report.

But the major reason for a large bill was that S. 659 had become a vehicle for a number of separately sponsored pieces of legislation touching on many aspects of higher education but also ranging far afield from higher education. With only one education subcommittee in the Senate—and a quorum of the members usually difficult to come by—the tendency is to package bills to expedite committee business. Moreover, Senator Pell faced a tough re-election campaign in 1972 and had made a clear-cut decision that he wanted to take one comprehensive bill through committee, to the floor, and to conference with the House. Rather than treating higher education, community colleges, vocational education, Indian education and other pending legislation piecemeal, he preferred to handle all of it in one package—and as early as possible to free his time for the upcoming campaign.

Once the bill had become bipartisan in character, it could scarcely be thrown open only to some members of the committee and not others. Thus many ideas were accommodated and S. 659 widened in scope and dimensions.

In part, this was a case of "padding" the bill. In folding more and more items into the measure, the members and staff knew well that not all of the extra baggage would survive eventual bargaining with the House. But having a bill of this kind, with many provisions that could potentially be traded away, would maximize the Senate's flexibility and options in conference. Also, some features of the committee bill were more symbolic than anything else. An example was the lid that would be clamped on tuition charged by institutions receiving cost-of-instruction allowances; here the Committee wanted to make a point of its concern about escalating tuition levels but knew that such a limitation was unrealistic and would probably have to be dropped out of the bill when it went to conference.

The cost estimates in the Committee Report constituted the "bottom line" in terms of what the Senate panel had wrought. The estimates indicated the magnitude of the bill in dollars: a total of more than $19 billion in new spending authority. The Basic Grants program alone, according to the Committee's projections, would require about $1 billion a year to be fully funded for all potentially eligible students.

By a cumulative process the Committee had produced a bill and a report that some observers likened to a Sears Roebuck catalog. The legislation had a grab-bag quality. Yet, the focus of the measure remained higher education, and at its core were several fundamental themes of significance for the future of federal policy.

The most important theme was the removal of financial barriers facing students who seek to continue their education beyond high school. The Committee Report marshalled data documenting the low college enrollment rates of minority and low-income populations and spoke of "the need for a comprehensive student assistance program which can guarantee each high school graduate an opportunity to seek a postsecondary education without regard to the economic circumstances of his or her family."[20] The "comprehensive program" proposed in the bill was actually a series of programs assembled under Title IV of the Higher Education Act. It began with the Basic Grant as a foundation, followed by Supplemental Educational Opportunity Grants, and supplemented further by the new State Student Incentive Grants program, College Work-Study assistance, and finally, both direct and guaranteed loans.

There was also a new recognition and emphasis on forms of higher education other than the traditional four-year academic curriculum. The Report pointed out that federal legislation had always sought to preserve diversity in higher education by treating the large and small, public and private institution even-handedly, but that now

. . .there is a new kind of diversity which the Committee believes ought to be encouraged. . . .[T]he federal approach to postsecondary education ought to be broad enough to encompass the entire spectrum of options for students,

including technical training and career-oriented programs.[21] Thus the Committee took the step of extending eligibility for all of the student aid programs in S. 659 to students in accredited proprietary vocational schools.

Moreover, the Report placed the Committee squarely behind the movement for innovation and reform in postsecondary education. While lauding the successes of American higher education, the Committee warned that the performance and management of the system left much to be desired, and urged "bold alternatives" such as those advanced by the Carnegie Commission and the Newman Report. The Committee noted that the federal government "has done much to encourage only one type of entrepreneur in postsecondary education—the research entrepreneur with his government grants, his laboratory and his staff." The proposed National Foundation for Higher Education, by contrast, would encourage the "educational entrepreneur" who is devoted to improving the process of teaching and learning.[22]

The Solidarity of the Committee's Position

All seventeen members of the Labor and Public Welfare Committee signed the report on S. 659 and asked to be listed as cosponsors of the bill. Such unanimity virtually assured smooth passage on the floor. It also meant that the Senate would be bargaining from a position of solidarity when the legislation went to conference with the House.

Consensus at the Committee level was not unusual in itself, but the strength of the consensus and the degree of commitment to this particular bill was extraordinary.

Many of the Members, of course, had a direct stake in S. 659 because it incorporated bills or amendments they had originally sponsored or personally believed in:

Pell was dedicated to the Basic Grants provision and had a stake in the entire bill because it came out of his Subcommittee.

Williams had the community college title.

Kennedy had Indian education, plus the knowledge that S. 659 was in broad outline much like the "Higher Education Bill of Rights" he had sponsored in 1969.

Mondale could also find much in the bill that was consistent with his own thinking, and he gave it his full support, even though he had been unsuccessful in putting across a different version of the Basic Grant in Subcommittee.

Javits personally contributed the state scholarship incentives plus several other provisions, and he persisted in behalf of the Administration's Foundation proposal.

Prouty was responsible for the Prouty amendment to the cost-of-instruction allowance program.

Dominick had nailed down the Student Loan Marketing Association.

Schweiker had ethnic heritage studies.

Beall had the emergency bail-out provision.

In their supplemental views contained in the Committee Report, the Committee's minority members collectively claimed credit for thirty-one distinct programs or provisions in S. 659.

An omnibus bill is an effective device for political coalition-building. But the Committee's enthusiasm for S. 659 was something more than the sum of individual commitments to portions of the bill. Whether or not they could claim private authorship of any piece of the legislation, the members sensed that this was an important measure advancing important principles. They believed in the core philosophy of S. 659, namely, in Senator Pell's words, "that the Federal government has an obligation to people rather than to institutions." This means placing top priority on aid to students; institutions would receive assistance only "if they serve the people, and adapt to their needs." It meant putting "the decision-making in the hands of the 'consumer' of educational services rather than in the 'conduits' of those services."[23] This basic rationale and other themes of the bill had been hammered out and reaffirmed on several occasions by the members and staff. "We talked philosophy from beginning to end,"according to a staff aide. Strong convictions and feelings about the bill had resulted.

The strength of feeling was reinforced by the Senators' disenchantment with the higher education establishment. Not only Pell and his staff but others on the Committee had been put off by the associations at One Dupont Circle. Their perception was that (a) the associations representing institutions of higher education were closed-minded to any new approaches other than their own recommendation of broad-based institutional aid, and (b) the associations were not presenting cogent arguments and evidence but were merely asserting their position. One of the dynamics of the Committee situation, therefore, was that the members and staff felt challenged to come up with something that in their view was more defensible than what the higher education lobby was asking for. They believed they had this in the cost-of-instruction allowance provision, linking institutional support to the objective of equalizing opportunity. And the Prouty Amendment dramatized the Committee's attitude by in effect holding the institutional funds hostage to the funding of student aid programs.

The Senators were also miffed at a specialized constituency within higher education—the professional organization of college officials who administer student assistance programs—because of this group's lack of support for Basic Grants. The National Association of Student Financial Aid Administrators favored expansion of the existing federal student aid programs operated through institutions but was not enthusiastic about a new national entitlement program, as in S. 659, that presumably would operate independently of institutions. The Senators considered this a parochial point of view not in the best interests of students.

A few days after the Committee reported the bill, Senator Pell took advantage of an opportunity to express publicly his dissatisfaction with the role the higher education groups had been playing. Speaking to the American College Public Relations Association, he charged that the representatives of higher education had "ignored what was going on in the Senate." He added:

I believe what we have seen up to this point in time is a lack of willingness on the part of the higher education community to look at new ideas. It is the same spirit. . .that has caused the educational community to bristle at the Newman Report or even at the concept of cost accounting in education institutions.[24]

For their part, the higher education groups perceived the situation conversely: that Senator Pell had ignored *them* because he was unwilling to listen to ideas that did not conform to his own. The mutual antagonism was plain. The higher education establishment and the key Senate education policymakers were at odds, and this fact seemed to strengthen the resolve and cohesion of the Committee as it staked out a position and reported S. 659.

An additional factor that helped cement bipartisan consensus on the bill was the close personal and working relationship between Pell and Prouty. The Senators had not previously known each other well, but their similar convictions on this particular legislation had brought them together and created mutual respect. Pell continued to consult Prouty during Prouty's hospitalization, and Pell took the unusual step of offering an amendment in Subcommittee on behalf of the absent Senator. Following the Subcommittee mark-up, Prouty was able to return briefly to his Senate work and in a floor speech lauded Senator Pell's leadership of the Education Subcommittee. The Chairman and the ranking minority member of the education panel had both invested themselves personally in the development of S. 659, and the bond between them was strong.

Squeeze Play Before the August Recess

The sponsors wanted to go to the floor as soon as possible rather than letting the bill sit for any length of time. At the staff level, this decision was candidly explained:

You never leave a bill lying around, particularly a big bill, over a recess. If you do, then some [expletive deleted] staffer will hear from Siwash State College and come in with some picky amendment to [expletive deleted] the whole thing.

Senator Pell pressed the Senate leadership for a slot on the calendar before the Senate went home for its August vacation. S. 659 was considered by the Senate on August 4, 5, and 6, 1971.

There were no surprises on the floor. Most of the proceedings followed a script. Pell, Williams, Kennedy, Mondale, Prouty, Javits, Dominick and Beall offered general statements explaining and extolling the provisions of S. 659. A number of Senators not on Labor and Public Welfare also registered support for the bill and praised the Committee's hard work. Time and again the measure was described as "historic" legislation in the tradition of the Morrill Act of 1862 or the National Defense Education Act of 1958.

But in Washington's midsummer doldrums, the Education Amendments of 1971 attracted little public attention. Aside from a highly favorable editorial in the *Washington Post*, the bill seemed to escape notice. Senator Prouty in his floor statement queried:

Can it be that there is no longer time or space for good news? This bill is good news for millions of young Americans who need the assurance that their aspirations will not be limited by their economic circumstances. This bill is good news for schools which are committed to expanding educational opportunities for all Americans. This bill is good news to those who realize that there is much to be learned about how we learn and how to teach. The bill is good news to those who see strength in a diversified educational system and wish to expand education and training options. This bill is good news to those. . .who are constantly seeking new ways to make government responsive to the aspirations of the people. This is good news for the Nation. . . .[25]

Even the interested public—the educational community—was largely inattentive to the imminent passage of such a major bill. The absence of publicity, however, was in one sense a boon to the Senate sponsors because it helped to assure routine treatment of the legislation and minimized the risk of disruptive debate or delay on the floor.

The few amendments offered on the floor were largely unrelated to the higher education provisions of the bill. Senator James Allen of Alabama won acceptance of an amendment to extend vocational education programs for three years instead of one as provided by the Committee. Also readily accepted was an amendment by Senator Abraham Ribicoff of Connecticut providing for the establishment of federal safety standards for summer youth camps. And the Senate agreed to incorporate Senator Hubert Humphrey's "Interns for Political Leadership Act," designed to give students interested in a political career the opportunity to work with elected officials in government. All three amendments passed by voice vote. On the floor, as in Committee, S. 659 served as a convenient vehicle for assorted legislative ideas.

Senator Dominick, however, failed in his attempt to add a provision for educating a select cadre of students for government careers in the field of foreign affairs. As a separate measure, his Foreign Service Scholarships Bill had been reported unfavorably by the Foreign Relations Committee and was vehemently opposed by Chairman William Fulbright.

One major piece of S. 659 was deleted by unanimous consent—the Indian education provisions. The leadership requested that these provisions be reintroduced as a separate bill and considered by both the Interior and Labor and Public Welfare Committees before floor action.

The only floor amendment with major implications for colleges and universities was a proposal by Senator Birch Bayh of Indiana to bar sex discrimination in public or federally supported institutions of higher education. Dubbed by Senate wags the "Bayh-sexual amendment," the proposal generated considerable debate. Senator Strom Thurmond of South Carolina worried aloud that the amendment would force The Citadel, his state's military college for men, to become coeducational. Others questioned the extent of coverage—whether it would bar separate dormitories or athletic programs for men and women. Finally, the Chair sustained a point of order that the amendment was not germane to the bill. Germaneness is not a standing rule of the Senate, but the unanimous consent agreement under which S. 659 was brought to the floor required that all amendments to this particular bill be germane. The Chair's ruling of nongermaneness was upheld 50-32 on a roll-call vote, and the anti-sex discrimination amendment was put aside.

There was virtually no other debate on the bill. However, antispending conservatives such as Senator Harry Byrd of Virginia did raise concerns about the bill's $20 billion price tag, and Senator Warren Magnuson of Washington, Chairman of the Senate appropriations subcommittee handling education, warned that actual appropriations for the programs would fall far short of the authorized levels. Magnuson, himself liberal-leaning yet realistic about fiscal constraints, admonished his colleagues:

The members of the Committee on Labor and Public Welfare are great authorizers. . .but I want it clear when this bill is passed, and I am going to vote for it, that there is another story when we get down to the problem of annual appropriations.[26]

Indeed, the reality of the appropriations process was difficult to reconcile with the rhetoric and the promise of the legislation that was about to be passed. In several areas the bill spoke of "entitlements"—most notably, an entitlement for needy students under the Basic Grants program. But did the term "entitlement" create a claim that the individual could legally enforce against the federal government? Was the government legally obligated to satisfy full entitlements, as under the GI Bill? Senator Norris Cotton of New Hampshire, ranking Republican on the Magnuson appropriations subcommittee, asked Senators Javits and Pell a series of questions on the floor to clarify the meaning of the bill in this respect. They responded that the level of funding for Basic Grants, as for most programs, would be determined by annual appropriations, and if the level in any given year fell short of the amount needed for full funding of entitlements, then entitlements would have to be ratably reduced. The individual would have a vested right only to his pro rata share of the amount of money available, not to his full "entitlement." Thus the guaranteed floor of resources promised by S. 659 for financing a college education was symbolic and not necessarily real.

But Magnuson's warning and the clarification of "entitlement" could not diminish the bloom on S. 659 as it neared final passage. The symbolism and the positive potential of the legislation dominated the moment. "For the first time in the history of our Nation," Senator Pell declared in a last brief statement before the vote, "there will be established the right to a postsecondary education."[27]

With barely a quorum to conduct business, the Senate finally voted on the entire bill early Friday evening, August 6. S. 659 passed by a roll-call vote of 51-0. Moments later the Senate formally adjourned for the August recess.

Thus the Senate expeditiously completed its work on a higher education (turned omnibus) bill in 1971. The other body of Congress, meanwhile, was trying to come to grips with a bill of its own. In the House, higher education legislation followed a more harrowing course.

Notes

1. *Congressional Quarterly Almanac*, 1971, p. 579.

2. Woodrow Wilson, *Congressional Government*, World Publishing Company, Cleveland, 1961, p. 76.

3. George Goodwin, Jr., *The Little Legislatures: Committees of Congress*, University of Massachusetts Press, Amherst, 1970, p. 46. See, also, on the institutionalization of subcommittees, Thomas R. Wolanin, "Committee Seniority and the Choice of House Subcommittee Chairman: 80th to 91st Congress," *The Journal of Politics*, Volume 36, (August, 1974), pp. 688-689.

4. Quoted in F.N. Khedouri, "Claiborne Pell, Democratic Senator from Rhode Island," *Ralph Nader Congress Project: Citizens Look at Congress*, August, 1972, p. 1.

5. Ibid., p. 2.

6. Ibid., p. 12.

7. Quoted in Douglass Cater, *Power in Washington*, Random House, New York, 1964, p. 158.

8. Ralph K. Huitt, "The Internal Distribution of Influence in the Senate," in *Congress and America's Future*, ed., David B. Truman, The American Assembly, 1965, p. 97.

9. Quoted in Khedouri, p. 12.

10. *Congressional Record*, April 25, 1969, pp. 10434-10435.

11 *Congressional Record*, April 14, 1969, p. 8779.

12. Quoted in Ed Willingham, "Education Report: Nixon's Approach to College Aid Meets Opposition in Crucial Hill Committees," *The National Journal*, May 22, 1971, p. 1091.

13. *Congressional Record*, March 25, 1970, p. 9299.

14. Remarks by Senator Claiborne Pell at the Annual Meeting of the College Entrance Examination Board, New York City, Tuesday, October 26, 1971.

15. *Hearings on the Higher Education Amendments of 1970*, Subcommittee on Education, Committee on Labor and Public Welfare, U.S. Senate, 91st Congress, 2nd Session, Part 1, p. 448.

16. Ibid., p. 459.

17. *Hearings*, Part 2, p. 1234.

18. *Congressional Record*, March 4, 1971, p. 5041.

19. *Hearings*, Part 1, p. 579.

20. Senate Report No. 346, 92nd Congress, 1st Session, p. 21 (1971).

21. Ibid., p. 29.

22. Ibid., p. 84.

23. Remarks by Senator Claiborne Pell at the Annual Meeting of the College Entrance Examination Board, New York City, Tuesday, October 26, 1971.

24. Speech by Senator Clairborne Pell to the National Conference of American College Public Relations Association, Tuesday, July 20, 1971.

25. *Congressional Record*, August 4, 1971, p. S13166 (daily ed.).

26. Ibid., p. S13651 (daily ed.).

27. Ibid., p. S13652 (daily ed.).

6

The House: Wrangling and Discord

When House Speaker John McCormack gaveled to order the first session of the 91st Congress in January, 1969, legislation to authorize new programs for higher education was not on the agenda. There was no need for it to be. The existing legislation was scheduled to run for another few years, the Nixon Administration had scarcely begun to establish its policy positions, and the Democratic House, accustomed to leadership from the executive branch for the previous eight years, was not yet prepared to initiate on its own, especially in the absence of any deadline.

The Preliminaries

However, as in the Senate, much preliminary legislative groundwork took place in the House in 1969-1970. In addition, as a result of the upheaval on the nation's campuses, higher education was the subject of hot debate in the House during the 91st Congress, and this debate influenced the politics that would shape the next higher education bill.

The Battle over Bills to Curb Campus Unrest

If one mentioned higher education in the House in 1969, it evoked one thing above all: campus unrest. Congress had already in 1968 enacted several provisions cutting off federal aid to student disrupters, but, in 1969, the pressure mounted in the House (less so in the Senate) for broader and tougher federal action to curb the wave of campus disruptions and riots.

Legislation toward this end was bitterly contested in the Education and Labor Committee. Within the Committee the major supporter of legislation to deal with campus unrest was Representative Edith Green, who chaired the House subcommittee with jurisdiction over higher education. In early 1969, Mrs. Green introduced a bill that would require colleges to file with the Commissioner of Education formal plans for dealing with campus disturbances, or forfeit their right to receive any federal funds. During several months of hearings before her subcommittee, Mrs. Green argued that her bill was moderate and reasonable, would effectively curb campus unrest, and would also forestall more severe measures that might threaten the rights of students and the

117

independence of colleges. One observer characterized Mrs. Green's bill as the "shoot-em-in-the-legs bill" in contrast to the "shoot-to-kill bills" being offered by other Members of Congress to deal with student demonstrators.

But Mrs. Green encountered stiff opposition on her subcommittee from Congressmen John Brademas (D-Indiana) and Ogden "Brownie" Reid (R-New York). With a coalition composed largely of the Democrats on the subcommittee (other than Mrs. Green), John Brademas took control of the situation and blocked the Green bill. The Washington higher education associations, fearing federal intervention in internal university affairs, supported Brademas and Reid.

Having failed to move a campus unrest bill out of her subcommittee, Mrs. Green persuaded Education and Labor Committee Chairman Carl Perkins (D-Kentucky) to have her bill considered by the full committee. Chairman Perkins' assent reflected his usual deference to Mrs. Green on higher education matters even when, as in this case, he disagreed on the merits of her proposal. Although she came very close to succeeding, Mrs. Green was frustrated in this new forum. Once again Brademas and Reid led the opposition, stalling the bill by filibustering, calling for additional hearings and witnesses, absenting themselves to prevent a quorum from being established, and raising the specter that the language of the bill could be applied against picketing and other activities by labor unions. This latter change was particularly disturbing to strongly prolabor Democrats on the committee who might otherwise have enthusiastically supported the Green bill. Following a month of complex maneuvering and frequently acrimonious debate, the committee voted 18-17 to send the bill back to the Green subcommittee, thus killing it.

As a result of this fight, Mrs. Green's previously cordial and cooperative relationship with the representatives of higher education was temporarily ruptured. She compared the attitude of higher education officials to that of college students who write their parents: "Don't worry. Everything's fine here. Send money."[1]

Another fallout of the 1969 campus unrest imbroglio was a deterioration in the relations between Mrs. Green and John Brademas, the two senior Democrats on the Education and Labor Committee with the most interest, experience, knowledge, and political clout concerning higher education legislation. The relations between Mrs. Green and Committee Chairman Perkins were also strained since he voted to kill the Green bill.

Later in the summer Perkins played a key role in averting further controversy in the House over the campus unrest issue. Responding to the apparent crisis in the Guaranteed Loan Program, Mrs. Green's subcommittee quickly reviewed and approved the Administration's proposal for a special allowance to participating lenders. However, the bill ran into troubled waters in the House, and Chairman Perkins faced a dilemma. He knew that if he went through the Rules Committee and brought the bill before the House under normal procedures, there would be a floor fight over campus unrest amendments and the emergency bill might be delayed or sidetracked. Thus Perkins tried to bring the bill before the House under suspension of the rules, a procedure precluding floor amendments but requiring a two-thirds vote on final passage. The first and third Mondays of each month are designated for consideration of legislation under suspension of the rules. Bringing legislation before the House under suspension of the rules at any other time requires unanimous consent. On four occasions before the congressional summer recess, Chairman Perkins requested unanimous consent to consider the Emergency Insured Student Loan Amendments of 1969 under suspension of the rules on a day other than the first or third Monday of the month. Each time objection was heard from Members who were dissatisfied because the House would be denied the opportunity to debate campus unrest amendments.

Finally, on the third Monday in September, Perkins again made the motion to suspend the rules and pass the bill, and this time only a two-thirds vote was needed. The bill passed overwhelmingly.

A floor fight over campus unrest had been averted. However, objection was heard on a normally routine unanimous consent request that would have enabled the Senate to accept the House bill without the need for a House-Senate conference. A conference had to be held delaying the bill for another month. The principal point of disagreement was a provision in the Senate bill requiring that lenders not discriminate in favor of students whose families had a prior business relationship with the lender. The conferees finally agreed to delete this provision and to mandate a study of the problem.

The Emergency Insured Student Loan Amendments of 1969 forecast an important aspect of the process of enactment of the Education Amendments of 1972: the exploitation of the legislative rules and procedures for political advantage. The bill also highlighted the chronic difficulties of the Guaranteed Loan Program which would re-emerge as a difficult and time consuming problem in the debate over the Education Amendments of 1972.

The Battle over Education Appropriations

Action on education appropriations was the other major battleground involving higher education in 1969. The Administration's fiscal year 1970 budget request for education, submitted to the Congress in early 1969, was about $500 million less than the amount available in fiscal year 1969. A coalition of more than seventy organizations—primarily elementary and secondary and higher education groups along with organized labor—was formed in Washington to lobby for increased education appropriations. Naming itself the "Emergency Committee for Full Funding of Education Programs," the coalition adopted the goal of funding all federal education programs to their full authorization levels.

Focusing most of its energy on the traditionally more fiscally conservative House of Representatives, the Full Funding Committee mobilized a large cadre of educators to lobby on Capitol Hill. They won a major victory when an amendment to the education appropriation bill sponsored by Congressman Charles Joelson (D-New Jersey) passed decisively on the House floor, adding nearly $1 billion for the most politically popular education programs. Despite some skittishness about becoming partners in a professional lobbying effort, the higher education associations joined and supported the Full Funding cause but were not the dominant or driving force.

Caught in political cross-currents, the fiscal year 1970 education appropriations bill did not finally reach the President's desk until late January of 1970. President Nixon promptly vetoed the bill, denouncing it as inflationary in a nationwide radio and television address. The House upheld the President's veto, and the President did not sign an education appropriations bill until March, only four months before the end of the fiscal year.[a]

The 1969 fight over appropriations confirmed the suspicions of the higher education associations in Washington and of many Democrats on Capitol Hill that the Nixon Administration was committed more to fiscal restraint than to aid for education. This suspicion was reinforced by their lack of access to the tight circle of Administration decision-makers in contrast to the easy entree they had enjoyed during the Johnson years. From the Administration's point of view, higher education appeared to be just another greedy special interest with no appreciation for national problems like inflation. Higher education was also perceived to be blindly clinging to old programs and stubbornly resisting any tough re-examination of programs and priorities.

A First Round of Hearings

In 1969, campus unrest and education appropriations took center stage in the House. Only in mid-December of 1969 did Mrs. Green's subcommittee begin very preliminary hearings on new higher education authorizing legislation.

Initially, the subcommittee had before it only two bills. One was the "Higher Education Bill of Rights," cosponsored by Representatives Reid and Brademas and based on the Carnegie Commission recommendations. It paralleled Senator Kennedy's bill of the same title. Also before the subcommittee was the Comprehensive Community College Act of 1969 sponsored by Representative Frank Thompson of New Jersey, third-ranking Democrat on the Education and Labor Committee behind Chairman Perkins and Mrs. Green. Thompson's bill was identical to the measure developed and introduced in the Senate by Harrison Williams.

---

[a]On the full funding committee, see Lucille Eddinger, "Full Funds for Education," *National Journal*, Volume 1, November 1, 1969.

The hearings continued into early 1970, rambling over assorted topics: conditions in the District of Columbia public schools, the Rivlin Report, manpower needs for college graduates, Veterans Administration education programs, and institutional aid. Then in mid-February Mrs. Green introduced the Omnibus Postsecondary Education Act of 1970, basically an extension of existing higher education programs. It also included Mrs. Green's unsuccessful campus unrest proposal of the previous year, and a title creating a new Department of Education and Manpower. Some observers speculated that Mrs. Green introduced her bill primarily as a stop-gap to keep attention from being focused on the Reid-Brademas bill until the Administration's proposals reached Capitol Hill.

By the end of April, the Subcommittee had three more bills for its consideration. Congressman John Erlenborn (R-Illinois), a member of the subcommittee, introduced the Student Loan Marketing Association Act of 1970. Like Senator Dominick, Erlenborn advocated a government-sponsored private corporation to serve as a secondary market and warehousing facility for federally insured student loans. Congressman Albert Quie (R-Minnesota), the ranking minority member on the Green subcommittee, introduced his Higher Education General Assistance Act of 1970. Also introduced in the other body by Senator Dominick, the Quie bill proposed to distribute federal funds to colleges based on the number of baccalaureate degrees they awarded. The bill was aimed at helping undergraduate institutions rather than those specializing in graduate studies. Quie, an alumnus of St. Olaf in Minnesota, was especially concerned about the financial plight of small private colleges. He also believed that basing the institutional aid formula on baccalaureate degrees awarded would serve to tie the federal funds to the performance of higher education institutions. Alternatively, he felt, distributing institutional aid on the basis of enrollments would encourage colleges to lower their admission standards to increase their share of the federal dollars.

The long-awaited presidential initiatives in higher education arrived in March and immediately became a target of criticism in the Green subcommittee hearings. From the Democratic side, Mrs. Green led the attack on the Administration's bill, charging it provided no relief for hard-pressed middle-income students and their parents. Reflecting the widespread suspicion that the Administration's special concern for low-income students was only a cover for reducing federal budgetary commitments, Congressman Brademas observed, "[I]t is the Bureau of the Budget that has written this higher education program rather than educators."[2]

On the Republican side of the subcommittee, there was also far from overwhelming enthusiasm for the Administration's proposals. Quie, who introduced the Administration bill, did so largely as a courtesy. He was lukewarm toward the student aid proposals, was concerned about the lack of an institutional aid program, and opposed the termination of the academic facilities programs.

The Problem of Identifying the Issues

After the Administration bill "bombed," the hearings drifted from topic to topic through the middle of July. The basic problem was that there was no consensus on what were the major issues in higher education to which the House higher education policy-makers ought to address themselves.

There were a great many candidates for the "major issue": the general financial crisis in higher education (the higher education associations); the financial crisis in the private sector of higher education (Representatives Quie, Green and Brademas); the needs of students from low-income families (the Administration); the financial squeeze on middle-income students and their families (Green and Brademas); and the need to preserve excellence and stimulate innovation and reform in higher education (Moynihan). There was also the view that no new programs were needed, that federal higher education programs were generally working well and needed only a little fine tuning and extension. This was the general view of Mrs. Green and the higher education associations (with the exception of the push for an institutional aid program in the latter case). In 1970, the subcommittee was not at the point of searching for solutions to problems; it was still groping toward an understanding and consensus on what were the top priority problems. The subcommittee did not arrive at any *answers* in 1970 because the members had not yet identified the *questions*.

The cross-currents on the subject of institutional aid reflected the lack of consensus. The higher education associations had made clear their support for general federal aid, but beyond this general level of agreement there was no common view on the most equitable formula for distributing federal institutional aid. In fact, the associations seemed reluctant to confront this thorny and potentially divisive issue.

Among the members of the Green subcommittee, there was also a generally sympathetic disposition toward federal institutional aid. But again the consensus went no deeper. Congressman Quie had his baccalaureate degree bill, reflecting a concern for private higher education and a desire to reward performance. Congressman Brademas, who had taught at a small women's college, whose district included Notre Dame, and who was educated at Harvard, was also concerned about the financial health of private institutions. However, he was the cosponsor of the Reid-Brademas bill that incorporated an alternative approach to institutional aid, namely, cost-of-education allowances tied to the flow of student aid funds to needy students—the approach favored and eventually adopted by the Senate subcommittee.

Though her omnibus bill did not include institutional aid, Mrs. Green was sympathetic and open-minded on the question. Like Quie, she was concerned about the plight of private higher education, but she resisted the idea of simply throwing open the federal treasury to bail out all of higher education. She was also troubled by the problem of devising a sensible formula.

The Decision Not to Report a Bill in 1970

While the focus and priority of policy issues in higher education remained nebulous, the central political question in 1970 was clear: Was the House Education and Labor Committee to report a higher education bill or not? Reporting a bill in 1970 meant confronting again the problem of student unrest, still a front-burner issue. Not reporting a bill meant avoiding a repetition of the bloody brawl of 1969.

Mrs. Green was pushing forcefully to report a higher education bill from her subcommittee before the end of the 91st Congress. One of her motivations was to provide the opportunity for advance funding of higher education programs, especially student aid. She had long been a critic of the dislocation caused by the vagaries of the yearly appropriation process, which often left students and college administrators uncertain about their federal funds until well into the fall term of each year. To establish the advance funding concept beginning in the academic year 1971–1972, higher education legislation would have to be extended a year before it was scheduled to expire, that is, in 1970, in time for the inclusion of funds for the new law in the fiscal year 1971 appropriation bill.

Given Mrs. Green's concern about advance funding and the apparently clear track ahead of her in the Education and Labor Committee, the higher education associations began to repair their relations with Mrs. Green that had been ruptured during the 1969 student unrest fight. They naturally wanted to be in on the action, if there was to be any.

Mrs. Green's ardor to do something about student unrest had not cooled despite her defeat in the committee in 1969. She made it clear that this would be an important component of any higher education bill. "It is my judgment," she said during the subcommittee hearings,

that no higher education bill is going to pass on the floor, without some reference to campus unrest because it is a widespread concern. So it seems to me that really what we are faced with is working out the best possible legislation in this regard.[3]

She failed to mention another option altogether, which was to have no higher education bill in 1970.

Congressman Brademas was firmly committed to this latter option. He felt that another fight over campus unrest, this time in an election year, would put House liberals on the spot and endanger their re-election chances. Despite being an incumbent in his sixth term, Brademas faced his own tough biennial fight in his marginal Indiana district.[b] The election-year dangers to Brademas

---

[b] On Brademas' district and electoral problems, see Jack H. Schuster, "An 'Education Congressman' Fights for Survival: Congressman John Brademas' Bid for Reelection, 1968," in *Policy and Politics in America*, ed. Allan P. Sindler, Little, Brown, Boston, 1973.

and his friends were magnified in 1970 by the slashing attacks of Vice President Agnew on the "radical-liberals" in Congress and by the determination of the Administration to purge the Congress of its ideological enemies.

Brademas and his allies still had the votes to control legislative action in the Green subcommittee. This coalition was reinforced by the ranking minority member of the subcommittee, Congressman Quie, who changed his mind on the subject of federal anti-campus unrest legislation—from support for such legislation in 1969 to opposition in 1970. The Administration remained steadfast in opposing additional federal legislation. Brademas also assumed that the higher education associations would understand the dangers inherent in bringing out a higher education bill in 1970, and that they would again support him in resisting any such move in the subcommittee. He was therefore disturbed and somewhat miffed to learn that the associations had begun a rapprochement with Mrs. Green.

After the Subcommittee hearings had run their meandering course, the subcommittee agreed to begin marking up a bill in mid-August, using the Quie bill as a starting point. A procedural motion proposed by Congressman Brademas was adopted providing that any section of the bill approved by the subcommittee would still be open to later amendments. This meant that "you could sit there forever" without reaching agreement on a bill.[4] Mrs. Green's hope of reporting a bill by May 1 had been long forgotten, and the election was looming ever nearer. The other members of the subcommittee did not share Mrs. Green's intense concern for advance funding and thus did not perceive an immediate deadline as she did. And though most members were concerned about the financial plight of higher education, they did not sense a crisis requiring immediate legislative action. Whether to deal with student unrest legislation was the overriding political question in the subcommittee, and on this question the Brademas forces had the votes to block action.

When the 91st Congress adjourned, one legacy that it left the 92nd Congress, therefore, was the job of producing new higher education legislation. The delay meant lost opportunities for some participants and new opportunities for others. The House policy-makers were still groping toward a definition of the major issues. Political alliances were in a state of flux. The associations had opposed Mrs. Green on student unrest in 1969 but began to collaborate again with her in 1970. Brademas had worked closely with the associations in 1969 but was irritated with them for being amenable, despite the risks he perceived, to legislative action on higher education in 1970. In recent years Mrs. Green and Congressman Quie had worked closely together on many issues, but as Quie changed his mind on campus unrest legislation and appeared not to share fully Mrs. Green's concern about protecting the interests of middle-income students, this tie began to loosen, and Quie and Brademas seemed to be inching together. Green and Brademas had opposed each other strenuously during the 91st Congress, but neither had given up all hope of working with the other on the major review of higher education legislation slated for the 92nd Congress. The Administration and the associations, two hostile and isolated camps for most of the 91st Congress, had at least begun talking to each other under the new Secretary of HEW, Elliot Richardson. In short, the legacy of the 91st Congress in the House was a fluid situation—neither the politics nor the issues had as yet congealed. A year later they would be set in concrete.

The 92nd Congress: Organizing for Action

When the 92nd Congress convened in January, 1971, higher education legislation was clearly on the legislative agenda, but it was not a high priority for either Congress or the Administration. Debates over economic controls, Vietnam, revenue sharing and welfare reform would dominate the headlines through June, 1972, when the Education Amendments were signed. Ironically, while the 92nd Congress was extremely active in legislating for higher education, higher education was not in the national spotlight as it had been in 1969-1970. Demonstrations on the campuses abated. The President no longer found it either necessary or advisable to veto education appropriations.[c] As Congress proceeded to legislate for higher education over the next eighteen months, there would be no fast-paced sequence of dramatic events to rivet public attention. The busing of elementary and secondary school children to achieve desegregation replaced student disruption as the gut social issue. There would be a mighty harvest for higher education in the 92nd Congress, but it would be a hot-house crop developing largely in isolation from the climate of public opinion except for the indirect effects of the storm over busing.

At the beginning of each Congress a significant amount of time is devoted to what the press usually characterizes as "routine organizational matters." For the careers of Congressmen and for the fate of many bills, these matters, like committee and subcommittee assignments, are far from routine. The organization of the Education and Labor Committee at the beginning of the 92nd Congress was no exception. Having seen her initiatives repeatedly frustrated by the majority of her subcommittee in the 91st Congress, Mrs. Green was determined to change its membership. In the hope of getting a subcommittee more congenial to her views, Mrs. Green pursued a two-prong strategy.

The first part of her strategy was an attempt to knock her chief antagonist, John Brademas, off the subcommittee. To achieve this objective, Mrs. Green apparently enlisted the cooperation of Congressman John Dent (D-Pennsylvania), a veteran labor Democrat from the coal mining area east of Pittsburg and fourth-ranking Democrat on the Education and Labor Committee. In the organizational

---

[c]In 1970 President Nixon had again vetoed the appropriations bill for education, but in August, as the election drew near, both houses overrode the veto.

caucus of the Democratic members of the Education and Labor Committee early in the 92nd Congress, Dent proposed a new rule for the allocation of subcommittee assignments among the Democrats on the committee. Each Committee member would be limited to two subcommittee assignments, one on one of the Committee's four labor subcommittees and one on one of the three education subcommittees. John Brademas was chairman of one of the two education subcommittees in addition to Mrs. Green's, so the effect of this rule would be to force Brademas to give up his membership on Mrs. Green's subcommittee. Because of his strong interest in the upcoming deliberations on a higher education bill, Brademas protested vehemently against the proposed Dent rule. The rule was rejected, and the first part of Mrs. Green's strategy failed. The only result was to widen the gulf between her and Brademas.[d]

The second part of Mrs. Green's strategy was to fill vacancies on the subcommittee with Democrats she found more congenial. Several of Brademas' frequent supporters had left the Green panel to take other assignments at the beginning of the 92nd Congress. To replace them, Mrs. Green recruited Congressmen Dent, Dominick Daniels of New Jersey and Roman Pucinski of Illinois. Each of these new members of the Green subcommittee was also a subcommittee chairman, Dent and Daniels of labor subcommittees, and Pucinski of the third education subcommittee. Mrs. Green assumed correctly that they would have neither the time nor the interest to participate actively in her subcommittee and would defer to her wishes out of comity for a fellow chairman. Thus the second part of Mrs. Green's strategy was more successful.

A unique situation existed on the Democratic side of the Green subcommittee. Of the seven Democrats other than Mrs. Green, five were chairmen of other subcommittees on Education and Labor: Dent, Daniels, Pucinski, Brademas and Frank Thompson of New Jersey, Chairman of a labor subcommittee and close friend of John Brademas.

On the Republican side of the subcommittee, Ogden Reid, Brademas' ally, left for another subcommittee assignment. Congressman John Dellenback of Oregon became ranking minority member, succeeding Al Quie who moved into the position of ranking minority member on the full Education and Labor Committee. In this capacity Quie served as ex officio voting member on all subcommittees, as did Chairman Perkins, and Quie would remain particularly active and interested in the affairs of the Green subcommittee.

Higher Education Subcommittee—92nd Congress

Democrats	*Republicans*
Edith Green (Ore.), Chairman	John Dellenback (Ore.)
Frank Thompson, Jr. (N.J.)	John Erlenborn (Ill.)
John Dent (Pa.)	Marvin Esch (Mich.)

---

[d]The explanation for the Dent proposal and its modification are more complex than the Green-Brademas dimension that is emphasized here for the purpose of our narrative.

Roman Pucinski (Ill.)
Dominick Daniels (N.J.)
John Brademas (Ind.)
James Scheuer (N.Y.)
Philip Burton (Calif.)
Carl Perkins (Ky.), ex officio

William Steiger (Wis.)
Earl Ruth (N.C.)
Albert Quie (Minn.), ex officio

Mrs. Green Prepares a Bill

As Mrs. Green looked forward to beginning hearings on higher education, she had reason to be optimistic. She could expect cooperation and deference on the higher education issues from the new members, Dent, Daniels and Pucinski. Neither Burton nor Scheuer were recognized experts or intensely interested in higher education legislation and would probably also go along with her. Opposition was possible from Brademas and Thompson, but by no means certain. Given her past history of working closely with the Republicans on a number of issues before the Education and Labor Committee, collaboration with the minority seemed feasible. Thus from Mrs. Green's point of view, the political line-up on the subcommittee seemed to auger well.

In addition, the campus unrest issue that had stifled subcommittee action in the 91st Congress had moved to the back burner, and the deadline for legislative action on higher education was drawing nearer. There was some question in early 1971 about whether the statutory provision for an automatic one-year extension of education programs technically applied to the higher education laws. If it did not apply, the legislation would expire on July 1, 1971. If it did apply (as it was soon agreed), the legislation would not expire until July 1, 1972. Whichever the case, it was clear that the 92nd Congress would have to act on higher education.

Competing with higher education for the attention of the full Education and Labor Committee was the Administration's Emergency School Aid bill, which was designed to help school districts that were in the process of desegregating. Secretary of HEW Elliot Richardson told Chairman Carl Perkins that it was the Administration's first priority in education, ahead of a new higher education bill. Some observers speculated that the Administration's enthusiasm for the Emergency School Aid bill was born of a desire to use it as a vehicle for antibusing amendments and as a means to confront Democrats with the now-inflamed busing issue. Whether to avoid embroiling the Education and Labor Committee in the busing issue or because of a genuine desire to move on higher education, Chairman Perkins made it clear to Richardson and the Committee that the higher education legislation would, instead, be the top priority. As evidence of his commitment and to set higher education in motion in the Committee, Perkins introduced H.R. 32, the Comprehensive Higher Education Act of 1971, in January. H.R. 32 was an extension of all of the expiring higher education programs with a few additions like a secondary market for student loans and a cost-of-instruction allowance program for institutions.

A month later President Nixon's second message on higher education was dispatched to Congress, and once again Congressman Quie accepted the responsibility of introducing the Administration's proposals. Quie also simultaneously reintroduced his baccalaureate degree bill.

The Administration's offerings received even shorter shrift in the House in 1971 than they had in 1970. On March 2, the first day of hearings on higher education in the Green subcommittee, before Secretary Richardson had a chance to utter a word in behalf of the Administration's program, Mrs. Green said:

I hope that in your statement you will give some attention to two areas which seem to me to be conspicuous by their absence in the administration bill. The first, as I see it, is a blindness to the financial needs of the sons and daughters of middle income families and, secondly, a blindness to the great needs of the private institutions of higher education.[5]

Congressman Quie was also no warmer in his support of the Administration's legislation than he had been the previous year. In fact, during nine days of hearings before the subcommittee in March, the dominant thrust was the identification of flaws and faults in the Administration's program.

The most active members of the subcommittee, Mrs. Green and Brademas on the Democratic side and Quie and Dellenback on the Republican side, had a rather clear idea of what they did not like. However, there was still only a general consensus on what they affirmatively wanted: a student aid program that did not cut out the middle class and a federal program to assist financially troubled institutions, especially the privates. The subcommittee members expected and anticipated that Mrs. Green as the chairman and expert on higher education would introduce a bill. Her bill, they hoped, would provide a specific alternative to the Administration's proposals, replacing the criticism of the Administration with concrete proposals that would embody the consensus on the subcommittee and be the basis for action.

One thing had changed by the end of the first month of hearings. Whereas, in 1970, Mrs. Green had been skeptical of the cries of financial crisis in higher education and the pleas for federal assistance, she was now convinced that the crisis was real and that some form of federal institutional aid was needed. Helping to convince her and other members were two reports, William Jellema's *The Red and the Black*, and Earl Cheit's *The New Depression in Higher Education*. Both authors testified in the March hearings, emphasizing that, in Jellema's words, "Most colleges in the red are staying in the red and many are getting redder, while colleges in the black are generally growing grayer."[6] Both stressed the plight of private higher education, and their views were buttressed by testimony from the higher education associations and university presidents.

Mrs. Green had delayed developing and introducing her own higher education bill beyond the beginning of the subcommittee hearings because of her uncertainty on how to handle the question of institutional aid. By March she was fully convinced of the need for such a program, so she cast about for a suitable formula. She publicly chided the associations, as she had the previous year, for their unwillingness or inability to offer a specific recommendation.

Privately, Mrs. Green invited the associations to present a set of alternative formulas for institutional aid and to recommend one. Her primary contacts with the associations were John Morse, a former aide to Mrs. Green in the early 1960s, now higher education's senior lobbyist as Director of Federal Relations for the American Council on Education (ACE); and Ralph Huitt, Executive Secretary of the National Association of State Universities and Land-Grant Colleges, a highly respected political scientist and former HEW Assistant Secretary for Legislation in the Johnson Administration. Lining up the alternatives was the easy part of the job for the associations. The ACE had already collected and analyzed half a dozen formulas in a booklet, and these were combined with two or three others that had been developed. The formulas prepared for submission to Mrs. Green included: using baccalaureate degrees as the basis for grants to institutions as in the Quie bill; a cost-of-instruction formula like the Reid-Brademas bill of 1969 and the Pell bill being developed in the Senate; capitation grants based on the number and level of instruction of enrolled students; and variations on these basic themes.

The real hurdle was to reach consensus on a preferred formula, something the associations had not yet achieved. But Mrs. Green's invitation was a command performance. Morse and Huitt consulted with other higher education representatives in Washington as well as college officials. Agreement was reached on a capitation formula weighted for enrollments at different instructional levels—more money per student would be paid for more advanced students. The consensus formula also had a special bonus for institutions based on the number of disadvantaged students they enrolled.

The view among the higher education representatives was that a capitation formula was best because it was the simplest. It could be easily understood in Congress. It also avoided the question of determining the relative financial need of individual institutions. Institutional aid based on the need of an individual school might lead the federal government into deciding what kinds of educational programs and activities should survive as well as monitoring and inspecting the fiscal management of colleges and universities. This raised the spectre of federal control of higher education.

In meetings with Morse, Huitt and other association leaders, Mrs. Green agreed with their conclusion that a capitation approach was best on the grounds of its simplicity. However, she was dissatisfied with certain specifics of the recommended formula, particularly the special weighting for disadvantaged students. It was dropped. She also felt that the weighting for graduate students was too large, especially given the apparent oversupply of Ph.D.'s. So she substantially decreased the payment for each student at the doctoral level. In addition, because of her particular concern with the financial plight of small private colleges, Mrs. Green augmented the formula as it applied to these institutions.

The representatives of higher education were not entirely pleased with the final version of the Green formula. New York University President James Hester, who had been closely involved in the discussions leading to the associations' recommendation, voiced his concern about the high cost of graduate education and the need to reflect this more adequately in the formula. This and a few other reservations not withstanding, the higher education establishment agreed to support the modified formula that Mrs. Green was now ready to sponsor in her bill.

The Alliance of Mrs. Green and the Associations

Both in and out of Washington, college and university educators who concerned themselves with federal policy not only supported the Green institutional aid formula but soon became fervently committed to it. Capitation grants became an article of faith within the higher education establishment. The Washington higher education associations in particular forged a united front for the cause of the Green formula.

There were several reasons for the intensity of higher education's commitment to the capitation grants. First, it was unique for the associations to have achieved agreement on a specific formula for institutional aid given the diversity of interests and potential for conflict on this issue in higher education. Having once achieved a consensus, there was strong pressure against reopening old wounds and exposing latent divisions.

Second, a united front seemed to be a sound general strategy in dealing with Congress. There was almost a patronizing attitude about the intelligence and sophistication of Congressmen and Hill staff. Airing the issues publicly, it was believed, would leave Congressmen and staff confused, and if they were confused, they might throw up their hands and not adopt any institutional aid program.

Third, for several years higher education had supported institutional aid to relieve the financial pinch. But in 1971 the financial situation in higher education seemed to be reaching crisis dimensions. Well known major institutions like Hester's N.Y.U. seriously contemplated the prospect of closing their doors. The pinch had become a squeeze and for some a strangle hold. Thus fervor was born in part out of a perception of widespread and desperate financial need.

An extra measure of enthusiasm came from the fact that the associations were supporting *their* formula. While Mrs. Green had modified the formula, it was still, in its basic form, their first preference. It seemed to promise something for everyone with a minimum of government control.

Moreover, "putting all of the chips on Edith Green," as one association representative put it, seemed to be a sensible political strategy. She was an effective legislator, and she chaired the relevant subcommittee in the House. In contrast to Senator Pell who was making his first major effort on higher education, Mrs. Green had "a long track record of getting what she wanted" in higher education legislation, dating back to the early 1960s.

Unwavering support for Mrs. Green also had the advantage of ease and simplicity as a political strategy. Adopting this strategy meant that the higher education representatives did not have to involve themselves in complex political bargaining and coalition-building.

Finally, zealous commitment to Mrs. Green not only made sense to higher education but was demanded by Mrs. Green, whose personality and political style required strict loyalty from her allies. One of her committee colleagues remarked, "With Edith it is kind of like marriage. You can't play the field."

Introduction of H.R. 7248

Mrs. Green worked exclusively with the higher education associations in reaching a decision on institutional aid. Other members of the subcommittee were not consulted. Once the bill was drafted, she asked them to cosponsor it on a take-it-or-leave-it basis.

Whether to cosponsor was a sensitive question for John Brademas. He had reservations about aspects of the bill, especially the institutional aid provisions. There was also the history of mutual antagonism with Mrs. Green. Yet Brademas finally decided to put his name on the Green bill, hoping to hold open the door to accommodation.

H.R. 7248 was finally introduced on April 6 with the cosponsorship of all the other Democrats on the subcommittee with the exception of Frank Thompson. But Mrs. Green's failure to consult with other members of the subcommittee had offended some of them. Thus the introduction of H.R. 7248 was not totally auspicious.

While the higher education representatives were disappointed that some of the other members of the subcommittee, especially Brademas, did not immediately accept the validity of the capitation approach to institutional aid, they nonetheless felt confident. After all, Green, Brademas, Quie, Dellenback and the rest seemed to be in favor of institutional aid. Only the details, it seemed, remained to be worked out.

Mrs. Green's Philosophy and Style

Mrs. Green's bill reflected a strong personal philosophy of education rooted in a deep commitment to meritocratic values. A former classroom teacher who entered Congress in 1955, she believed that access to higher education should be available to those who, by reason of their talent, hard work and motivation, demonstrate a capability for academic achievement and success. Arbitrary barriers such as race, sex and income should be removed, but academic quality should not be sacrificed to the goal of more egalitarian access. Thus Mrs. Green opposed open admissions or compensatory treatment for the poor and disadvantaged in higher education.

This philosophy implied support for institutions of higher education to insure a quality education and enough places for all the meritorious, and it explains her leaning toward the capitation principle rather than cost-of-instruction aid to institutions based on their enrollment of disadvantaged students.

In the area of student aid, her philosophy implied generous support for those of proven ability, support adequate to provide the highly qualified but poor student not only *an* education but the best education for which he qualified, even if it was costly. But Mrs. Green had come to the view that too much federal student aid was being targeted on low-income or minority students simply because they were low-income or minority and were able to gain entry to a postsecondary institution, not because they had superior qualifications. Also, in the late 1960s Mrs. Green had soured on federal aid for disadvantaged students because she was convinced they fomented much of the unrest on college campuses.

The Green bill proposed to extend all of the existing federal student aid programs administered through the colleges—Educational Opportunity Grants (EOG), College Work-Study, and National Defense Loans—but with certain modifications. The EOG program was amended to de-emphasize the income of a student's family as the principal basis for awarding the grant and to place greater discretion in the hands of the student financial aid officer. The bill also proposed to modify the EOG program by making it clear that a student who receives this grant is not automatically entitled to receive it in subsequent undergraduate years. Symbolically at least, this change meant that continued aid would be based on a sustained demonstration of merit as well as need. Under College Work-Study, the preference for "students from low-income families" was changed to those "with the greatest financial need." Thus students from middle- to high-income families who attend expensive private colleges and universities might become eligible. Showing "evidence of academic or creative promise" was also added as a criterion for selecting Work-Study students, again reflecting Mrs. Green's meritocratic values. Finally, eligibility for all the student aid programs was broadened, as in the Senate bill, to include those attending less than full-time; those who demonstrated the virtues of self-help by attending part-time and working their way through school would no longer be excluded.

Not surprisingly, Mrs. Green was strongly opposed to a new student aid entitlement based on uniform national standards related primarily to income, as proposed in different versions by both Senator Pell and the Administration.

In fact, she bridled at such proposals. A uniform national program, she believed, would fail to treat each student individually by weighing his merit and need. Such a system would also be administered in all likelihood by the Office of Education, which she considered a morass of bureaucratic incompetence. In her view, federal student aid was best administered through colleges and universities where ideally the student financial aid officer could sit down with each student and "package" the available aid to fit the student's individual situation.

Thus the Green bill contained no new thrust in student aid comparable to either Pell's or the Administration's. As a principal architect of the existing federal student aid programs, Mrs. Green naturally did not want to see them diminished or overshadowed by a new program. It was also her strong conviction that nothing could be accomplished by a new program that could not be more simply and efficiently achieved through more adequate funding of the existing programs. Moreover, if there was to be a major new departure in federal support for higher education, Mrs. Green had decided to place first priority on institutional aid rather than student assistance.

Other facets of H.R. 7248 clearly had their origin in Mrs. Green's special concerns. A title prohibiting discrimination on the basis of sex in federally supported education programs stemmed from her interest in women's rights as well as her philosophy of removing arbitrary barriers in the path of the meritorious. A title of the bill authorizing the General Accounting Office to study and evaluate federal education programs stemmed from her dissatisfaction with the Office of Education.

Most of the rest of the Green bill consisted of the extension with minor changes of the federal categorical aid programs like college library support and academic facilities. The bill also included two new titles clearly intended to buy support from two of the Democratic members of the Green subcommittee. At the request of Congressman Dent, who had worked with Mrs. Green on the rules governing membership on subcommittees, a mineral conservation education title was added. Dent represented coal mining country in Pennsylvania. A title granting the College of the Virgin Islands and the University of Guam the status of land-grant colleges was included at the request of Congressman Burton, chairman of the Subcommittee on Trust Territories of the House Interior Committee. At this early point, the legislation in the House, like its counterpart in the Senate, was already taking on a Christmas-tree character.

Two additional aspects of Mrs. Green's political philosophy and style significantly colored her role in the process. First, during the decade of the 1960s and into the 1970s, Mrs. Green became more conservative in comparison to her Democratic collegues on the Education and Labor Committee. Whereas, in 1961, the percentage of times she supported the Conservative Coalition was zero, in 1972 she supported the Conservative Coalition 48 percent of the time. By way of contrast, Brademas supported the Conservative

Coalition 4 percent of the time in 1961 and 6 percent of the time in 1972.[e] The turning point for Mrs. Green from a liberal Democrat to a moderate-conservative Democrat came in about 1967-1968, the era of urban unrest and campus disorder. Speculation abounds concerning the reasons for her change, or whether she changed at all, or if she remained faithful to her beliefs while the issues changed and others changed with them. Whatever the explanation, the fact remains that she found herself working more closely with the Republicans and southern Democrats on the Committee and in the House on a range of social issues. During the early 1960s when the landmark higher education bills were passed, her close allies were the liberal Democrats. In 1971 this was no longer true.

Second, compounding her problems on the Committee was a personal style that galled many of the other members. Like any very successful politician, she could be charming, cordial and agreeable, but she could also be stern and caustic. During hearings she usually held other members closely to their time limit for questioning and frequently interrupted both members and witnesses. Impatient, arbitrary, petulant, vindictive and mercurial are adjectives both friends and foes used to describe Mrs. Green. Subcommittee colleagues described working with her in such terms as: "You may get along fine with her for awhile, then she'll turn around and kick you in the teeth;" or "With her it's razor blades." Mrs. Green's style had won her a number of opponents who were motivated in part by a desire to get satisfaction for what they perceived to be personal abuse at her hands.

A Change of Strategy by the Administration

Following introduction of the Green bill, the focus of the hearings shifted from flogging the Administration to examining the Green bill. Brademas, Quie and Dellenback raised hard questions concerning the Green institutional aid approach and its lack of any relation to the relative financial needs of higher education institutions. Supporters of the Green formula answered that determining the financial need of individual institutions and tailoring a formula to deliver money in proportion to that need were a practical impossibility. Father Henle, President of Georgetown University, noted, "University accounting is one of the mysteries of the world, and the effort to evaluate exactly the financial situation of an institution is extremely difficult."[7] While the Green formula, they argued, did not provide perfect equity, it had the merits of being fairly

---

[e]The definition of the Conservative Coalition and these scores are to be found in *Congressional Quarterly Almanac*, 1961, Congressional Quarterly, Washington, D.C., 1962, pp. 650-651; and *Congressional Quarterly Almanac*, 1972, Congressional Quarterly, Washington, D.C., 1973, pp. 68-69.

simple and administratively feasible, and it would help those in need since it helped everyone.

The subcommittee hearings ended without a consensus on institutional aid. The members were persuaded that a financial crisis existed in higher education, but the question of the extent of that crisis and how best to meet it through federal action remained open. After almost two years of intermittent deliberations, Mrs. Green and the associations had decided on the priority of institutional aid and had agreed on a specific formula. Other members of the subcommittee were still wondering whether this was either the right priority or the right program.

The Green panel formally began mark-up on June 8, but through the end of June the situation remained fluid. The lines had not formed. Mrs. Green continued to search for an alliance that could command a majority on the subcommittee. Meanwhile those opposed to her institutional aid formula had yet to unite behind an alternative.

Given the constraints on free-wheeling and candid discussions imposed by having open hearings and open mark-ups, Mrs. Green held informal discussions in her office involving both Democratic and Republican members. But again no agreement emerged. Mrs. Green also sent out feelers to the Administration for a deal in which the Administration would support the Green institutional aid formula in return for Mrs. Green's support of the Administration's entitlement grant for students. This idea stirred a brief flurry of interest in the Administration but did not go very far.

The key events that began to crystallize the situation were a switch in strategy by the Administration on institutional aid and a switch by Quie, the ranking Republican, into alignment with the Administration. Through the spring hearings, Quie's position, at least formally, was to support his baccalaureate degree bill although he harbored reservations about it. The Administration remained set against any institutional aid. This meant that the Administration was in the increasingly uncomfortable position of having no program to deal with what was widely perceived as a financial crisis in higher education.

Prior to the introduction of the Green bill the political wisdom in HEW was that the Administration could get away with opposing all institutional aid because of the inability and unwillingness of the associations to agree on a specific formula and the divisions within the House subcommittee. However, when the associations and Mrs. Green agreed on the capitation formula, HEW saw a real danger that the worst form of institutional aid from the Administration's point of view, capitation grants, might be passed in the House. This threat, along with the political embarrassment of appearing unresponsive to a crisis, moved HEW to begin considering alternative forms of institutional aid. Secretary Richardson persuaded Mrs. Green to delay the beginning of subcommittee mark-ups until the Administration could formulate its position.

Within HEW the question was what form of institutional aid was least objectionable. Secretary Richardson felt this was an important enough question to require a personal decision by the President, and he forwarded a memorandum to the White House setting forth the political situation on institutional aid and outlining the alternatives. Capitation grants were not one of the options, but the cost-of-education allowance was. After several weeks delay, the decision finally came down from the White House in late May. Given the need for an Administration position to head off the Green formula, the President chose the cost-of-instruction approach to institutional aid, the approach that most closely tied institutional aid to students. President Nixon personally and strongly favored aid to students rather than institutions as the first priority. This presidential decision was the only instance of White House involvement in higher education in the 92nd Congress prior to the final bill reaching the President's desk. In 1971-1972 White House interest in education was largely confined to the questions of busing, desegregation assistance and overall budgetary levels.

On receiving the White House decision, Secretary Richardson requested a meeting on the Hill to brief House and Senate Members and staff. The decision was revealed much to the satisfaction of Senator Pell and his Senate colleagues, who found the Administration endorsing their position on institutional aid. Neither Mrs. Green nor Quie had been consulted in the formulation of the Administration program and both were outraged. The Administration was announcing support for the type of institutional aid which Mrs. Green least preferred. So far as the associations were concerned, their long series of conferences with Secretary Richardson had come to naught, and active contacts with the Administration ceased now that their number one priority was a lost cause in the executive branch.

Quie's Conversion

Congressman Quie was upset at the meeting with Richardson and openly displayed his anger, a rarity for the mild-mannered Minnesotan. He was philosophically opposed to cost-of-instruction institutional aid for reasons quite different from Mrs. Green's. Since President Kennedy first proposed a version of the idea in the early 1960s, Quie felt that cost-of-instruction allowances were like a bounty or a bribe being offered by the federal government to higher education institutions for each disadvantaged student they admitted. He found this no less morally objectionable than the wealthy parent of a not-so-bright student giving a donation to a school with the understanding that his progeny would be admitted.

Before too long, however, Quie converted to the Administration's position on institutional aid. One reason for Quie's realignment was that he had just become ranking Republican on the Education and Labor Committee and thus the Republican Administration's chief spokesman on the issues before the

Committee. While by no means simply a water carrier for the Administration, he did not relish the prospect of being publicly opposed to the Administration on a major issue. So party loyalty and his position as ranking member led him to look for a way to reconcile himself to the Administration's proposal.

Also, one of the strong points of the baccalaureate degree bill from Quie's point of view was that it provided substantial aid to private colleges for which he had a special concern. He was persuaded by HEW officials that the cost-of-education approach would provide as much institutional aid to these schools as his own bill.

Third, Quie wanted an institutional aid formula that made grants in some way related to the need of an institution for assistance. The Green formula seemed clearly defective in this regard. On the other hand, schools that admitted disadvantaged students bore an additional burden in educating these students and thus could be seen to have special need. Although the Administration's approach was not linked necessarily to the overall financial health of an institution, it seemed better than the Green formula's complete lack of discrimination among institutions.

Finally, Quie felt that enrollment-based institutional aid could easily become an expensive and inflexible commitment by the federal government. The analogy that he and his staff frequently applied was the impact aid program, which made grants to local school districts based on their enrollments of elementary and secondary school students from families employed by the federal government. A generation of Republican and Democratic administrations had struggled unsuccessfully to repeal or amend impact aid and distribute the large number of dollars it represented in some more rational way. Capitation grants, Quie feared, would be as immovable and irrational as impact aid. Capitation grants were based on something that the higher education institutions controlled and could count—their enrollment. Cost-of-instruction allowances would be based on a variable controlled by the federal government, federal student aid, and this seemed to promise greater flexibility.

So given a predisposition not to oppose the Administration, Quie found sufficient merit in the cost-of-instruction approach to allow him to go along with it. In fact, he soon became one of its more vigorous and enthusiastic supporters. For many of the same reasons Congressman Dellenback, ranking Republican on the Green subcommittee, also found himself sympathetic to the cost-of-education approach proposed by the Administration.

The Brademas-Quie Alliance

Congressman Brademas also found cost-of-education allowances acceptable. A Rhodes Scholar and Harvard Overseer, Brademas prided himself on being an intellectual in politics. New ideas and fresh approaches to problems appealed to him. Proposals nurtured and supported in the academic community caught his attention. Cost-of-instruction allowances seemed to be an innovative and creative idea, even though it was not actually new. The Carnegie Commission on Higher Education supported the idea, and it was a key feature of the 1969 Reid-Brademas bill that was based on the first major report of the Carnegie Commission. Prestigious academics like Alice Rivlin, Frank Newman, and Ben Lawrence all shared Brademas' reservations on the Green formula and encouraged consideration of alternative approaches.

Brademas was also frustrated and angered by the inability or unwillingness of the associations to present what he considered a cogent case supported by adequate data for capitation grants. While he was not completely closed to the capitation approach, it ran contrary to his style to accept it as an article of faith simply because the associations had agreed on it. In addition, though he was a cosponsor of the Green bill, he had no stake in capitation grants. In fact, since he no longer counted Mrs. Green among his allies and had crossed swords with her on a number of issues in recent years, one reason to be against capitation grants was because it was the *Green* formula.

Thus Brademas had supported cost-of-instruction in the past and found those he respected in favor of it. A strong analytic case for capitation was not being made in his opinion; and it bore the imprint of his antagonist, Mrs. Green. Moreover, he agreed with Secretary Richardson's argument that capitation grants would simply shore up the status quo while providing no incentive for reform in higher education.

Once the Administration settled on cost-of-instruction, Quie had converted and Dellenback and Brademas found it appealing, there was the basis for a bipartisan alliance on institutional aid. There was a similar convergence of views on the other key higher education issue, student aid.

Republicans on the Education and Labor Committee were not wedded to the Administration's student aid proposals, but they liked the concept of an entitlement for needy students. It represented a practical application of some cherished principles. It promised the targeting of federal money on those with real need rather than indiscriminately throwing money at a problem. It was designed to strengthen competitive forces in higher education by enabling students to shop in the education marketplace with a guaranteed minimum amount of resources.

On the Democratic side, Mrs. Green had no enthusiasm for an expansive new grant program for students from low-income families. Brademas, on the other hand, wanted to help students from both middle-income and low-income families. He remarked during the hearings:

. . . I think it is most unfortunate that our subcommittee has been put in the posture of appearing to have to choose between poor and middle-income students. I am strongly in favor of helping both groups of students and I don't want to trade off poor kids for middle-income kids, and vice versa. . .[8]

Thus Brademas found himself in agreement in principle with Quie and the Republicans on more student aid for low-income students, but the issue of curtailing or terminating existing student aid programs more beneficial to students from middle-income families remained open.

With their broad agreement on the two key issues, institutional aid and student aid, an alliance between Brademas and Quie was a naturai. Given the changed membership of the subcommittee in the 92nd Congress, Brademas could not control the subcommittee, as he had previously, with a coalition of Democrats and one Republican defector. For Quie to be successful, he had to find someone among the Democrats to work with. As a Republican staff aide put it, "The basic rule if you are in the minority is that to have some impact on the final legislation you have to work with someone in the majority." The previous philosophical agreement and working relationship between Quie and Mrs. Green having broken down on the higher education issues, Quie was looking for an alternative partner among the Democrats. Both political logic and agreement on the issues favored a Brademas-Quie alliance. But the time was not yet right, particularly from Brademas' point of view, for full and open collaboration. Brademas was nurturing major bills on child care and the National Institute of Education in his own subcommittee. He needed some cooperation from Mrs. Green to get the former through the Committee and the latter into the higher education bill. A decisive break with Mrs. Green would have been imprudent. When the first round of mark-ups ended on June 30, the Brademas-Quie relationship was at the point of courtship and engagement, but they were not yet married and in bed together.

Distractions and a New Issue

The June mark-up sessions ended cordially but indecisively. In addition to a lack of agreement on the issues, action was slowed by the problem of generating interest and establishing quorums to do business. Several of the new members of the subcommittee were not overly concerned or informed on higher education. The five Democrats on the Green panel who were chairmen of their own subcommittees often found it difficult to attend. Congressman Dent, for example, was working on minimum wage, coal mine safety, black lung benefits and equal employment opportunity in his subcommittee during the spring and summer of 1971. Mrs. Green, Brademas, Quie and Dellenback were the most informed and active members. Others like Steiger and Erlenborn played lesser but significant roles.

Higher education was temporarily put on the shelf in July as the Education and Labor Committee engaged in a bruising battle over legislation to amend and extend the Office of Economic Opportunity and create a broad new child-care program. Also during this interim period the debate over institutional aid was further complicated by constitutional questions raised in a Supreme

Court case. All the institutional aid proposals included eligibility for church-related private colleges, so the question was: What form of institutional aid was most consistent with constitutional standards concerning the separation of church and state? While this problem had been lingering in the background throughout the debate over institutional aid, it came to the fore when the Supreme Court handed down its decision in the case of *Tilton* v. *Richardson* on June 28. The question before the Court was the constitutionality of federal grants for brick and mortar construction to church-related colleges and universities under the Higher Education Facilities Act of 1963. By a vote of 5-4, the Court found the Act constitutional with the exception of a provision allowing the prohibition against the use of the facilities for religious purposes to lapse after twenty years.

The main constitutional standard applied by the majority was to ask "whether excessive entanglements characterize the relationship between government and church under the Act." The Court found that "excessive entanglement" did not exist in the case of the HEFA program because it provided "a one-time, single-purpose construction grant" in "the absence of any intimate continuing relationship or dependency between government and religiously affiliated institutions." The majority opinion as well as the close division of the Court raised serious questions about institutional aid that would be provided yearly and for general purposes.

To consider the implications of the *Tilton* decision for institutional aid, a panel of legal experts was invited to testify in late July in an additional day of hearings. As might have been expected, there was no clear consensus among the experts. Mrs. Green was bolstered by their unwillingness to assert that capitation institutional aid was clearly unconstitutional by the Court's standards. Meanwhile Brademas and Quie, like the Senate Committee, came to the conclusion that if any form of institutional aid was constitutionally acceptable, it was likely to be cost-of-instruction allowances, on the grounds that such a program would primarily serve the legitimate federal purpose of opening access to higher education for disadvantaged students.

Following this brief flurry of interest as a result of the *Tilton* decision, the constitutional concern once again receded into the background. Only the Supreme Court could make the final determination and no one could confidently predict what the Court would do. Thus the feeling seemed to be that Congress should go ahead and legislate without trying to divine what a future Court test might bring.

Subcommittee Mark-up

The Senate passed its higher education bill, S. 659, on the final day before the August recess. When the Congress reconvened in September, the pressure was on the House subcommittee to move. The Senate had already acted, Chairman Perkins and the House leadership were growing impatient waiting for the long-promised higher education bill, and it was getting into the year when the higher education programs would expire. For the subcommittee, the luxury of debate and disagreement without decisions had passed. When the subcommittee held two more days of mark-ups on September 22 and 23, the mood had clearly changed from the June mark-ups. The lines were being drawn as the members had to choose up sides and decide on a bill to report to the full Education and Labor Committee.

The development of a bill in both the subcommittee and subsequent full committee mark-ups involved two interrelated processes. First, there was the process of amendment and modification of the Green bill, which was used as a starting point. Second, there was the growth from the large bill of fourteen titles introduced by Mrs. Green in April to the massive omnibus bill of twenty titles sent to the House in October.

One reason the bill grew was that Senator Pell had made it clear he intended to work on only one education bill in the 92nd Congress. Thus all of the subcommittee chairmen on the Education and Labor Committee felt that the education legislation they were developing would have to be included in the Green bill or be lost in the 92nd Congress. In addition, it was argued that if the House went to conference not having its own provision on some subject, it would have to consider the Senate provision on a take-it-or-leave-it basis. Thus specific pieces were added to the Green bill to match what was in the bill that had already been passed by the Senate.

There was no systematic attempt, however, to have something in the House bill corresponding to everything in the Senate bill—only an attempt to match in areas of particular concern to members of the House committee. Otherwise, there was almost no consideration of the Senate bill, even after it had passed the Senate. The House and Senate bills ended up with many broad similarities largely because they were both extending and amending the same expiring legislation, not because either body paid much attention to what the other was doing. A House committee staffer remarked, "They do their thing, we do ours, and someday we will put it all together."

The bill also grew because of the addition of "sweeteners." Mrs. Green bargained for support by allowing many of the members of her subcommittee to have their own pet titles and provisions in the bill. In particular, she acceded to the demands of the other subcommittee chairmen to include their education legislation in H.R. 7248. So Mrs. Green's decision at the beginning of the 92nd Congress to bring a number of fellow subcommittee chairmen on to her own subcommittee to more easily control it had the unanticipated consequence of creating strong pressure for an omnibus bill.

Among provisions added by the subcommittee was the National Institute of Education. This Administration initiative had been adopted by Congressman

Brademas and nurtured in his subcommittee. Brademas had a long-standing commitment to improving the quality of education research, and getting the NIE into the Green bill was one of his highest priorities. He succeeded in doing so despite Mrs. Green's lack of enthusiasm for the proposal. She viewed federal education research as an irretrievably hopeless disaster and was lukewarm at best toward the NIE.

A program to promote postsecondary occupational education was also added during the subcommittee mark-up. It came out of Congressman Pucinski's subcommittee and had his support as well as Congressman Quie's. Pucinski had also been developing an ethnic heritage studies bill comparable to a feature of the Senate bill sponsored by Senator Schweiker. Both Pucinski bills became titles of H.R. 7248.

Also to match a provision in the Senate legislation, the Green subcommittee added a youth camp safety title sponsored by Congressman Daniels. Daniels had been working on this legislation in his subcommittee.

In contrast to the Senate measure, the House subcommittee bill did not incorporate a community college title. Congressman Thompson, the primary House supporter of this idea, happened to be out of the country when the subcommittee mark-up was called, and those interested in such legislation in the higher education community, primarily the American Association of Junior Colleges, were caught off guard and preoccupied with the Pucinski-Quie occupational education title. The Administration's National Foundation for Higher Education also got nowhere in the subcommittee. Quie was unenthusiastic. Mrs. Green was wary of giving a large amount of discretionary money to federal education bureaucrats, and Brademas saw the Foundation as a possible competitor to his cherished NIE.

On the key issue of student aid, Mrs. Green's bill emerged intact from the subcommittee, without a broad new entitlement grant program and with all the amendments to existing programs she had wanted. On the other key issue, institutional aid, Mrs. Green was less successful. A majority of the subcommittee including Brademas, Thompson and the Republicans opposed the Green capitation formula. But when one of the Republicans, John Erlenborn, was unwilling to support cost-of-instruction allowances, this approach to institutional aid also failed on a tie vote. Thus the bill reported by the subcommittee did not contain a program of general institutional aid. Only a small temporary program sponsored by Steiger of Wisconsin and comparable to the Senate bail-out provision was in the bill.

Full Committee Mark-up

The full committee moved expeditiously to its mark-ups on September 28, 29, and 30. In this new context, the alliance revolving around the now consummated marriage of Quie and Brademas operated more publicly. From Brademas' point of view the alliance could be more overt because his NIE was fairly safely lodged in the higher education bill. Also, the child development bill, which Brademas had guided through the Committee with a delicate and fragile coalition of Democrats and Republicans, had been reported to the House.

However, this alliance was less effective in the full committee than it had been in the subcommittee. Quie offered a proposal analagous to the Senate Basic Grant program with one major difference. The Quie Basic Grant would have replaced an existing program, Educational Opportunity Grants, while the Pell Basic Grant was added to the existing programs. Thus the Quie proposal was known as the EOG Substitute. But it failed in the full committee.

On institutional aid, the Committee adopted a compromise which provided that two thirds of the institutional aid would be awarded on the basis of the Green capitation formula and one third on the basis of the Quie-Brademas-Administration cost-of-instruction formula. Where Mrs. Green had failed on institutional aid in the subcommittee, she got two thirds of what she wanted in the full Committee.

The Role of the Black Caucus Members

Mrs. Green gained an important element of support on student aid and institutional aid from the four Democratic members of the Committee who were members of the congressional Black Caucus: Augustus "Gus" Hawkins of California, William "Bill" Clay of Missouri, Shirley Chisholm of New York, and Herman Badillo, Puerto Rican from New York, who also counted himself a member of the Caucus. Among the participants and observers of the role played by the Black Caucus members in the full committee mark-up, there is a strong consensus on two points: First, the Black Caucus Members held the balance of power that could have tipped the two issues either way. Second, they squandered the opportunity that this strategic position gave them and got very little out of supporting Mrs. Green. One observer remarked, "This was the first time on a major piece of social legislation where the Black Caucus held the balance of power, and they failed to use it effectively."

When Quie offered his Basic Grant in the full committee, Gus Hawkins, the most senior member of the Caucus on the Committee, was the only Caucus member present. He cast his vote and the votes of the other Caucus members by proxy against the Quie amendment, providing the margin of defeat. At a subsequent meeting of members of the Caucus with several black educators, it was agreed that it might have been a mistake to oppose the Quie amendment, but it was too late to change. They hoped, however, to recoup by supporting cost-of-instruction allowances rather than the capitation form of institutional aid.

Only a few hours later, through a chance conversation with a Caucus member's legislative assistant, an Education and Labor Committee staffer who was close to Mrs. Green learned of the intentions of the Black Caucus members on institutional aid and relayed the information to her. Realizing that she would have to strike a bargain with the Black Caucus members, Mrs. Green delayed the Committee vote on this issue and asked for a meeting in Congresswoman Chisholm's office. After some negotiation, agreement was reached on a formula that would provide two thirds of the funds on the basis of capitation and one third in the form of cost-of-instruction allowances. In addition, Mrs. Green offered to support an increase in the authorization level for the Developing Institutions program, which primarily benefits Black colleges.

It was widely assumed that the Basic Grant, which was targeted on students from low-income families, and the cost-of-instruction allowances, which went to schools admitting economically disadvantaged students, would be particularly advantageous for Black students and the colleges they attended. And these interests were expected to guide the decisions of the Black Caucus members. Yet the Caucus settled for the one third cost-of-education slice of institutional aid and the few millions in increased authorization for Developing Institutions. Thus the Black Caucus members seemed to be acting contrary to the "objective" interests of their clientele.

Several factors may account for this. The Black Caucus members had some realistic concerns on the merits of Quie's Basic Grant proposal. Quie was proposing to *substitute* the Basic Grant for an existing student aid program. While the Caucus members knew that the existing programs were inadequate, they also knew that they did deliver benefits to Black students and Black colleges. The Basic Grant promised more for Black students, but the Caucus members were by long experience wary of trading dollars in hand for a promise. Mrs. Green, in fact, frequently characterized the Basic Grant as a "false promise."

While one would expect the Caucus members to be concerned about the interests of Black students in America, they were also attentive to the needs of their individual districts, as is every Congressman. Messages from the University of Southern California, a prestigious private university in Hawkins' district, and the financially distressed schools in New York in the case of Mrs. Chisholm and Congressman Badillo, strongly supported the Green institutional aid formula and were relatively indifferent to the Basic Grant. Thus by supporting Mrs. Green, the Caucus members were acting like good representatives of interests being articulated back in their home districts.

The Black Caucus members were inevitably handicapped in analyzing and understanding the issues of both student and institutional aid. In the 92nd Congress, no member of the Caucus served on the Green subcommittee. Moreover, the Caucus members were overwhelmed with work in their dual role as representatives of their home districts and representatives of the Black community at large—a national constituency. The Caucus members were deeply involved with a number of other controversial and complex issues—the poverty program, child care, emergency school aid and busing. Their staffs were as overburdened as they were.

Faced with the difficult issues of student and institutional aid, the Caucus members naturally relied on their political instincts. One instinct was not to trade existing programs for the "promise" of a new program. Another instinct was to go along with the majority of their fellow Democrats and Mrs. Green, especially since Chairman Perkins was asking for their help to get a bill out of committee. Finally, it was their instinct to distrust Quie and the Republicans and to be skeptical of their commitment to disadvantaged students. The Republicans were the party of Richard Nixon, Spiro Agnew, the Silent (white) Majority, law and order, and benign neglect for Blacks. Perhaps a good liberal Democrat like Brademas could have been expected to persuade them that it was all right to go along with the Republicans this time. However, his credibility with the Caucus members diminished as a result of the fight over the child development bill. They were dissatisfied with some aspects of the bill as reported by the Education and Labor Committee, and they correctly attributed the unsatisfactory provisions to Brademas' compromising with the Republicans to get the bill through the Committee.

The Caucus members may also have been overimpressed by the fact that someone as senior and influential as Mrs. Green would walk over to one of their offices to make a deal. This may have seemed a concession by Mrs. Green rather than a sign of their potential strength.

The New York Delegation

Part of Mrs. Green's success in the full Committee, especially on institutional aid, was attributable to the presence of seven members from New York, the largest delegation from any state. The financial crisis in higher education was particularly acute and visible in New York, and strong representations in favor of the Green institutional aid formula were made to the delegation by Hester of N.Y.U. among others. Guided by home-state interests, most of the New York delegation supported Mrs. Green on institutional aid.

Deference to the Subcommittee Chairman

Mrs. Green also enjoyed more success in the full committee because in this forum she was the subcommittee chairman and spokesman for the bill before a group of members who were generally interested and informed about higher education but not deeply concerned or expert on the issues. In this situation, given sharp and mostly party-line divisions among the subcommittee members, the tendency on the part of the committee Democrats was to go along with the subcommittee chairman, following the norms of reciprocity among subcommittees and deference to a recognized expert.

Perkins' Support

Finally, Mrs. Green's victory in the full committee relied on the support of Carl Perkins, the Committee Chairman. Perkins' top priority in 1971 was to clear a higher education bill. This was his responsibility as chairman—to see that a bill was passed before the existing legislation expired. Also, Perkins wanted to focus the Committee's attention on higher education to head off the Administration's emergency desegregation assistance to elementary and secondary schools. Consideration of such a bill risked involving the Committee in an acrimonious fight over school busing.

Perkins indicated his interest in moving a higher education bill and focusing the attention of the Committee on higher education by introducing H.R. 32 early in the 92nd Congress. He was not, however, wedded to his own bill, and tried to help Mrs. Green expedite H.R. 7248. He also participated as an ex officio voting member of the Green subcommittee during its mark-ups, trying to move the bill out of subcommittee. From the Chairman's point of view, supporting Mrs. Green fit with his goals as chairman and his personal style. Generally low-key, soft-spoken and conciliatory by nature, the Chairman sought to oblige Mrs. Green's strong views on higher education and her forceful personality.

In addition to resolving the issues of institutional aid and student aid largely in favor of Mrs. Green's views, the full committee added a weak and vague title for federal support of comprehensive state planning for postsecondary education, with a special emphasis on community college programs. This gave the House a position to match the state planning provisions in the Senate bill and was also a slight nod in the direction of Frank Thompson's community college bill.

On September 30 the Education and Labor Committee voted 35-1 to order the bill reported to the House. Such an overwhelming vote was not necessarily an accurate index of enthusiasm for the bill. Among some of the members not deeply involved in higher education, a favorable vote probably reflected a finding that there was nothing especially obnoxious in the bill, and that it was time to get the measure out of committee so attention could be turned to other issues. Among those more closely involved, Mrs. Green and her supporters were generally satisfied with the outcome of the Committee's deliberations. On the other hand top Republicans on the Committee faulted the bill for its lack of a new entitlement grant program for students, cost-of-instruction institutional aid, or the Administration's Foundation proposal. Yet these Republicans, as well as others like John Brademas who were unhappy with some of the key decisions, could vote to report the bill for two reasons. First, most of them found things in the legislation about which they were especially enthusiastic; as in the Senate, almost every member of the relevant subcommittee had some personal stake in the bill.

Democrats

Chairman Perkins: a bill

Mrs. Green: institutional aid, student aid, sex discrimination

Frank Thompson: state planning commissions

John Dent: Mineral Conservation Education

Roman Pucinski: Occupational Education, Ethnic Heritage Studies

Dominick Daniels: Youth Camp Safety

John Brademas: National Institute of Education, one third of institutional aid

James Scheuer: National Commission on Financing Postsecondary Education, Work-Study for Community Service Learning

Philip Burton: Land-Grant Status for the College of the Virgin Islands and the University of Guam

Republicans

Albert Quie: Occupational Education, one third of institutional aid

John Dellenback: one third of institutional aid

John Erlenborn: Student Loan Marketing Association

Marvin Esch: Interns for Political Leadership, library program amendment

William Steiger: Emergency bail-out

Second, reporting the bill out of committee was not the final decision. Those who had lost in the Committee could look forward to fighting another day on perhaps more favorable terrain, either the House floor or the conference committee. In particular, those wanting to adopt the Basic Grant, cost-of-instruction allowances and the Foundation knew that even if they failed on the House floor, the positions they preferred were already embodied in the Senate-passed measure.

A major bill is both a legal mechanism to meet public problems and a political document embodying a structure of bargains, compromises, and trade-offs. At this point H.R. 7248 was an ideal bill politically because, as the saying goes, nobody was completely happy with it, but everybody could live with it.

Notes

1. Quoted in *Congressional Quarterly Almanac, 1969*, Congressional Quarterly, Washington, D.C., 1970, p. 729.

2.   "Higher Education Amendments of 1969," *Hearings Before the Special Subcommittee on Education of the Committee on Education and Labor*, 91st Congress, First Session, 1969-1970, p. 1153; see also, p. 1818.

3.   Ibid., p. 1292.

4.   Robert Andringa quoted in Ed Willingham, "Education Report/Nixon's college student aid plan criticized as blow to middle-class families," *National Journal* Volume 2, August 29, 1970, p. 1861.

5.   "Higher Education Amendments of 1971," *Hearings before the Special Subcommittee on Education of the Committee on Education and Labor,* 92nd Congress, First Session, 1971, p. 81.

6.   Ibid., p. 150.

7.   *Hearings* (1971), p. 867.

8.   Ibid.

7

On the Floor: New Forces and New Actors

H.R. 7248 reached the House floor on October 27, 1971. The outcome, after four days of debate and the consideration of forty-one amendments, was to accept the major policy choices made by the Education and Labor Committee. With the full committee chairman and the subcommittee chairman united and vigorous in their support of the measure, the House only marginally modified it. The House did not and perhaps could not basically recast this complex omnibus bill. Amendments were offered that represented minority positions in the full committee. Most lost. Other amendments represented special concerns of members that had not been articulated fully in the Education and Labor Committee. Some were successful, but none seriously altered the bill. The attention the bill received, the amendments that were offered, and the outcome were typical of House floor action on controversial, major pieces of legislation. The House massaged the bill but essentially reaffirmed the decisions of its specialized committee.

However, two new dimensions were added to H.R. 7248. First, and most important, the bill became the vehicle for the House to express itself on busing elementary and secondary school children to achieve racial desegregation. To most members of the House, the press and the public, an important but not highly visible measure was moved into the spotlight and transformed into the busing bill. While those in the higher education policy arena considered the busing issue an extraneous and unfortunate subplot, for the general public, the higher education issues were the subplot.

Second, up to this point, the procedural history of the bill in both houses had been rather routine. But from the time the bill reached the floor of the House until it was signed by the President, its progress was marked by extraordinary manipulation of the legislative rules and procedures.

Four Days in the House

The first order of business in considering almost any major bill by the House is passing a rule from the Rules Committee, which generally works with the majority party leadership to ensure an orderly and steady flow of legislation. The Rules Committee reported a rule within a month after the Education and Labor Committee completed its work. An open rule permitting amendments was proposed, typical in the case of controversial domestic legislation on which the House would like to work its will.

149

The rule also included a highly unusual provision. It waived some types of points of order, but it specifically allowed points of order to be raised on the grounds that parts of the bill were properly within the jurisdiction of committees other than Education and Labor. If a point of order is raised and sustained against part of a bill, then the offending part is stricken. While such points of order are usually waived to preclude jurisdictional squabbling on the floor, the diversity and scope of H.R. 7248 led chairmen of other committees to demand that their committees' prerogatives be protected by the opportunity to raise this type of point of order. Despite vigorous protests from Chairman Perkins who said the rule would set an unfortunate precedent and make it difficult for the House to act on comprehensive legislation, the rule was adopted.

On the floor members from six House committees raised twelve points of order that their jurisdictions were being violated. Eight were either sustained by the Chair or conceded by the managers of the bill from the Education and Labor Committee. In some cases the offending sections of the bill were restored in a modified form by an amendment. While these eight successful challenges to the bill on jurisdictional grounds did not result in any basic changes, the Rules Committee action had the effect of allowing a new controversy, the defense of committee turf, to be injected into the consideration of the bill.

Having devoted the first day to adopting the rule plus four hours of general debate, the process of amendment began on the second day, and the battle over student aid occupied center stage. Congressman Quie tried to forge a Republican-liberal Democrat alliance in the full House comparable to his working relationship with John Brademas in committee. This time he offered his Basic Grant substitute with the cosponsorship of Congressman Fraser, a liberal Minnesota Democrat. But Quie's strategy was even less successful in the House than it had been in committee. The Quie-Fraser amendment lost by better than two to one. Old habits die hard and voting alliances among traditional enemies cannot be created overnight. A majority of Republicans supported the Quie-Fraser amendment, but Fraser could only bring twenty Democrats along with him.

Some supporters of the Basic Grant felt strongly that to offer the Quie-Fraser amendment was a major mistake because the House was put on record rejecting it. Conferees typically feel an obligation to defend strongly those parts of a bill on which the will of their house has been decisively expressed. Thus rejection of the Quie-Fraser amendment could lessen the chance that the Basic Grant in the Senate bill would survive the conference committee.

Institutional aid was the focus of debate on the third day when Congressman Erlenborn proposed to strike this feature from the bill entirely. As in Committee, he found both the capitation grants and the cost-of-education approach defective. His amendment was defeated, 84-310. No Democrat and only five Republicans on the Education and Labor Committee supported the amendment; less than a majority of all House Republicans and only twelve

Democrats voted in favor. The vote reflected the Education and Labor Committee's success in forging a viable compromise and in sensing the mood of the House. There was an apparent consensus that federal action was needed to alleviate the financial distress of higher education.

Mrs. Green was delighted with the outcome. Institutional aid, largely based on the capitation approach that she preferred, was accepted by the House. The supporters of the cost-of-instruction approach, on the other hand, were satisfied for now with the foothold they had in the House bill. They were willing to put off further battle on this subject until the conference committee, where they would be aided by the Senators whose entire institutional aid program was based on cost-of-instruction.

Congressman Buchanan of Alabama proposed another unsuccessful institutional aid amendment, which would have denied funds to higher education institutions supported by religious groups. The failure of the amendment to excite enough interest even to get a record vote reflected one of the basic assumptions about federal policy making for higher education, namely, that distinctions should not be made between classes of institutions like public versus private or church-supported versus non-church-supported.[a]

The busing leviathan first stirred when Congressman Pucinski announced his intention to offer the Emergency School Aid Program (ESAP) as an amendment. He noted that his amendment, about which "so many Members have inquired," would include a "total and complete prohibition against busing."[1]

The final day of House action began like the previous days, tinkering with the higher education programs. Another chapter was written in the see-saw battle over sex discrimination. Mrs. Green's bill, as first introduced, had included a strong anti-sex discrimination title that was watered down in the subcommittee mark-up. Then, through the efforts of Mrs. Green, it had been strengthened in the full committee mark-up. On the floor it was again weakened. The primary bone of contention was the inclusion of undergraduate admissions in the prohibition against sex discrimination in education programs. On two separate votes, by five-vote margins, an amendment by Congressman Erlenborn exempting undergraduate admissions was accepted. In contrast to student aid and institutional aid, the winning side in committee on the closely contested issue of sex discrimination failed to receive overwhelming support on the floor. The issue remained close and would be finally resolved in conference.

John Brademas' National Institute of Education was knocked out of the bill on a point of order because specific provisions of the NIE title infringed on the jurisdiction of the Post Office and Civil Service Committee. Although Brademas appeared ready to concede on the provisions in question, the point

---

[a]The only caveat is that federal support may not be used for religious training and education at church-related schools. Also profit-making institutions are not eligible for all federal programs.

of order was raised against the entire title. The point of order came from Congressman H.R. Gross of Iowa, the savvy and crusty Treasury watchdog, who in all likelihood wanted to kill the NIE at least as much as protect the jurisdiction of his committee. After the point of order was sustained, however, Brademas managed to restore the NIE with the objectionable provisions deleted. The Brademas amendment was adopted 210-153, a surprisingly close vote given the bipartisan support for the NIE in committee.

The close margin was largely attributable to Mrs. Green's active opposition. She remarked to her colleagues, "May I just suggest that in my judgment if you want to save money, if you want to put money into the colleges and universities, if you want to improve education, and if you are going to cut funds this is the place to cut them."[2] Most of the votes against the NIE came from conservative Republicans and southern Democrats concerned with the growth of federal spending. The support of the Administration probably saved the NIE as Republicans voted almost two to one for the Brademas amendment.

The NIE episode convinced Brademas that any further attempts at accommodation with Mrs. Green would be futile. Their split originated in ideological divergence in the mid-60s, and also in a natural rivalry for preeminence in the House in the field of higher education. The 1969-1970 fight over student unrest, Mrs. Green's effort to exclude Brademas from her subcommittee, and the conflicts over student aid and institutional aid had all widened the breach. Now Brademas saw his fellow Democrat and fellow education subcommittee chairman try to kill his major legislative initiative on the floor of the House. This was the final straw. The split between the two leading experts on higher education in the House was now irreparable.

When the reading of the bill for amendment reached the twentieth and final title, H.R. 7248, as a higher education measure reported by the Education and Labor Committee, had emerged largely unscathed. The student and institutional aid positions of the Committee were reaffirmed. The extension of existing higher education programs and the addition of a few new programs and other Christmas-tree ornaments were accepted with almost no dissent.

Here Comes the Bus

After a full day on higher education, the House finally reached the last title at about eight o'clock in the evening. Then the pent-up flood of concern over the issues of busing and emergency aid to local schools burst through, and the House began a bitter and passionate debate that extended for six hours.

The busing issue was another dimension in the divisive national debate over race relations.[b] Attention was now focused on busing for several reasons.

---

[b]The essence of the busing debate is captured in the title of a study by the NAACP Legal Defence Fund, "It's not the Busing, It's the Niggers."

Prodded by the Supreme Court, federal district courts in the South began requiring that previously segregated schools do more than admit Black students. They had to remedy the effects of segregation by affirmatively acting to integrate their schools. This frequently involved busing students from previously all-black schools to previously all-white schools and vice versa.

Second, busing and desegregation moved North. The federal courts began to widen the definition of *de jure*, legally imposed, segregation to include some of the less overt practices used in the North to achieve a separation of the races in the public schools.

Third, in both the North and South, most notably in Detroit and Richmond, federal courts entertained the idea of mandating that suburban school districts be combined with the center city district to achieve racial desegregation. This idea outraged many suburban parents who had moved to the suburbs to avoid integrated schools and/or to escape poor quality urban schools.

Fourth, the Supreme Court in its carefully worded April 20, 1971, decision, *Swann* v. *Charlotte-Mecklenburg*, said

. . .we find no basis for holding that the local school authorities may not be required to employ bus transportation as one tool of school desegregation. Desegregation plans cannot be limited to the walk-in school.[3]

Thus the Supreme Court upheld the use of busing as one remedy in cases of *de jure* school segregation. Those who had hoped that the Supreme Court would curb busing now sought a legislative remedy from Congress.

The Nixon Administration pledged to help end school segregation and to abide by the decisions of the federal courts. However, the President attempted to redefine the issue, posing the achievement of quality education for all as an alternative to busing to attain an arbitrary racial balance in the schools.[c] The Administration's initiative was the Emergency School Aid proposal, which would provide federal funds to assist school districts desegregating under order from a court or the Department of HEW. But, in its rhetoric, enforcement policies and legislative proposals, the Administration was clearly on the anti-busing side of the desegregation debate.

For all of these reasons, by November, 1971, the continuing national debate over race relations had become a debate over busing, and had reached crisis proportions in the minds of federal legislators. Three antibusing amendments were successfully added to the higher education bill. There was no "probusing" side in the debate. Rather it became a struggle between those who wanted to moderate or stall the progress of desegregation, the antibusers, versus those who

---

[c]See President Nixon's statement, "Desegregation of America's Elementary and Secondary Schools," March 24, 1970, *Weekly Compilation of Presidential Documents*, Volume 6, pp. 424ff.

wanted to continue or accelerate federal desegregation efforts, the "anti-anti-busers."

As the debate continued into the night, the Members grew irritable and short tempered, creating a highly charged atmosphere. A veteran civil rights lobbyist compared the ugly mood to lynch mobs he had seen in his youth in the South. Given the antibusing stance of the Administration and the outcry against busing in both the North and South, the results were a foregone conclusion as soon as the amendments were offered. All three passed by margins of almost two to one.

Representative Broomfield, a Michigan Republican, offered the first anti-busing amendment, which provided that the implementation of federal district court orders requiring busing to achieve "racial balance" would be delayed until all appeals, or the time for all appeals, were exhuasted.[d] Ohio Republican John Ashbrook and Mrs. Green offered the other two antibusing amendments, which prohibited the federal government from spending education funds for busing "to overcome racial imbalance . . . or . . . in order to carry out a plan of racial desegregation," and from requiring state or local education agencies to spend their funds for busing.

Having concluded action on busing, the House turned to Pucinski's Emergency School Aid Program (ESAP), a direct descendent of the Emergency School Aid Act recommended by the Administration in May, 1970, to implement the "quality education" strategy announced by the President.

In the previous Congress, despite many obstacles, Pucinski had succeeded in guiding a modified version of the Administration's bill through his subcommittee and the House, only to see it die in the Senate. Undaunted, the Pucinski subcommittee again tackled this legislation in the 92nd Congress. Through a process that included at least as many cross-currents as the higher education bill, ESAP was reported in October, 1971. However, the Rules Committee refused to grant a rule, citing a deadline of October 1 which it had established for considering legislation in the first session of the 92nd Congress. While the Rules Committee had treated this deadline flexibility in other cases, ESAP was denied a rule on a straight party vote with the Democrats responding to their leadership who hoped to avoid a fight on busing. The Rules Committee was acting in its classic role of regulating legislative business in line with the priorities of the majority party leadership.

Having failed in the Rules Committee, Pucinski brought the bill before the House under suspension of the rules, the procedure usually reserved for non-controversial bills and requiring a two-thirds majority for passage. But the bill

---

[d] In the late night confusion, the "anti-antibusers" seem to have missed an opportunity to challenge the Broomfield amendment on the grounds of its lack of germaneness. This challenge might have been successful because the Broomfield amendment dealt with the implementation of court orders rather than the funding and adminstration of education programs. See *Congressional Record*, daily edition, November 4, 1971, pp. H10407-H10408.

did not even get a majority. Bills considered under suspension cannot be amended, so many members voted against it because they wanted the opportunity to add antibusing amendments. Thus twice having failed to pass ESAP as a separate bill, Pucinski successfully offered it as an amendment to the higher education bill on the night of November 4.

Busing and ESAP had an important impact on the higher education bill. First, the higher education issues, rarely front-page news, would now be almost completely obscured. The major decisions concerning higher education would remain a largely private debate within the higher education policy arena rather than attracting wider public attention and discussion as the bill came into the home stretch.

Second, it was clear that reconciling the numerous and important differences between the House and Senate bills in conference posed a severe test. The possibility of irreconcilable differences on the higher education issues clearly existed. However, now there was a new and even more dangerous threat to the life of the bill. At this point the Senate bill contained neither antibusing nor an emergency school aid program. Even if the Senate were to graft on its own counterparts, as it shortly would, the entire bill could founder over House-Senate differences on these explosive issues.

Third, the congressional process was obviously going to take longer than anticipated. The June 30, 1972 deadline for the expiration of all higher education programs began to loom on the horizon. The hopes of having the new higher education programs in place to be implemented by the fall semester of 1972 would soon fade.

Mrs. Green, an antibusing leader, understood the risks to her prized higher education bill if it were linked to busing and ESAP. Nevertheless, she concluded there was no way to keep these issues separate, and she sponsored one of the busing amendments. From this time on, Mrs. Green's commitment would be not only to the bill's higher education programs but also to the House busing provisions.

The House voted final passage of the bill as amended, 332-38. Despite the addition of the busing curbs, only one member of the Black Caucus, Congressman Bill Clay of Missouri, and only three other Democrats, who might fairly be characterized as liberals, voted against the bill. Most votes against the bill were from the rock-ribbed conservatives who oppose almost all new domestic programs. When the House finally adjourned at 2:32 a.m., it was not to see the bill again for six months. Now the size of a small phone book, the bill again went to the Senate.

Back to the Senate

The normal procedure at this stage would have been for the Senate to insist on its bill and to agree to a conference with the House to resolve differences.

Instead, the measure was referred to the Senate Labor and Public Welfare Committee, largely to add the Senate version of ESAP. Having allowed ESAP to die at the end of the 91st Congress, the Senate had passed it early in the 92nd Congress. Now the Senate sponsors of ESAP, especially Senator Walter Mondale of Minnesota, wanted to have their version attached to the Senate higher education bill to match the Pucinski ESAP amendment that had been added to the House higher education bill.

Meeting in executive session in early December, the Senate Labor and Public Welfare Committee unanimously reported S. 659, including Mondale's ESAP, to the full Senate. The Committee also added the Indian Education Act that had passed the Senate as a separate bill, and some very mild antibusing language. The inclusion of additional programs again reflected Senator Pell's determination to have one education bill and one education conference in the 92nd Congress.

Busing Again

Since S. 659 had been amended in committee, the Senate would have to pass the bill again, and it would have the opportunity to amend it. With the busing controversy at white heat, the House having passed a bill with antibusing amendments, and the spring presidential campaigns imminent, it was inevitable that S. 659 would be transformed in the Senate from the higher education bill to the busing bill by the larger forces in the political environment. Anticipating a long struggle over antibusing amendments, the Senate leadership decided to postpone floor consideration until January.

S. 659 was finally brought before the Senate on February 22, and it was the principal item on the agenda for almost two weeks. As when the Senate considered the bill in August and when it had been passed by the House in November, the higher education recommendations of the legislative committee were reaffirmed. Busing dominated the debate. This was the second time around for the bill on the Senate floor, and the higher education issues were pushed even further into the background than on the House floor.

In the Senate, the House Rules Committee's function—setting the time limits and terms of the debate—is performed through unanimous consent agreements negotiated by the leadership of the two parties and all interested Senators. Where the House Rules Committee often acts to structure floor action to further the policies of the majority party leadership, the Senate unanimous consent agreements seek to accommodate fairly all shades of opinion. Because it takes only one objection to defeat a unanimous consent agreement, and the threat of a filibuster is available to any Senate faction that feels ill used, this agreement must be a device for accommodation rather than leadership. The unanimous consent agreement illustrates the contrast between the more hierarchical House and the more collegial Senate. As one Senate aide remarks, "The Senate is not

100 Senators from fifty sovereign States; it is 100 sovereign Senators from fifty States."

In this case, the unanimous consent agreement provided for six hours of debate on the bill per day for seven days, almost all for the purpose of considering the twenty proposed amendments dealing with busing and desegregation. The busing language produced by the liberal Labor and Public Welfare Committee did not placate the antibusing sentiment in the Senate. The arena for fighting out the busing issue in both houses was the floor.

In contrast to the House, however, the Senate busing debate was far less acrimonious. The more dispassionate Senate approach reflects the style of the Senate, where norms of collegiality and moderation predominate in this smaller body with members serving six-year terms. The practice of conducting business by unanimous consent both reflects and necessitates this style.

Also in contrast to the House, the Senators concerned about busing did not have to jump on the first busing amendment that came alone. There was a choice. The Minority Whip, Robert Griffin of Michigan (where the busing controversy was hottest), offered a set of stringent amendments. On the other hand, the Senate Majority Leader, Mike Mansfield of Montana, and the Minority Leader, Hugh Scott of Pennsylvania, cosponsored a package of busing amendments which were weakened versions of the House provisions. Thus the Senate party leadership played a creative role in tempering the busing conflict. In the House, there had been no moderate alternative.

Through a complex series of parliamentary maneuvers typical of the Senate, both the Scott-Mansfield and Griffin amendments were adopted. Then this entire package was defeated by one vote, the Griffin amendment was defeated by three votes, and the Scott-Mansfield amendment was again adopted.

Other Senate Issues

An important issue of legislative-executive prerogative also emerged during the Senate floor debate. The Office of Education was moving toward implementation of an "educational renewal site strategy," which involved the consolidation and coordination of several federal elementary and secondary education programs with the aim of achieving a more focused and effective impact on educational services at the local level. Commissioner of Education Sidney Marland, supported by HEW Secretary Richardson, maintained that the plan was simply a new "administrative procedure." Several Democrats on the Labor and Public Welfare Committee countered this was a new "program" without legislative authorization and that it modified existing programs contrary to the intent of Congress.

In an attempt to resolve the dispute, high-level negotiations were carried on between Secretary Richardson, Senator Javits and Senator Cranston of

California. Faced with a deadline on the only education bill likely to come along in the 92nd Congress and aware of the strong desire of many Senators to reassert legislative prerogatives, Richardson finally agreed not to oppose Senator Cranston's amendment dealing with the issue. The Cranston amendment, which was adopted, authorized a limited renewal program, undid much of the reorganization of the Office of Education undertaken to implement the renewal strategy, and, most importantly, stringently prohibited any consolidation of education programs and appropriations unless specifically authorized by law. Richardson, Javits and Cranston further agreed that if they could reach an agreement "spelled out in writing" that was satisfactory to the Senators who had expressed concern on the matter, then Cranston "would not press in conference for the adoption of this amendment."[4]

Senator Birch Bayh of Indiana offered a weaker version of his sex discrimination amendment that had been ruled out of order in August. This time it was accepted without opposition.

In the House Again

On March 1, 1972, the Senate adopted 88-6 the amended S.659. It was now up to the House to go through the normally routine procedure of disagreeing with the Senate and requesting a conference. But when Chairman Perkins took the House floor and asked for unanimous consent to do this, Congressman Joe Waggonner objected.

Waggonner and other antibusers wanted the opportunity to instruct the House conferees not to yield to the Senate on the House busing amendments. Such a move—a house instructing its conferees—is a rare occurrence. It reflects a lack of confidence in the committee members handling the legislation and limits their bargaining freedom in conference, making agreement on a bill more difficult.

But the antibusers were intent on instructing the House conferees. Four months had passed since the House had had an opportunity to vote on busing. The national debate over the issue had not abated, and the antibusers were anxious for another occasion to demonstrate their fervor. Moreover, looking at the list of prospective conferees, the antibusers noted that these Members had voted for the Broomfield amendment by a slim margin but that a majority of them had voted against both the Green and Ashbrook amendments. Because the House had adopted the three amendments by more than 2-1, passing instructions was a way to protect the House busing amendments from what seemed the natural tendency of the House conferees to abandon them in conference for the weaker Scott-Mansfield amendment.

Perkins vainly protested that the instructions would complicate the conference and endanger the urgently needed higher education legislation. However, the motion to instruct was adopted, 272-139, with the support of Mrs. Green. Offering a motion to instruct the conferees was unusual. That it was adopted by almost 2-1 was extraordinary, and a good indication of how strong the antibusing tide was running in the House.

The Speaker then appointed the House conferees:

Democrats	Republicans
Carl Perkins (Ky.)	Albert Quie (Minn.)
Edith Green (Ore.)	Alphonzo Bell (Cal.)
Frank Thompson, Jr. (N.J.)	Ogden Reid (N.Y.)
John Dent (Pa.)	John Erlenborn (Ill.)
Roman Pucinski (Ill.)	John Dellenback (Ore.)
Dominick Daniels (N.J.)	Marvin Esch (Mich.)
John Brademas (Ind.)	William Steiger (Wis.)
Augustus Hawkins (Cal.)	Orval Hansen (Idaho)
Lloyd Meeds (Wash.)	
Philip Burton (Cal.)	
Joseph Gaydos (Pa.)[e]	
Romano Mazzoli (Ky.)	

On March 13, the Senate routinely continued to insist on its bill and agreed to a conference with the House. The following Senate conferees were appointed:

Democrats	Republicans
Claiborne Pell (R.I.)	Peter Dominick (Col.)
Jennings Randolph (W. Va.)	Jacob Javits (N.Y.)
Harrison Williams (N.J.)	Richard Schweiker (Pa.)
Edward Kennedy (Mass.)	J. Glenn Beall (Md.)
Walter Mondale (Minn.)	Robert Stafford (Vt.)[f]
Thomas Eagleton (Mo.)	
Alan Cranston (Cal.)	

The stage was now set for the effort to put it all together. In the conference committee, final legislative choices would have to be made on the higher education issues that had been debated and developed over the past three years. In

---

[e]James Scheuer of New York was appointed a conferee on March 8, but he dropped off before the first meeting of the conference to devote his time to re-election problems. Gaydos was appointed to replace him.

[f]Senator Stafford replaced the deceased Senator Prouty on the Senate Education Subcommittee.

addition, this overwhelmingly liberal group of House and Senate conferees would have to weigh principle and pragmatism to try to achieve an agreement on busing that could pass both houses.

Notes

1. *Congressional Record*, daily edition, November 3, 1971, p. H10292.
2. Ibid., November 4, 1971, p. H10380.
3. 402 U.S. 1 at 30.
4. *Congressional Record*, daily edition, February 28, 1972, p. S2711. This statement by Senator Cranston, beginning on p. S2710, gives his version of the controversy and his negotiations with Secretary Richardson.

8 The Conference Committee

The conference committee first met on March 15, 1972, in S-207, an elegant high-ceilinged room with a crystal chandelier, white marble fireplace, and rich dark wood-paneled walls on the Senate side of the Capitol. The conferees faced a staggering task. The basic working documents of the conference, four large volumes, contained 274 numbered explanations of the differences between the two bills.[a] Counting subdivisions of these items, the "Blue Books" listed 401 differences in the bills.

The 401 differences were not simple technical variations in legislative language. Many of the individual items dealt with large and complex programs like the Basic Grant. Other items described a major program in one bill followed by the statement, "There is no comparable House [Senate] provision." Thus, for example, with respect to the Basic Grant and National Foundation for Post-secondary Education, all of which were in the Senate bill but not in the House bill, the conferees had to decide on the inclusion of major programs. In many cases there were fundamental differences in approach and philosophy. The Senate cost-of-instruction provisions versus the House capitation institutional aid was one such basic policy difference. Another was the Senate Basic Grant versus the slight revision of existing programs by the House. Also, lurking in the wings was the busing issue.

The task was also formidable because of the basic decision-making rule in conference committees, which is that a majority of the conferees from each house must agree. This can occur in two ways. First, one house "recedes" and accepts the position of the other house. Second, the conferees from one house propose to the other side modified language, and if at least a majority of the other side accepts the proposal, agreement is reached, the side offering the proposal having "receded with an amendment."

The conference had the inherent difficulty of finding two majorities to agree with each other. In addition, it would be harder to get at least eleven members on the House side to agree with at least seven on the Senate side in contrast to the usual conference where three or four members would constitute a majority of the conferees from each house.

---

[a]In the "Blue Books" the House bill and the Senate bill were printed side by side lining up the sections of the two bills that corresponded to each other. These volumes also had a third column of explanations of the differences that were numbered and called "items." These numbered items served as the basic point of reference for discussing the two bills.

The large number of House conferees was due to two factors. First, major parts of the House bill came from each of the three education subcommittees of the Education and Labor Committee. Although the three subcommittees overlapped, the need to include significant representation from each expanded the House delegation to the conference. Second, within Mrs. Green's subcommittee almost every member had a personal stake in the bill. Thus all but two of the thirteen members of the Green subcommittee were House conferees. On the Senate side, though there were not multiple education subcommittees, each member of the Education Subcommittee also had personally prized provisions in the bill, and all twelve members became conferees.

As the conference opened, there were some widely shared expectations concerning the direction it would take. Particularly in the higher education associations and in HEW, there was a high regard for the political strength and legislative effectiveness of Mrs. Green. Chairman Perkins was not reputed to be among the strongest House chairmen and was expected to defer to Mrs. Green. His interests were primarily in elementary and secondary education and in issues, like the poverty program, that most directly affected his eastern Kentucky district. Senator Pell was perceived as a minor-league Senator with a modest legislative record. With Perkins and Pell heading the House and Senate delegations and with Mrs. Green's track record, many observers felt she would prevail in the conference.

On the specific issues, it was generally expected that some form of the Senate Basic Grant would be accepted. The vigor and unanimity of the Senators in support of this program, its endorsement by the Administration, and Senator Pell's determination to sit in conference indefinitely until it was accepted seemed to guarantee its survival.

Although a few thought that the Green capitation formula would prevail, most observers predicted that the institutional aid formula would be compromised. One view was that the formula would be split 50-50, 50 percent based on the Green capitation formula and 50 percent on some combination of the Quie-Brademas and Senate cost-of-instruction approaches.[b] All predictions foresaw the Senate institutional aid formula as the chief loser in any compromise.

The NIE was in both bills and was an Administration initiative. It seemed to be a sure thing. The Administration's Foundation was thought doomed because of the hostility on the House side from Green, Brademas and Quie and only lukewarm support from the higher education community. A brokered marriage with the Senate accepting the House's occupational education title in

---

[b]The Quie-Brademas one third of the House institutional aid formula based aid to an institution on the dollar volume of federal student aid received by students at the institution. The Senate cost-of-instruction formula, on the other hand, based aid to institutions on the number of Basic Grant recipients they enrolled.

return for House acceptance of the Senate's community college title was considered a natural, if not made in heaven.[c]

Other predictions were based on finely calibrated assessments of the position, commitment and political clout of various members and the Administration. For example, the strong commitment of both Congressman Pucinski and Senator Schweiker to the Ethnic Heritage Studies program, the relative indifference of the Administration, and the fact that this was a small program seemed to bode well for its survival, despite its having been eliminated from the House bill by a floor amendment.

It was universally felt that the conference would be long and difficult. Chairman Perkins, in a caucus of the House Democratic conferees before the first conference meeting, noted that it would be "a devil of a mean conference." There was even some gloomy speculation that the conference might fail. The headline of a preconference story in *The Washington Post* asked, "Is There Any Hope for the Higher Education Bill?"[1]

The Basic Dynamics of Reaching Agreement

Despite the magnitude of the task and some pessimism, agreement was reached on a bill. It took twenty-one conference meetings lasting approximately eighty hours over a two-month period. Three factors explain how this unusually difficult conference was brought to a successful conclusion. First, the choice of the conference members enabled two majority coalitions to be formed that agreed on the key issues; second, a process for decision making was established that facilitated agreement; and third, the key leaders, Perkins and Pell, were steadfastly committed to getting a bill and had the political skills required to achieve that objective.

The Composition of the Conference

There is a strong presumption that every conference will produce a bill. Conferees are by profession legislators and politicians. The arts of bargaining, compromise and negotiation are their stock in trade. However, despite the image of infinite malleability that is often associated with professional politicians, generally they

---

[c]In fact, before the conference began, a letter from a community college president presenting an intellectual rationale for combining the two programs was widely circulated. The letter argued that the community college title aimed at institution building while the occupational education title aimed at program development. Thus one title would help create the institutions, and the other would help provide programs at those institutions. Letter of January 27, 1972, from Frank M. Chambers, President, Middlesex Community College, New Jersey, to Congressman Dominick Daniels and other members of the New Jersey congressional delegation.

have strong basic principles concerning public policy questions. On most issues there are broad limits beyond which legislators will not go for the sake of expediency and compromise. Thus, in this case, where major differences between the House and Senate bills involved fundamental questions concerning the federal responsibility for higher education, as well as the busing issue with its bearing on racial justice, the choice of the specific individuals to make up the conference committee could determine whether agreement was possible.

On student aid and institutional aid, the Senate conferees unanimously supported the Senate position. On the other hand, the House subcommittee and full committee had been divided, with Quie, Brademas and their allies favoring something comparable to the Senate bill. Mrs. Green and her allies were successful both in the committee and on the House floor. They kept a Basic Grant program out of the House bill and obtained an institutional aid program based largely on the capitation principle. The divisions within the House committee would continue to be reflected by the House conferees.

The basic question was whether Quie and Brademas could put together a majority coalition among the House conferees and recede to the Senate on institutional aid and the Basic Grant, or whether the Green forces could stand fast for their position in the House bill. If the Green forces had the upper hand, the most likely scenario would be a grudging acceptance of the Senate Basic Grant in return for major concessions from the Senate on institutional aid. If a Green majority demanded both that the Senate give up the Basic Grant and make concessions on institutional aid, the prospect was deadlock and no bill.

The power to appoint House conferees is held formally by the Speaker, but in practice it is exercised by the chairman of the committee that considered the legislation. The committee chairman normally allows the ranking minority member of the committee to select the minority conferees. Thus this task fell to Congressman Quie. Quie put himself on the conference committee and picked all of the Republican members of the Green subcommittee with one exception, Earl Ruth of North Carolina, the most junior Republican. Ruth, a conservative, was out of step with his Republican colleagues on the Education and Labor Committee, and he agreed not to become a conferee on this bill in order not to cause problems for Quie. Ruth was also among the most outspoken antibusers, and his presence in the conference would have made compromise on busing more difficult.

In addition, Quie picked three Republicans as conferees who were members of the two other education subcommittees, Alphonzo Bell, Ogden Reid and Orval Hansen. These choices also artfully left out a number of possibly troublesome members from Quie's point of view, such as John Ashbrook of Ohio and Earl Landgrebe of Indiana, both extremely conservative.

Quie's careful selection produced a group of eight Republican conferees who were either sympathetic to Quie's position on the issues or at least uncommitted. John Erlenborn, who offered the unsuccessful floor amendment to delete institutional aid from the bill, and William Steiger, who preferred his emergency bail-out, were two possible exceptions. There was no guarantee that Quie could count on unanimous Republican support. Congressmen are open to persuasion from many quarters, and most will not blindly take directions from a legislative leader. The fact that the Republican conferees voted as a solid bloc on the key issues was testimony not only to Quie's shrewd choices but also to his skills as a leader.

In his late forties and relatively young to be the ranking minority member of a committee, Quie is a large boyish-looking man with a quick wit and sly sense of humor. A Minnesota dairy farmer from Lutheran Norwegian background, he has the easygoing directness of a Midwestern farmer. He is also a canny and resourceful politician, diligent in legislative work, and genuinely concerned about policy issues. Along with Mrs. Green and John Brademas, he was one of the House Members who consistently understood the details of legislation as well as the staff, if not better.

In the weeks before the conference, Quie sat down with the Republican conferees for frank discussions and was able to persuade his skeptical colleagues, like Erlenborn and Steiger, as well as those who were not expert on the issues, to support his position on the Basic Grant and institutional aid. There were naturally some mutual accommodations as well as perhaps a few *quid pro quo's*. Thus Quie was able to bring together and bring along the other seven Republican conferees. One of the Republican conferees remarked, "Quie deserves a great deal of credit for the unity of the House Republicans in the conference. He is a consensus-builder."

The united Republican conferees, of course, could not alone dominate the House delegation to the conference. They still were the minority. But the unity of the House Republican conferees maximized their impact in the conference and meant that they would have to work with fewer of the Democrats to form a majority. Also, the respect that the Republicans had for Quie allowed him to deal with the Democrats with some discretion and flexibility.

Chairman Perkins selected the twelve Democratic conferees, taking all eight Democrats from the Green subcommittee along with four others from the Brademas and Pucinski subcommittees.

It was clear from the outset that Democrats Brademas and Frank Thompson favored Quie's position on the major higher education issues. Brademas and Quie worked closely together during the committee deliberations with Brademas casting Thompson's proxy while the latter had been preoccupied with the Campaign Financing and Disclosure legislation in another committee. The other ten Democrats, including Perkins, either favored or were sympathetic to Mrs. Green's view. Thus if a solid bloc of eight Republicans were joined by Brademas and Thompson, there would be a stand-off at 10-10 among the House conferees on student aid and institutional aid.

The delicate balance of contending forces was almost upset early in the conference when Congressman Reid announced that he had switched from the Republican to the Democratic Party. He resigned from the Education and Labor Committee, since he was a member of its Republican delegation, and was given a different assignment by the Democrats. It might have been expected that he would also drop off the conference committee, which Mrs. Green strongly favored since Reid was perhaps Quie's most solid supporter and he had worked in partnership with Brademas going back to the Reid-Brademas bill in 1969. Quie would have had a difficult time finding a reliable replacement. Reid stayed, however, preserving the balance. He moved over and sat with the House Democrats and also caucused with them, but Quie continued to vote his proxy when Reid was absent.[d]

On the Senate side, the choice of the conferees did not entail the adroit juggling that was involved on the House side. There was no need. The Senate committee had not been riven by factions and was unanimous in support of the basic features of its bill.

The only issue which split the Senate conferees was busing. The presence of an unusually large group of twelve Senators at the conference provided the opportunity to try a number of different compromises on busing until one that commanded a majority could be found. A smaller group of Senators would have presented a situation of less flexibility. The same observation applies also to the size of the House delegation and its ability to reach a position on busing acceptable to a majority of the Senate conferees.

The Procedures

A second basic factor in reaching agreement on a bill was the set of procedures adopted for resolving differences. The procedures facilitated compromise, avoided deadlocks, and dampened conflict.

A key procedural decision was unnoticed at the first conference session, when Perkins, who was Chairman of the conference committee, opened Volume 1 of the Blue Books and began a discussion of Item 1 on page 1. Having concluded with Item 1, he proceeded to Item 2 and so on. This meant that the higher education issues would be dealt with first. Busing and the Emergency School Aid Program (ESAP) were printed at the end of the Blue Books and would be confronted only much later. It also meant that the most controversial higher education issues would not be taken up immediately. The first three titles of the Higher Education Act were relatively noncontroversial. Only then did one reach Title IV, student aid, which contained the Basic Grant.

---

[d]For those with a simplified view of parties and party loyalty in the legislative process, here is a case of a Republican leader, Quie, working to retain on the conference committee a turncoat Republican who had become a Democrat and whose presence increased the overrepresentation of the Democrats.

A second procedure aimed at avoiding unproductive deadlocks. As the conference committee reached each item, generally there would be some discussion with one delegation either offering to recede or suggesting that the other side recede. When agreement was not reached quickly and the discussion began to drag, the item would be passed over to be resolved at a later date. The conference would then move on to other issues on which agreement could more easily be obtained. In this way the conference moved through all of the higher education provisions settling the differences that could be most quickly and easily resolved. It took eight meetings of the conference over a period of almost a month between March 16 and April 13 to make this first pass at the higher education provisions. Then the conferees worked through the higher education provisions a second time focusing on those issues still in disagreement and settling all but the most controversial. This second pass at the higher education issues took seven more conference meetings and another two weeks between April 18 and May 2. Only then were five meetings between May 3 and May 16, devoted to ESAP, the still-remaining higher education issues, and finally busing.[e] An alternate procedure would have been to try to crack the tough nuts, like busing, first. If agreement were reached, then the conference could mop up the easy issues. If there were no agreement, everyone could pack up and go home or just sit and see who would break first.

A third aspect of the format was a distinct preference for dealing with the issues on a technical and pragmatic basis. Discussions of philosophy were avoided. The conferees addressed themselves not to questions of abstract truth but to the task before them, reconciling the language of two different bills.

This partiality for pragmatic solutions was established by Chairman Perkins' conduct of the first session. A contrast to his approach was provided at the second meeting, which Mrs. Green chaired in Perkins' absence. Mrs. Green had not been at the first meeting when Titles I and II had been disposed of item by item on narrow grounds. Mrs. Green began with a philosophical discussion contrasting the House approach to Title III, the Developing Institutions Program, with the Senate's. There were several objections, and she was informed that the procedure that had been agreed on and had worked successfully the day before was to go item by item rather than discuss the philosophical differences between the two versions of entire titles. The conference then continued as it had on the previous day.

The procedures facilitated agreement for several reasons. First, the conferees gained experience in communicating and bargaining with each other before they confronted the toughest issues. Many of the House and Senate conferees were meeting for the first time. Personal rapport and working relations

---

[e]The general sequence of handling the items of differences was not strictly adhered to. The most important exception was the Basic Grant that was settled once during the first pass through the bill and then reopened and not resolved until the final stage when the most difficult higher education issues were acted on.

were established as they dealt with the easy items. When confronted with the tough issues, the chances for misunderstanding were lessened, and the potential for cooperation was increased with the legacy of successful collaboration. Settling these hard issues later did indeed strain relations among the conferees almost to the breaking point. If this wrenching experience had occurred early, without the background of rapport among the members, the conference might have crumbled. Even if the conference had succeeded in handling the big issues early, the atmosphere might have been poisoned, making the resolution of the rest of the differences much more difficult.

Second, moving through the higher education bill twice, skipping the most difficult issues, meant that by the time busing, ESAP and the key higher education issues were up, most of the active conferees had a dual investment in the bill. Each had invested time and effort over a six-week period. Also, almost all of them had by this time some programs to which they were personally strongly committed already lodged in the bill, the differences having been resolved. Not wanting to see their grueling efforts wasted and their personally favored programs die, most conferees were likely to be a little more accommodating when the conference reached the thorniest items.

Third, skipping controversial items averted logjams early in the conference. During the first six weeks, the conference continually moved forward. It resolved issues. A feeling of momentum developed. The conferees grew confident in their ability to successfully handle ever more difficult problems. The sweet smell of success began to permeate the conference as the weeks went by.

Finally, confronting the task item by item in pragmatic fashion also facilitated agreement. It would have been more difficult to compromise differences in philosophy both because they touch on the deeply held views of the members and they lack concrete referents that make reasoned argument and compromise easier.

Chance also affected the decision-making procedures. If Mrs. Green had been at the first conference session, she might have set a different tone for the deliberations. Instead, when she was chairing in Perkins' absence on the second day, the procedures were already established, and her attempt to proceed by a more philosophical and comprehensive method was rebuffed.

The operation of the conference fit the conferees' mood. At the first session, there was a sense of relief and tranquility, like that of the crew of a ship who have passed through a typhoon and are now returned to business as usual navigating in calmer waters. This bill, the product of more than two years of painstaking and often tedious efforts by the group of Congressmen who were now conferees, had been buffeted and almost overwhelmed by the maelstrom over school busing. Now the Members were in a closed session largely isolated from these environmental effects to discuss the higher education issues that were their primary concern. Nearly all of them viewed busing and ESAP as extraneous and unfortunate appendages to the higher education bill. Through at least the first month of the conference there was almost a taboo against discussing, even informally, the problem of reconciling the House and Senate busing amendments.

Choosing Perkins as the chairman of the conference was another key procedural decision made at the first session. The chairmanship of successive conferences dealing with a given subject normally alternates between the House and Senate. Before the conference began, however, there was some uncertainty over whose turn it was to chair. Upon learning that Perkins was interested, Pell gracefully obliged and proposed that Perkins be the conference chairman. The handling of this issue was important because it avoided a potentially unpleasant debate which personal and institutional pride could have made difficult to resolve. It also smoothed the path for amicable and cooperative relations between Chairman Perkins and Senator Pell.[f]

The Commitment and Political Skill of Perkins and Pell

Chairman Perkins focused with unflagging zeal on the single objective of getting a bill reported by the conference. He said at least a hundred times publicly and privately, "We're going to get a bill." This statement became a cliche of the conference. There were three reasons for Perkins' singleminded determination.

First, throughout his entire congressional career Perkins had been a liberal supporting federal domestic social welfare programs. Perkins' political beliefs and his perception of the interests of his constituents made him an advocate of federal aid-to-education legislation.

Second, it is the role of committee chairmen to produce legislation to meet salient public needs in their areas of jurisdiction. To preserve and build his reputation within Congress as an effective legislative leader, Perkins had to produce a bill. There were rumblings of dissatisfaction among the House Democratic leaders because of the extended amount of time this bill was taking. Perkins risked both the ire of the leadership and a loss of face among his fellow committee chairmen if he failed to deliver. One higher education lobbyist remarked, "Perkins was losing standing among the dukes [the other committee chairmen]. They were pressing him to get his troops together and to get a bill out."

Third, the intensity of Perkins' commitment was a matter of personality. A big, soft-spoken, kindly man, Perkins usually looks slightly rumpled and walks with a shambling gait. Some of his more urbane colleagues consider him

[f]Senator Pell, the subcommittee chairman, was the chairman of the Senate conferees even though Senator Williams, the chairman of the full committee, was a conferee. Perkins, the chairman of the full committee, chaired the House delegation rather than Mrs. Green, whose position on the Education and Labor Committee was analogous to Senator Pell's. The fact that Carl Perkins rather than Mrs. Green was the chairman of the House conferees had an important bearing on the outcome of the conference.

something of a country bumpkin. His appearance belies not only his skill as a legislator but also his capacity for hard work. A staff member observed, "When Carl Perkins undertakes to do something, he generates phenomenal psychological drive to get it done. This is his Baptist-Calvinist-Puritan ethic. He drives and drives and drives. If there are frustrations and roadblocks, far from defeating him, they just energize him even more."

With few exceptions, Perkins was not troubled by the substantive issues. No matter how they were worked out, there would be a bill that continued all the existing programs and added some new programs. What he was after was agreement in the conference and, looking down the road, passage of the conference report in the House and Senate.

Perkins' political skills were displayed in the way he structured and facilitated the conference. One of his colleagues remarked, "Perkins handled the conference like Bobby Fisher."

Of major importance was Perkins' sense of political timing. Most politicians recognize that, having determined a course of action, it is often not what you do that decides your success as *when* you do it. A sense of political timing is a unique and finely tuned clock ticking in the head of every skillful politician. Perkins' canny political timing was crucial in presiding over the conference, particularly his handling of the sequence of items and the pace of the conference as a whole.

Perkins moved swiftly through the first two titles of the higher education bill on the first day. This had the effect of institutionalizing the procedures of the conference, in particular that of skipping items. Sometimes he used his prerogative as chairman to skip over some items without debate when he wanted to move along. Or he would intercede when the debate on an item seemed to be exacerbating differences rather than producing agreement.

He also exercised some discretion in scheduling the business for each session of the conference. He could suggest that the conference return to an item previously skipped over or jump ahead to take up an item. He used scheduling discretion to accommodate individual members, especially the busy Senators. Because many of the conferees were interested in only one or a few programs and rarely attended the conference sessions, Perkins would have the conference take up their pet items when they found it convenient to attend. This accelerated the process of vesting individual conferees in the bill. It also helped create an atmosphere of cooperation. If Perkins learned or felt that an agreement had been reached among the conferees interested in some previously skipped or not yet reached item, he would call it up to nail down the bargain before it had a chance to break down. He also sensed that the members needed to discuss some particularly difficult items several times before they were ready to decide. Perkins would call up these items, let the debate go on, and ask that they again be deferred, until they were fully ripened.

In addition, the chairman used scheduling to modulate the temper of the conference. After a closely fought or difficult issue had been settled, he might bring up a string of relatively easy items to restore the spirit of cooperation and recharge the momentum of the conference. He could even use scheduling as a subtle form of punishment. On the day after Mrs. Green made a speech in the House criticizing the House conferees for selling out to the Senate, Perkins brought up the sex discrimination title. Because the Senate title was stronger than the House version, Mrs. Green, a champion of the cause of women's rights, was put in the awkward position of leading the charge to sell out to the Senate.

The chairman also exercised discretion in calling for votes. With the exception of busing, most of the votes were among the House conferees as they searched for a position to present to the Senators or as they decided on the acceptability of Senate proposals. When Perkins sensed that a consensus existed among a majority of the House conferees that was acceptable to the Senators, he would intervene and call for a vote before further discussion muddied the issue. He also would occasionally push for votes among the House conferees on tentative proposals that were under discussion so that the contending sides could get an accurate reading of their strength.

While Perkins' first goal was to get a bill out of conference, he was also looking ahead to passing the conference report, especially in the House where the busing fervor and the instructions to the House conferees were a clear warning of the dangers faced by an unsatisfactory bill. Given the major differences between the two bills and the unity of the Senators in defense of their bill, it was clear that some major concessions would have to be made by the House. This risked alienating some support in the House. It was also clear that some compromise on the busing amendments would have to be worked out. The House conferees were not going to be able to preserve the House busing amendments intact and thus would not be able to live up to the letter of the instructions. This risked arousing the ire of the House antibusers.

Perkins perceived that to pass the conference report in the House, it had to appear to be the best deal that could be obtained, the product of a long and tough fight. Thus while Perkins wanted the House and Senate conferees to resolve their differences, he did not want the agreement to seem to come too easily. He therefore tried to set a pace for the conference best described as measured urgency. He pushed the Senators from the very beginning for more and longer conference sessions. There was never a feeling of marking time or deliberate stalling. On the other hand, he exerted his influence to make major issues, especially the Basic Grant, institutional aid and busing, the subject of long deliberations. On learning that an accommodation had been reached on one important issue, Perkins got the interested parties to agree to hold off formally ratifying their compromise. He asked on a few occasions that House conferees vote contrary to their beliefs to uphold the position of the House on a controversial item in a pro forma vote. Thus before the hard bargaining to finally settle the controversy, the House conferees would be on record refusing to give in to the Senate.

Some conferees, understanding Perkins' long-range perspective and his commitment to getting a bill, also got into the spirit. When a compromise had been worked out privately and was certain to command a majority of both delegations, they would sometimes stage a series of proposals and counter-proposals that ended up at the agreed point. Thus rather than simply pushing through the agreement on the strength of their votes, an exchange of offers was arranged. The result was the same, but hopefully it would look better when the conference report reached the House.

Perkins also played an important role in facilitating the emergence of a majority coalition on the House side that could reach agreement with the Senators on institutional aid and other issues. This facet of his role will unfold below.

Senator Pell was also committed to bringing a bill out of conference. He, like Perkins, was a liberal Democrat favoring expansive federal social welfare programs. However, Pell had a special commitment to this legislation. It was the most important bill yet to come out of the Senate subcommittee during his tenure as chairman, and he took personal pride in the Basic Grant, which he and his staff often referred to as the "Pell Grant."

Pell had another reason for wanting the conference to end successfully. He was up for re-election in 1972 and faced a stiff challenge. In fact, in the spring of 1972, during the conference, he was rated a distinct underdog. Part of his re-election problem was his record of legislative accomplishment, which, at least to the public eye, looked rather scanty. Guiding the Education Amendments, with the "Pell Grants" included, into law would be an important achievement bolstering his record. In their pessimistic moments, Pell and his staff spoke of the higher education measure as his "legacy" if he should be defeated.

Pell's personality also contributed to the intensity of his commitment. Aristocratic and low-key, Pell could also be stubborn. Like Perkins, he was simply not willing to let this bill fail.

Pell was neither chairman of the conference nor chairman of a divided delegation, so his tasks were not as difficult as Perkins', but he too made important contributions from his position as chairman of the Senate delegation. It was up to Pell to alert Senators when the programs in which they had a special interest were being considered and to protect their interests when they were absent. As long as he protected the special interests of his Senate colleagues, which he did with care and diligence, they were willing to let him speak for the Senate on most issues. This gave Pell considerable flexibility and a position of strength in bargaining with the House.

He also worked to accommodate the Senate Republican conferees. He would not allow a conference session to begin until at least one Republican Senator had arrived, and he always conferred with the senior Republican Senator present, usually Javits or Dominick, and got their agreement before responding to a proposal from the House or making an offer on behalf of the Senate. Often sitting in the conference as the only Democratic Senator and holding the proxies of all of the other Democrats, Pell could have acted unilaterally, outvoting the Republicans any time he chose. Instead, he elected to maintain the bipartisan unity that had characterized the history of the Senate bill.

Pell made a conscious effort to preserve in the final bill the programs with which the Republican Senators and the Nixon Administration were identified. This not only added to his bargaining ability in the conference, but was designed with an eye toward passing the conference report in the Senate. In addition, Pell was looking even further down the road to the time when the bill would reach the White House to be signed or vetoed.

The Process of Conference Committee Decision Making

Given the basic dynamics of the conference, how did the thirty-two conferees resolve the 401 differences?

Minor and Technical Differences

In many areas there was a basic consensus, and action proceeded rapidly. Discussion centered around which alternative would strengthen the program that everyone agreed on. This pattern was evident with respect to the National Institute of Education (NIE).

The thirteen differences between the House and Senate versions of the NIE were all resolved during part of one afternoon session of the conference. In fact, the NIE seemed to be something of a breather which Chairman Perkins turned to between more controversial issues. The NIE was never skipped over as a controversial or difficult issue, and there was no need for extensive private negotiations before it was brought up. Of the thirteen differences, the House receded on six, the Senate receded on six, and one was settled by combining the language from both bills. Of the seven differences where a provision in one bill had no counterpart in the other bill, five were accepted, indicating the objective of strengthening the NIE by adding language one house had overlooked.

Special Interests and General Indifference

Another group of items that yielded to expeditious action were those on which one or a few members felt strongly and everyone else was indifferent. Once the few concerned members worked out their disagreements, the conference ratified their agreement. This process applied, for example, in the cases of Mineral Conservation Education and Indian Education.

Congressman Dent of Pennsylvania and Senator Randolph of West Virginia, both representatives of coal mining areas, were the only members with a strong interest in Mineral Conservation Education. They agreed to drop the program, which was in the House but not the Senate bill, with the understanding that separate legislation was well on its way to acceptance in both the House and Senate. The conference went along without a murmur.

On Indian Education, the Senate bill had a major program while the House bill had nothing, although similar legislation was being developed in a House committee. In this case, Congressman Lloyd Meeds of Washington and Senator Kennedy worked out an agreement by which the House would accept the Senate program with amendments proposed by Congressman Meeds. Again the conference committee passively acceded.

Another example was the action among the House conferees on the less controversial aspects of ESAP. Looking toward floor action on the conference report, Chairman Perkins and other House conferees wanted to enhance the credibility of ESAP among House liberals and the Black Caucus. Thus they tried when possible to follow the lead of Congressman Hawkins, the only Black conferee. On one occasion, Chairman Perkins called for a voice vote on the House side on an ESAP item. The result was uncertain. Perkins asked, "How did the gentleman from California [Hawkins] vote?" Hawkins responded, "Aye." "The ayes have it," announced Perkins, bringing appreciative laughter from the group.

Bargaining on the Merits

While perhaps a majority of items were settled by the two means described above, they were not the dominant mode of operation in terms of time and effort. Most action and discussion within the conference, as well as a great deal conducted informally outside, involved tough bargaining. Generally speaking, these bargains were of two types. First there were trades, "We will accept *A*, if you will accept *B*." Second, there were compromises on language, "We will accept *A* if you will modify it to read. . . ." Frequently, especially on the major issues of student aid, institutional aid and busing, proposals were made for packages of trades and compromises, "Our version of the bill contains *A, B, C,* and *D*, whereas your version of the bill contains comparable provisions *E, F, G,* and *H*. We propose that you accept *A* and *B* from our bill receding on *E* and *F* from your bill; we will accept *G* from your bill and recede on *C* from ours, and we further propose that to deal with *D* and *H* language be accepted that reads as follows. . . ." Offers from one delegation of trades, compromises and packages would often be answered by counteroffers from the other side. Thus there might be a series of proposals and counterproposals made until there was one before the conference that a majority of both sides could accept or until it was decided that further bargaining was fruitless, at which point the issue would be skipped until a later date. In addition, in a two-month conference negotiating hundreds of differences, a member might agree to a proposal one day, even though he did not feel it was the best bargain he could get, with the expectation that later, on items about which he felt more intensely, other members who got the better deal this time would be willing to come more than halfway to accommodate him.[g]

One of the more important decisions of the conference was the bargain struck with respect to the occupational education and community college titles. It will be recalled that the Senate bill contained a program for the improvement of community colleges, with no counterpart in the House bill. On the other hand, the House bill had a program of federal grants for occupational education for which there was no Senate counterpart.

The expectation of a major trade in this area was made plain at the second session of the conference in an interchange between Congressmen Frank Thompson and Al Quie. Thompson had introduced a community college bill analogous to the one in the Senate bill. Quie was a sponsor of the House occupational education program. During the consideration of Title III, Developing Institutions, attention was focused on a special earmarking of some of the Developing Institutions funds for community colleges. Quie objected to trying to take care of the community colleges in Title III because there was a separate community college title later in the bill. Thompson responded by offering to forego special treatment for community colleges in Title III in return for a commitment of support from Quie for the community college title in the Senate bill. Quie said he would be happy to support the community college title if the Senate would accept his occupational education program.

While the community college and occupational education titles were not strictly complementary, accepting both titles presented no major difficulties. However, another issue was entwined with community colleges and occupational education—state planning. The House bill included federal grants and technical assistance to the states for comprehensive postsecondary education planning. If states chose to apply for funds, they were to designate or create a "broadly and equitably representative" agency to do the planning. This agency could also establish a committee to concentrate specifically on community colleges. In addition, the occupational education title of the House bill required that states establish or designate a state agency to administer the program and to draw up state plans for occupational education.

The Senate bill also contained state planning. It required that as a precondition for receiving federal assistance under programs that required planning, a

---

[g]The types of bargains described here are analogous to those suggested by Lewis A. Forman, Jr., *The Congressional Process: Strategies, Rules, and Procedures*, Little, Brown, Boston, 1967, pp. 22-33.

single state agency would have the planning responsibility. In addition, this "State Higher Education Commission" could apply for grants from the Commissioner of Education to undertake comprehensive statewide planning for postsecondary education. Finally, the Senate community college title required, as a condition of receiving federal funds under the community college title, that this state commission establish a community college committee and that it "develop and adopt a statewide plan for the expansion and improvement of postsecondary education programs in community colleges."[h]

State planning complicated the packaging of the occupational education and community college titles. One reason was that the planning provisions were very complex. Second, state planning mandated by the federal government raised the fundamental issue of federal and state roles in the control of postsecondary education. There was broad agreement that the federal government could legitimately require states to plan as a condition of receiving funds under specific programs, and federal encouragement of comprehensive planning by the states was considered desirable. The philosophical issue came down practically to the question of how much "flexibility" the states would be allowed. A mandatory requirement that the state consolidate in a single agency all federal higher education planning would force many delicately balanced state administrative arrangements to be reconstructed. Some felt this was a federal infringement on the states' jurisdiction. In addition, the provisions under consideration specified who should or must be represented on the state planning agencies. Specifying by federal law the membership of the state agencies seemed to some beyond the boundary of legitimate federal action.

In the first round on the higher education provisions, this whole complex of problems was skipped. As the conference worked through the higher education issues a second time, occupational education, community colleges and state planning came up again. There was agreement on the trade outlined in the conversation between Thompson and Quie a month earlier. It was clear, however, that it would be difficult and time consuming to do the required pruning and grafting in the conference. Congressman Meeds suggested that "the staff" be instructed to prepare a draft blending the provisions of the two bills into a single proposal. This suggestion was readily agreed to.

With the aid of scissors, paste and the Xerox machine, the staff produced a document by the next afternoon. The staff could not agree on whether each state should be required to consolidate its federally mandated planning for postsecondary education in a single state agency, and this issue was left open for the members.

---

[h]For a detailed comparison of state planning in the two bills, see the testimony of Aims McGuinness, Jr., in "Oversight Hearings on Administration of Section 1202 of the Higher Education Act," *Special Subcommittee on Education, House Education and Labor Committee*, 93rd Congress, First Session, 1973, pp. 22-43.

Alerted that the community college title was due to be taken up, Senator Williams made one of his rare appearances at the conference. The community college title was one of his major legislative initiatives. But being the busy Chairman of the full Senate committee, Williams expected that the usual Senate pattern would be followed; that is, he expected to preside over the ratification of an agreement worked out by the staff. Williams was therefore surprised to find that the skids had not been greased and that Representative Quie was raising difficult and detailed questions. The Senator did not know the staff draft well enough either to defend it or to work out further compromises. There was an inconclusive discussion centering on the unresolved state planning question, and it was finally agreed to send the staff back to the drawing board.

The staff produced another, technically smoother proposal for consideration by the conference the next week. Some conferees seemed ready to disassemble the staff proposal and start again from scratch, but Williams was better prepared this time. He perceived quickly that the problem was not disagreement over the substance of the staff draft but rather the uneasiness and suspicion of many members at swallowing in one bite a 22-page staff document. Thus, rather than trying to discuss the document as a whole, Williams adopted the procedure that had been successfully used by Chairman Perkins. He opened the staff document to page 1 and asked if there were any amendments or discussion. The most controversial issue, state planning, appeared first, and three amendments to page 1 were adopted. The consideration of the staff proposal continued with amendments on almost every page. By the time they reached page 14, the conferees felt they had discharged their responsibility as legislators and made their mark. The rest of the staff document was accepted without amendment.

On the controversial issue of mandatory consolidation of all state planning for higher education required by the federal government, the staff and the conferees reached a compromise described by one of the staff as "an artful legislative creation." To receive federal funds under the community college or occupational education programs, a state would have to create a planning agency or designate an existing agency that met the requirements set out for representativeness. The 1202 Commission, taking its name from the section of the bill, would then undertake the planning required to receive funds under these two programs. The agreement also included grants to the 1202 commissions for comprehensive statewide postsecondary planning. With respect to federal planning required for other higher education programs, states were given the option of either consolidating it in the 1202 Commission or leaving it where it was in other state agencies.[i]

The conference actions in this case illustrate the roles of staff and lobbyists.

---

[i]The way the planning provisions from the two bills were combined can be seen in specific detail in "1202 Oversight Hearings," pp. 26-41.

Setting up a staff task force that produced a document considered as a *staff* document was unusual. The staff usually worked in smaller and more informal groups. Otherwise, the role of staff in this case was typical. They operated with a mandate from the legislators. They tried to represent the views and interests of their members. Most staff have a cameleon-like ability to take on the political coloration of their boss. When the staff exceeded their mandate, or misperceived the wishes of the members, their leash was pulled up short and their efforts were cast aside. The legislators always had the final say. Indeed the legislators were wary of being dominated by the staff, as the massaging of the second staff draft clearly indicates. The final package produced in this case was not a staff creation. The staff acted as faithful surrogates.

As the state planning provisions were developed in the House and Senate committees, they were largely unnoticed even within the higher education community. The Education Commission of the States (ECS) and the State Higher Education Executive Officers Association (SHEEO) testified in both houses in favor of federal support for strong state planning. They also endorsed the idea of a federal requirement that all state planning for postsecondary education mandated by the federal government be consolidated in a single state agency. But during the conference these two groups did not closely follow the issue.

Meanwhile Don McNeil, the Chancellor of the University of Maine, had taken note that the state planning provisions might have unsettling effects in his state. He directed his executive assistant, Aims McGuinness, to study the precise impact of the provisions on Maine.

Early in the conference, McGuinness sent his analysis to the conferees and followed up with personal contacts in Washington. One result of his efforts was a letter from Congressman William Hathaway of Maine, who had formerly been on the House Education and Labor Committee, to the conferees. The letter urged "that maximum flexibility be given to the states to work out the precise administrative mechanism for planning and coordination which will fit within the context of unique state structures, laws and traditions." In leaving the consolidation of federally required state planning optional and allowing states to designate existing state agencies for the new federal planning, the conference agreement came down more on the side of Maine than ECS and SHEEO. Whether this was the result of the relatively modest lobbying efforts of McGuinness is impossible to tell. What is clear is that his impact was maximized in the vacuum created when the other higher education associations left the field. Sporadic efforts by one or a few lobbyists when some parts of the bill were being considered while most of the higher education associations sat on the sidelines was typical during the conference.

In addition to compromising over the actual words in the law, another technique was sometimes used to reach a compromise. In a conference report, the bill agreed on is accompanied by a "Joint Explanatory Statement of the

Committee of Conference," which not only explains what the conferees did, but sometimes includes their "understanding" or "intent" concerning how a provision of the law will be interpreted and implemented. Thus in resolving differences the conferees sometimes agreed, as part of a bargain, to include specific supplementary language in the explanatory statement, rather than trying to write all of their views into the statutory language. An offer to include specific language in the report as part of a proposal was often used to bridge the final distance between two sides or to take care of problems perceived by a few conferees but which were not significant enough to warrant inclusion in the law itself.

The bargaining thus far described involved reconciling the differing views of the conferees on the substantive merits of the issues. Substantive considerations were clearly predominant in the actions of the conference. However, some actions of the conference were based on more pragmatic political considerations. A particularly interesting example of political bargaining, as well as a case study in the norms of congressional politics, is the conference action on the Political Interns and Youth Camp Safety programs.

The Political Interns Program had been added to the Senate bill by a Humphrey floor amendment. A similar program in the House bill had been knocked out on the House floor. Senator Mondale pushed vigorously in conference for adoption of the program on behalf of fellow Minnesotan Humphrey. Among the House conferees, there was little enthusiasm for the program on its merits and some also felt an obligation to uphold a House position expressed in a record vote. The first time Political Interns came before the conference, the House conferees unanimously refused to recede, and the item was skipped. After it was skipped a second time, Senator Mondale proposed a compromise that substantially scaled down the program. The House again refused to recede, but this time by a vote of 9-11. Congressman Thompson was among the House conferees willing to accept the Mondale proposal, and he set out to try to round up two more votes on the House side. Thompson persuaded his friend and ally John Brademas and Congressman Daniels to switch so that the vote would be 11-9 in favor of accepting the program. Both Brademas and Daniels were willing to go along if Mondale would compromise still further. Thompson spoke informally with Mondale, who accepted the required compromise to get the support of Brademas and Daniels.

Political Interns was brought before the conference the next day. However, Mrs. Green asked that action be postponed because she had strong views on the program and had to leave. In deference to Mrs. Green, the issue was put aside. An opportunity to culminate the deal slipped away.

At the next meeting of the conference, Political Interns was again brought up with Mondale offering the more modest version of the program that was supposed to get the support of Brademas and Daniels. A vote was taken among the House conferees. Daniels was not present, and Mrs. Green voted his proxy against the Mondale proposal. Thompson explained to Mrs. Green that Daniels had agreed to vote for the latest Mondale compromise, but Mrs. Green responded that Daniels had changed his mind. The House conferees refused to accept the Mondale proposal, and Political Interns was skipped again. Mondale was shocked and Thompson was outraged.

Later the same day Youth Camp Safety came up. This program had also been added to the Senate bill on a floor amendment, by Senator Ribicoff of Connecticut. On the House side, it had been developed by Congressman Daniels in his subcommittee and tacked onto H.R. 7248 in the full committee to match the Ribicoff amendment in S. 659. On the House floor, an amendment by Congressman Pickle of Texas deleting the Youth Camp Safety program from the bill and substituting a study of the problem was adopted by a recorded vote. In the conference Daniels wanted the House conferees to accept the Ribicoff program that was similar to his own.

In the background of the deliberations on Youth Camp Safety was a strategic consideration related to passing the bill in the House. At a private meeting Chairman Perkins expressed the view that the House position on Youth Camp Safety should be maintained, that is, only a study. His reasoning was that it was important to defend, where possible, the positions of the House that had been taken by roll-call votes. But more importantly, said Perkins, Congressman Pickle had strong feelings on this issue, and Perkins had indications that if the Senate program was not adopted, it would be worth "seven or eight Texas votes" for the conference report in the House. In addition, Brademas recalled that Daniels had voted against his NIE in the House.

When Daniels appeared at the conference, Thompson asked him why he had gone back on his word on Political Interns. Daniels apologized, but Thompson was hardly mollified and informed Daniels that he was going to have to vote against accepting the Senate Youth Camp Safety program.

The House conferees proceeded to vote 11-9 against the Senate position on Youth Camp Safety, with Perkins, Thompson and Brademas voting in the majority. Thompson and Brademas were, in part, squaring their individual political accounts with Daniels as well as acting in what they perceived to be the long run interest of passing the conference report in the House. Following the House refusal, the Senate receded on Youth Camp Safety because there was no strong defender of the Ribicoff amendment among the Senate conferees. Congressman Daniels was bitterly disappointed at losing the program he most cared about in the bill. The next day Mondale gave up on Political Interns, and the Senate receded. Thus both Political Interns and Youth Camp Safety were dropped. Two positions of the House expressed in roll-call votes had been upheld, perhaps marginally improving the chances of the conference report in the House. Congressman Pickle later did in fact vote for the conference report along with six other Texas Congressmen.

The Basic Grant

While community colleges/occupational education/state planning was significant and controversial, all participants recognized from the beginning that the Basic Grant and institutional aid were the most important higher education issues.

As the conference began, the Quie-Brademas alliance was reactivated. Four things were established. First, Quie supported in principle the Basic Grant and cost-of-instruction institutional aid from the Senate bill. Second, he could count on the solid backing of the other seven Republican conferees on these two issues. Third, Brademas and Frank Thompson also favored the Basic Grant and cost-of-instruction institutional aid. Fourth, there were thus at least ten votes for this position on the House side, one less than a majority of the House conferees. Thus Brademas and Quie and their respective supporters resolved to work together to get these two programs incorporated into the conference bill. They agreed to compromise their own disagreements over specifics and to bargain to win Senate acceptance of some changes to get the support of at least one more House conferee.

The prospects for success of the Quie-Brademas alliance were enhanced in the new forum. Whereas in the House committee they had been a faction trying to override the subcommittee chairman, Mrs. Green, and lacking the votes to do it, in the conference they were half of the House delegation. In addition, and more importantly, in conference a majority of the House conferees and a majority of the Senate conferees had to agree, and the Quie-Brademas position enjoyed unanimous support on the Senate side. Thus Quie and Brademas were one vote away from accomplishing what the conference was supposed to accomplish, namely, to resolve the differences in the two bills. Mrs. Green and her allies had a deadlock, and any additional votes they might pick up would only harden the deadlock.

As the conference began, a three-cornered series of informal meetings were held among Congressman Quie and his staff aide, Bob Andringa, Congressman Brademas and his staff aide, James Mooney, and Senator Pell's staff, Steve Wexler and Richard Smith.[j] The purpose of these meetings was to reach agreement within the Quie-Brademas alliance and with Senator Pell on the "details" of the Basic Grant.

The most important question was how to calculate the grant to a student when inadequate funds were appropriated to pay every student the full amount for which he was eligible. At less than full funding, the Senate bill provided for a "ratable reduction" of each student's grant. This meant, for example, that if available appropriations were adequate to pay only 50 percent of all grants, each student would receive 50 percent of the grant for which he was eligible. Quie and Brademas objected to this on the grounds that it hit the neediest students, those eligible for the largest grants, hardest. Also, by spreading the funds thinly, ratable reduction would result in many students receiving very small and perhaps meaningless grants.

To take care of these problems, Quie proposed a "floating ceiling" through which the size of the maximum grant would be floated downward from $1,400

---

[j]Wolanin attended the meetings representing Congressman Thompson.

to the level where the available appropriation would be sufficient to pay fully all grants at the new lower maximum. This proposal was designed to concentrate the funds among the neediest students. Quie's advocacy of this approach was consistent with the Administration's objective of "targeting" education programs on the neediest. His proposal also had the effect of cutting the least needy students out of the program entirely. Cutting less needy students out to concentrate the funds on the neediest was disturbing to Brademas who had long opposed the idea of trading one class of students against another. In addition, Pell wanted the pool of grant recipients to be as large as possible with all feeling some pinch from inadequate funding. This, he reasoned, would create more political pressure for full funding of the program. The parties arrived at a complex compromise, a schedule under which no one would be dropped from the program, and the neediest students would be paid a larger proportion of their full grant eligibility.[k]

One minor issue in the Senate bill was the possibility of students receiving a grant that when combined with their parents' contribution, would give them more than they needed for their education. This was easily taken care of with an "antiwindfall" amendment. Another problem was that the Senate bill established a minimum grant of $200. It was apparent that with the reduction formula, a $200 minimum grant would again put many students out of the program. So it was agreed to add an amendment making the minimum grant $50 at less then full funding. By the third week of the conference, all were in agreement on these issues. Attention then focused on finding one additional House conferee to accept the Basic Grant.

The Basic Grant was considered for the first time at the third conference session in late March. Pell expressed determination to retain his pet program. Led by Mrs. Green those House Democratic conferees skeptical of the Basic Grant expressed reservations not so much about the merits of the program as the threat it posed to the existing student aid programs—Educational Opportunity Grants (EOG), Work-Study and direct federal loans. Their fears were not without foundation. The Administration's student aid proposals in 1970 and 1971 had proposed a new Basic Grant-type program but also a drastic curtailment of existing programs. Mrs. Green argued that if the Basic Grant were accepted without some protection for the other student aid programs, the Administration might try to achieve its original objective through the budgetary process. Quie did not view this prospect with particular alarm because his version of the Basic Grant, which failed in both the House Committee and on the House floor, had been a substitute for the EOG. Nor was Senator Pell overly concerned on this score because he wanted above all to maximize potential funding for the Basic Grant.

---

[k]This oversimplifies the reduction schedule. To gain an understanding of its full complexity, the reader is directed to section 131(b)(1) of PL92-318.

However, it became clear that, to win the necessary support of the one or more additional House conferees for the Senate Basic Grant, a guarantee was needed for funding the existing student aid programs. Among supporters of the Basic Grant, especially Brademas and Thompson, there was also interest in assuring that the existing student aid programs were not abandoned. The Basic Grant concept, after all, was to provide a foundation of aid to which would be added support from other federal programs as well as state and private sources.

A draft amendment was prepared specifying the amount to be available for EOG, College Work-Study and direct federal loans. So the Basic Grant issue had rapidly narrowed to the question of how much funding for these existing programs should be assured.

At the March 27 session, discussion centered among the House conferees as they sought agreement on a modified Basic Grant. A proposal by Mrs. Green requiring that the three existing programs be funded at 100 percent of their fiscal 1972 level before funding the Basic Grant was rejected on a tie vote. Brademas offered a proposal including the three items agreed on informally with Quie and Pell—the schedule for reducing Basic Grants at less than full funding, the antiwindfall provision and the $50 minimum grant at less than full funding. The Brademas proposal also required Work-Study and federal direct loans to be funded at 80 percent of their fiscal 1972 level and EOG at 50 percent before funds were available for the Basic Grant. The rationale for the lower percentage protection for EOG was that the new Basic Grant would fill much of the need for federal grant support to students. After the Brademas proposal was amended to boost the guarantee for Work-Study and federal direct loans to 100 percent and for EOG to 75 percent, it was then presented as an offer to the Senate side. Following Pell's lead, the Senate conferees rejected the House offer on the grounds that it would prevent the Basic Grant from getting off to a strong start. For the rest of the afternoon, the conference moved rapidly, resolving most of the differences on Sally Mae as a breather from the controversy over the Basic Grant.

After a break for dinner, the conference reconvened for its first evening session. The Senate side made a counterproposal that was identical to the original Brademas package, that is, protecting the existing student aid programs at 80-80-50 percent rather than 100-100-75 percent. The House conferees accepted this counteroffer 11-9.

The crucial eleventh vote did not come from the expected source. Since the beginning of the conference, Brademas and Thompson had been working assiduously to persuade Gus Hawkins, the only Black among the House conferees, to support the Basic Grant. The sentiment in the House Black Caucus seemed to be that the Caucus had been mistaken in opposing the Basic Grant in committee and the association of Black Colleges (National Association for Equal Opportunity in Higher Education) was supporting the Basic Grant. Thus

Brademas and Thompson reasoned that Hawkins was the most likely defector from Mrs. Green's camp.[1] To the chagrin of Brademas, Thompson and some Black educators, however, Mrs. Green continued to vote Hawkins' proxy on the Basic Grant.

The eleventh vote came instead from Congressman Phillip Burton. Burton rarely attended the conference and had shown no deep interest in the bill other than the provisions to grant land-grant status to the College of the Virgin Islands and the University of Guam. His proxy was also being voted by his subcommittee chairman, Mrs. Green. However, between the afternoon and evening consideration of the Basic Grant, he agreed to give his proxy to Brademas with respect to the Basic Grant. That morning Secretary of HEW Richardson had appeared before the Education and Labor Committee to defend the Administration's new antibusing legislation. Brademas led the attack on the Administration's program, pleasing Burton, a strong civil rights supporter, and at least temporarily making him more sympathetic to Brademas' position in the conference. Another factor was that representatives of the new National Student Lobby, many with roots in Burton's home state of California, had been vigorously arguing the case for the Basic Grant with Burton.

When Brademas voted Burton's proxy in favor of accepting the Senate Basic Grant counterproposal, Mrs. Green angrily charged that Burton's proxy was being voted for a position he did not support. She threatened not to sign the conference report.

Despite the victory for the Basic Grant, the issue was still far from being resolved. After the 11-9 vote, the conferees reached an informal agreement to accept additional "perfecting amendments" to the Basic Grant.

The next day Brademas and Thompson met with Chairman Perkins who said that he was not opposed to the Basic Grant but was concerned that the existing student aid programs might be curtailed before this untried program was working smoothly. He advocated more protection for the existing programs. Perkins also said it would be helpful in taking the conference report back to the House if agreement on this major program, rejected by a record vote in the House, were not reached early in the conference. He wanted a longer period of discussion and bargaining. Within the Quie-Brademas coalition there was also some uneasiness over the legitimacy of their narrow victory. Thus they were willing to go along with the Chairman both to enhance the prospects of the conference report in the House and to get a broader consensus for the Basic Grant. The meeting in Perkins' office ended with the chairman pledging to keep in close touch with Brademas and Thompson. Discussion on the Basic Grant now became four-cornered with the addition of Perkins.

As frequently happens when a major issue is left lying around only partly

---

[1]Hawkins attended the conference intermittently. When he was not present, Mrs. Green had been voting his proxy in the early sessions.

resolved, someone discovers additional problems. On the evening of the 27th, a Quie amendment had been accepted that deleted the limitation in the Basic Grant formula that no grant could exceed half the cost of attendance at the school of the student's choice. Quie wanted to eliminate this provision because he felt it unfairly penalized low-income students enrolled in low-cost institutions.[m] Quie's amendment was accepted by supporters of the Basic Grant not only because it cured the inequity that disturbed Quie but also because it expanded the program. However, a check with the House Parliamentarian indicated that this change might cause a problem when the conference report was before the House. The House rules for conferences allow only agreements that do not exceed what is in at least one version of the bill. In the Parliamentarian's view removing the half-cost limitation went beyond the Senate bill, and it could make the entire bill vulnerable in the House to a point of order.

Rather than restoring the half-cost limitation, Quie proposed to substitute for it a limitation based on a student's "need." He proposed that a Basic Grant be $1,400 minus family contribution not to exceed one-half of need, with need defined as the difference between family contribution and the total cost to the student of attending an institution. Quie believed the half-need limitation, a feature of his unsuccessful EOG Substitute, would result in greater equity among students. Senator Pell and his colleagues, however, opposed the half-need proposal because detailed analysis showed it would scale down the program even more than the original half-cost limitation in the Senate bill.

The Basic Grant was reopened on April 11, with the House members searching for agreement on the two outstanding issues—protection for the existing student aid programs and half-cost versus half-need. Brademas returned to the 100-100-75 percent guarantee for the existing programs, consistent with Perkins' wishes. He also proposed the Quie half-need limit. Mrs. Green countered with a substitute to guarantee 100 percent funding for all three of the existing student aid programs. The Green substitute was defeated on a 10-10 tie, and the Brademas proposal was adopted as an offer to the Senate on a voice vote, with Mrs. Green sounding the only nay. The Senate rejected this offer and made a counterproposal that the protection for the existing programs would decrease year by year, which was unanimously rejected by the House. The Basic Grant was now completely reopened, and the 10-10 vote indicated that Hawkins was still allied with Mrs. Green and Burton was back in her camp. However, the almost unanimous voice vote for the Brademas proposal signaled that there was a broad consensus among the House conferees to accept the Basic Grant if the Senate gave a little more.

---

[m]For example, with the half-cost limitation, a student whose family could contribute zero and who was attending a school costing $1,500 could only receive $750, while a student whose family could contribute $650 and who was attending the same school would also receive $750. Thus two students from different economic circumstances would receive the same Basic Grant.

In deference to Chairman Perkins' sense of timing, further counterproposals from the Senate side were delayed while the conference moved ahead on less controversial issues. The four-cornered discussions continued and finally on May 4 at the 17th of the 21 conference sessions, the Basic Grant was quickly accepted with virtual unanimity on both sides. The Senate conferees accepted the 100-100-75 percent guarantee. But they insisted that this guarantee be expressed in dollar figures, in which form they felt it stood less risk of being expanded later. It was agreed that a "need" limitation would apply to the Basic Grant at less than full funding, but that the original Senate half-cost limitation would apply if the program were fully funded. Perkins got the prolonged consideration that he wanted as well as the protection for the existing programs. Quie, Brademas and their allies won broad approval among the House conferees for the Basic Grant and agreement from the Senate conferees for some modifications that they felt improved the program. The Senate got acceptance for the Basic Grant without compromising its fundamental features.

Two aspects of the Basic Grant issue in conference merit special comment. First, because the House rules on conference agreements were stricter than the Senate's, agreements in the conference were checked frequently with the House Parliamentarian by Chairman Perkins. Such a check in the case of the Basic Grant injected an important new issue into the discussion and complicated final agreement. Chairman Perkins also used the House rules as one of his political resources. On some occasions, with or without checking with the Parliamentarian, he would state that the House conferees could not accept a Senate proposal because by so doing they would be exceeding their authority. It could then be claimed that the House side would happily go along with the Senate if it were not hamstrung by the House rules. In addition, frequent consultations with the Parliamentarian were intended to demonstrate to both the Parliamentarian and the House Speaker that the House conferees were making diligent efforts to abide by the House rules. This might lead the Parliamentarian and the Speaker to give the actions of the conference the benefit of the doubt if points of order were later raised on the House floor.

Second, Congressman Quie and his staff were intensely involved in the debate over a formula for reducing Basic Grants at less than full funding and half-cost versus half-need. The fact that they developed their own alternatives on these two complex questions exemplified Quie's activist legislative style and effective leadership of the Republican conferees.

Institutional Aid

On institutional aid, as on the Basic Grant, Brademas, Quie and their allies were committed to the approach in the Senate bill. A long series of informal negotiations between Quie, Brademas and Pell, with Perkins playing an active role primarily on timing rather than substance, produced an agreement that was then ratified by the conference committee. In contrast to the process with respect to the Basic Grant, there were no extended discussions in the conference. A verbatim record of the conference would give the impression that institutional aid was a minor issue that was disposed of without debate at the last session.

When the informal meetings between Brademas, Quie, Pell and their staffs began in late March, both the Basic Grant and institutional aid were on the agenda. Until the Basic Grant was resolved, discussion of institutional aid did not advance beyond general agreement on the cost-of-instruction approach over capitation grants. At this stage the Senate representatives seemed willing to compromise their cost-of-instruction institutional aid formula further in the direction of Mrs. Green's capitation approach than was acceptable to Quie and Brademas. Pell and his staff expected to have to compromise with Mrs. Green on institutional aid to win agreement for the Basic Grant. Later, when this did not prove necessary, they had to readjust their thinking to see the possibility of an institutional aid formula based on cost-of-instruction. In contrast to other features of the Senate bill, no Senate conferee felt strongly about cost-of-instruction. In the early meetings, Quie and Brademas were the most ardent defenders of the Senate approach.

On April 12, an event critical to the outcome of the conference occurred on the House floor. Mrs. Green made a brief speech expressing her "deep discouragement over some developments in the conference." Her discouragement stemmed, she said, from the fact that the House conferees were selling out to the Senate on items where the House had expressed itself in recorded votes. In addition, the conferees were "gutting or phasing out . . . existing [higher education] programs that have worked extremely well." Thus, she said, "I must report to my colleagues in the House that, in my opinion, the prospect of a higher education bill emerging from the present conference that would be acceptable to a majority of House Members is a darkening prospect."[2] Mrs. Green also introduced a bill to extend the existing higher education programs for one year.

Mrs. Green's speech enraged Chairman Perkins more than anyone else. He took it as a thinly veiled personal attack on his work as chairman of the conference. He also felt the charge that the House conferees had been giving in to the Senate on items where the House had taken a record vote was unfair and did not square with the facts. Above all, he was angered by Mrs. Green's failure to share his commitment to "get a bill" and by what he read as the intent to kill the measure in conference and substitute for it her one-year extension. Following Mrs. Green's speech, Perkins' role began to change. Where he had been neutral, willing to see either Mrs. Green or Quie and Brademas win and anxious only to move the conference to a successful conclusion, he gradually became an active partner in the Quie-Brademas alliance.

On the day after the Green speech, Perkins asked Frank Thompson to vote in favor of the House position on institutional aid to counter Mrs. Green's criticism. Thompson agreed, and Senator Pell was informed that, shortly before the conference adjourned, Perkins would call up the issue of institutional aid. Pell was simply to take the House vote under advisement. The plan went off and the House conferees voted 11-9 not to recede to the Senate on institutional aid, Thompson voting with Perkins, Green and other Democrats against Brademas, Reid and seven Republicans. This was the only time institutional aid was raised before the last conference session.

Toward the end of April Perkins, Brademas, Thompson, Pell and others focused on the scenario for settling the remaining issues and timing the conclusion of the conference. The understanding was that Perkins would go along with whatever agreements were worked out on the issues between Brademas, Quie and Pell. Brademas had a mandate from Perkins to compromise the substantive issues.

As the conference moved into May, the strategy-review meetings were eventually broadened to include about twenty participants and in effect became caucuses of the most active House and Senate conferees committed to bringing out a bill. In the face of this House-Senate alliance, the remaining difficult issues seemed to diminish to the status of details to be worked out rather than potential stumbling blocks.

Mrs. Green's speech made reaching a consensus on institutional aid substantially easier than on the Basic Grant. With Perkins joined to the Brademas-Quie alliance, there was no longer the problem of finding the eleventh vote among the House conferees. Also, on the assumption that Mrs. Green was committed to killing the bill, there was no longer any need to try to accommodate her.

As attention began to focus on institutional aid in the third week of April, Brademas informally circulated a proposal that was largely the brainchild of his administrative assistant, James Mooney. It was dubbed the "Mooney Cocktail." Under this proposal 45 percent of the institutional aid funds would be awarded to higher education institutions on the basis of the number of Basic Grant recipients they enrolled, that is, the Senate cost-of-instruction approach. A second 45 percent of the institutional aid funds would be distributed on the basis of the amount of student aid received by the institution's students under the EOG, College Work-Study, and direct federal loan programs, which was the Quie-Brademas cost-of-instruction approach from the House bill. Thus 90 percent of institutional aid would be based on the cost-of-education principle. Both of the 45 percent parts of the institutional aid formula included bonuses for smaller institutions in line with the general consensus in favor of providing special help for small private schools. The remaining 10 percent of the institutional aid would be granted on a per capita basis for each postgraduate student. This toehold for the capitation approach was retained for the pragmatic reason that without it the share of funds for public and private universities would be far smaller than their share of enrollments.

The Brademas proposal was basically acceptable to both Quie and the Senate side. Outside groups were asked to evaluate the distribution of funds by this formula among various categories of institutions, and the estimates indicated that private institutions and public community colleges would do somewhat better than under the House formula. This pleased community college supporters like Frank Thompson, and it also squared with the general desire to provide assistance for the privates. In general, the distribution among categories of institutions was not substantially different from the House bill.

The only problem that took time to iron out was linking institutional aid to the Basic Grant. In the Senate bill, no payments of institutional aid could be made in any year in which Basic Grants were not fully funded. This was the "Prouty amendment" expressing the Senate judgment that student aid rather than institutional aid was the first priority.

Discussion of the Prouty amendment revolved around the questions of whether it should apply to the entire institutional aid program or only one of the parts of it and whether it should be softened to permit some funding of institutional aid before the Basic Grant was fully funded. It was finally decided to water down the provision by applying it only to the 45 percent of institutional aid related to the Basic Grant and triggering payments under this part when the Basic Grant reached 50 percent of its full funding level.

About a week before the end of the conference, all parties in the House-Senate coalition were in full agreement on the institutional aid program. It was then set aside to be brought out for ratification at the last session of the conference. Remarkably, the 45-45-10 institutional aid formula remained a well-kept secret. Mrs. Green heard a report that such a proposal was under consideration, but she dismissed it as absurd. The major higher education associations, whose preeminent priority was capitation institutional aid, neither learned of it nor participated in its formulation. Administration officials who were monitoring the progress of the conference also did not have a hand in it. The institutional aid compromise, like most decisions of the conference, was reached without substantial input from the outside.

Busing Through the Night: The Final Session

The final conference session, an epic event, began in the afternoon of May 16, 1972. In the week preceding, attention had begun to focus intensely on busing. Institutional aid had been settled informally and quietly put in reserve. Caucuses were being held that included most of the active and influential House and Senate conferees with the exception of Mrs. Green and her allies. They began seriously trying to thrash out the busing issues. Quie had a pet scheme; others suggested a variety of compromise packages; Perkins focused on preserving the Broomfield amendment intact to win support from House Republicans to pass the conference report; and Mondale raised the possibility of a liberal filibuster against the conference report if stringent busing amendments were accepted. In short, there was no consensus on the issue.

These caucuses brought a sobering realization that the honeymoon was over. However intellectually and politically difficult the higher education issues had been, they were being resolved in the cozy intimacy of a conference committee where professional politicians were pragmatically settling the issues. With the exceptions of Senator Pell who saw this bill with the Basic Grant intact as an important asset in his re-election campaign and Perkins whose reputation as a chairman would be damaged by failing to get a bill out of conference, none of the members seemed to perceive any strong external constraints on their decisions on the higher education issues. Members' policy judgments and the internal dynamics of the Senate and House Committees were the most important factors determining the outcomes on higher education. Now, unavoidably facing busing, the members would have to cope with the intrusion of powerful passions from the national political environment.

The national controversy over busing had not abated since the stormy busing debates in the Senate and House. In fact, through the two months of the conference, busing had become even more salient nationally. The spring of 1972 was the season of presidential primaries, and busing was a hot issue in the vigorous Democratic nomination contest. Among Democratic contenders, Governor George Wallace of Alabama took the most adamant position against school busing and scored more impressively than had been expected in the primaries, topping the field in Florida and making very strong showings in Wisconsin, Pennsylvania, Indiana and West Virginia. A busing referendum was held in the Florida primary, and almost three fourths of the voters favored the antibusing alternative, a result consistent with national public opinion surveys.

The passions of the outside world seemed physically to intrude in the last conference session with the presence of Secret Service agents guarding Senator Kennedy. Governor Wallace had been wounded seriously in an assassination attempt in Maryland the day before, and President Nixon ordered Secret Service protection for all of the presidential contenders including Kennedy, who was frequently mentioned as a possible Democratic nominee.

President Nixon had also added to the busing debate with a nationally televised speech and a special message to Congress on March 17, the day after the conference began. Soon thereafter two bills embodying the Administration's antibusing program, euphemistically titled the "Student Transportation Moratorium Act" and the "Equal Educational Opportunities Act," were introduced in Congress. Both the Senate and House Education committees held hearings. Despite the public antibusing sentiment, the initiatives from the Administration, and the Congressional hearings, Congress did not act on busing during the conference. Thus it appeared that if the Congress were going to "do something" about busing in the election year of 1972, it was up to the conference. That the expectations of congressional antibusing action were focused on the higher education conference committee was apparent when, on May 11, the House conferees were instructed for a second time to preserve intact the House busing amendments.

As the conferees gathered on May 16 and the voluminous accumulation of conference documents was wheeled on carts into the room by the committee staff, there was the sense of being in the eye of a raging political storm. There was also a sense of historical drama, of writing another page in the saga of American race relations. As the presence of Kennedy's Secret Service agents underlined the national political forces impinging on the conference, the site and timing of this last meeting highlighted its historical dimension. The session was in the Old Supreme Court Chamber in the Capital, site of the landmark decision, *Plessy* v. *Ferguson* (1896), establishing "separate but equal" as the constitutional standard for judging state laws affecting nonwhites. This case had been the main constitutional justification for state segregation laws. As the conference dragged on into the next morning, May 17, the busing amendments were being argued on the anniversary of the Court's historic *Brown* v. *Board of Education* decision (1954), which had overturned *Plessy* specifically with regard to public education.

The Old Supreme Court Chamber itself added to the historical aura of the occasion. The two-story Chamber held with ease all of the participants. Entering, one immediately noticed across the room the raised bench at which the Supreme Court Justices had sat. A row of marble columns rose behind the bench. The tables for the conference were set up in front of the bench in the area that would have been occupied by lawyers arguing before the court. On scroll brackets attached high on the wall around the Chamber were stone busts of great Justices. The session proceeded before the bench and under the steady and solemn gaze of John Jay, John Marshall, Roger Taney, William Taft and their colleagues. Despite the image of politicians as cynical pragmatists, several of the Members remarked on the symbolism of the place and the date. Thus the participants in this low visibility conference, heretofore dominated by higher education issues, were now actors on the national political stage and at least bit players in American history.

The conference convened at 2:00 in the afternoon and recessed almost immediately so that the Senators could caucus. Chairman Perkins joined them to plead for more flexibility, especially from the liberal Senators on the busing amendments. But when the conferees went back into session, the Senate side stood firm and refused to accept the House provisions.

The attention of the conference then turned to unresolved higher education issues. Through the afternoon and well into the evening, following a break for dinner, the conferees arduously worked out agreements on the state-allocation formulas for student aid programs, a needs test for student borrowers under the Guaranteed Loan Program, and a prohibition against discrimination by banks using the Student Loan Marketing Association.

Finally in the waning hours of May 16, the conferees turned again to busing, this time in earnest. The conferees were juggling about a dozen issues relating to busing and school desegregation, trying to find a combination on which a majority of both sides could agree. Many of the Congressmen and Senators tried their hand, some more than once, at putting together a package. A blizzard of offers swirled through the conference. About twenty-five packages failed to enlist the support of the required two majorities.

Among the antibusers in the House there was a widespread belief that the House conferees would accept with only token resistance the weaker Senate Scott-Mansfield amendment. This belief was a major reason for twice instructing the House conferees, and to some extent also pervaded the conference as illustrated by an interchange a week before the final session. Congressman Romano Mazzoli, a freshman Democrat from Kentucky, rather innocently asked Chairman Perkins, "What is the impact of the House instructions?" Perkins responded, "Well, we'll try to follow the spirit of it." A roar of laughter swept the room. Perkins quickly amended his statement saying, "We'll try to follow the spirit and the letter of it." Mrs. Green then dryly observed, "I think we should follow the letter since the spirit is weak."

Despite the widespread skepticism, the House conferees at the last session fought vehemently to force the Senate to accept busing language closer to the House bill. The instructions and the political soundings Chairman Perkins and others had taken in the House made an important difference. The long struggle through the night over busing was not a charade. Many House conferees defended staunchly what they personally opposed because they wanted to pass in the House a conference report whose overall merit they saw as outweighing its antibusing defect. If they had been guided by their personal preferences, a large majority of the House conferees would have happily accepted the Scott-Mansfield Amendment, and busing would not have been a major issue in the conference.

The sequence of busing offers and counteroffers continued into the early hours of the morning. At around midnight, two higher education lobbyists who had been keeping a vigil in the hall, went out and returned with a large tray of coffee and cookies from a local carry-out. These were eagerly consumed. The smokers' supplies of cigarettes were exhausted. The room became hot and stuffy as the air conditioning turned off automatically at 10 p.m. Jackets came off, sleeves were rolled up and ties were loosened. Fatigue began to wear on everyone as the long hours of debate dragged on, and the members continued to talk in a half-shout to make themselves heard in the cavernous chamber. Some of the exchanges became acrimonious. Chairman Perkins, his voice uncharacteristically rising, said, "Senator Mondale, you'll be responsible for the defeat of this bill." Mondale, one of the Senators refusing to agree to stiffening the Senate busing language, heatedly responded, "I'll not be a party to selling out constitutional rights." The House Parliamentarian was rousted out of bed at about midnight to give an opinion about one of the busing proposals. Congressman Pucinski missed a plane for Illinois where he was to make an appearance in his campaign for the Senate. The results of the previous day's presidential primaries in Maryland and Michigan filtered in, showing Governor Wallace a decisive winner in both and giving the conferees a timely reminder of antibusing sentiment in the land.

The Senate and House delegations caucused without either one making much headway. The situation began to look grim. Some began thinking what before had been unthinkable—What if the conference failed to reach an agreement?

But gradually, through a combination of reasoned argument, pragmatic compromise, sheer exhaustion and stubborn unwillingness to let months of effort go to waste, a consensus began to emerge. As 3 a.m. approached, only two issues remained unresolved, both involving the Broomfield amendment in the House bill, which provided that the implementation of any Federal District Court order requiring the busing or transfer of students to achieve a racial balance would be delayed until all appeals, or the time for all appeals, had been exhausted. The Senate Scott-Mansfield Amendment contained a comparable provision that differed in including an expiration date of July 30, 1973, rather than the unlimited duration of the Broomfield amendment. The Senate provision also did not apply to court orders requiring the "transfer" of students within a school district to achieve a racial balance. The Senators insisted on the June 30, 1973, expiration date. The House members accepted in principle the idea of a time limit, but they were holding out for January 1, 1974. Many Senators also wanted to delete the word "transfer" from the Broomfield amendment, arguing it would cripple court-ordered integration efforts that did not include busing, for example, redrawing school attendance zones. House members insisted that the Broomfield amendment had to be retained intact if they were to pass the conference report in the House.

Congressman Brademas formally proposed setting the expiration date at January 1, 1974, and retaining "transfer." The Brademas offer was approved by the House conferees, 10-7.[n] The Senate conferees rejected the House proposal on a 5-5 tie vote. This was the first time the Senate conferees took a roll-call vote at the last session, and only the second time during the entire conference—an illustration of the politics by consensus that prevailed among the Senators.

Senators Pell, Randolph, Dominick, Beall and Stafford voted to accept the House proposal. They were the moderates on the busing issue who favored greater accommodation with the House position. Senators Mondale, Kennedy, Eagleton, Cranston and Javits voted to reject the Brademas offer. Senator Pell

---

[n]For Congressmen Brademas, Thompson and others, support for retaining the Broomfield amendment was based only in part on the pragmatic calculation of passing the conference report in the House. They were also convinced that the amendment would, in fact, have no legal effect because it would delay court orders to achieve "racial balance." Federal courts had been ordering plans to end *de jure* segregation but not to create racial balance in schools. Indeed, the Supreme Court expressly said in the *Swann* case that it would not find plans to achieve "racial balance" constitutional.

would usually have been in this camp, but he was most interested in getting the bill out of conference and enacted.

Two votes among the Senate conferees were unaccounted for—Senator Williams' and Senator Schweiker's. Schweiker had played almost no part in the conference. Williams, aside from his role in the community college/occupational education/state planning package, also had not been active. They were the only two conferees not present, and those who held their proxies did not feel confident that they would be voting as Williams and Schweiker themselves would vote. The Senate conferees were always fastidious in protecting the rights of their colleagues, insuring that their positions were not unrepresented or misrepresented.

If the two unaccounted for votes were not cast, it would be extremely difficult to break the deadlock. If one were cast on each side, the deadlock would also continue. If both votes went with Pell, the issue could be resolved. If both votes went with Mondale, the split between the House and Senate would be widened and the prospects for getting a bill would be even darker.

The gravity of the situation dictated trying to contact the two Senators. Senator Dominick held Schweiker's proxy, and Mondale was holding Williams'. Schweiker was reached and a queue rapidly formed at the phone to present to him the different perspectives. Schweiker agreed to support Pell. Thus Williams' decision became decisive. It took longer to reach Williams because he was in New Jersey, and several calls had to be made to track him down. When the Senator got on the line another queue formed. The Senator's staff aide, Nik Edes, outlined the situation and advised that rather than take any step backwards on civil rights, even a symbolic one, the Senator should let Mondale vote his proxy. Pell argued that the merits of the bill as a whole required more compromise with the House. He also put in a personal plea for the bill to help in his difficult re-election campaign. Frank Thompson, a fellow New Jersey Democrat, discussed the pros and cons in terms of New Jersey politics and emphasized the need to preserve the Broomfield amendment if the conference report was to have a chance of passing in the House. An anxious, tired and sweaty knot of people gathered around the phone and quietly listened to the arguments. Having heard everyone out, Williams decided to assign his proxy to Pell. He was perhaps feeling his responsibility as the committee chairman to get the legislation enacted and to support Pell, his subcommittee chairman.

Returning to the conference table, the Senate side finally agreed to both the January 1, 1974, date and the inclusion of "transfer." Temporarily aground and several times in danger of foundering, the bill had successfully navigated through the busing storm.[o]

---

[o]In addition to the modified Broomfield amendment, the other busing and desegregation issues in dispute on the final night were resolved as follows: The Ashbrook amendment prohibiting the expenditure of federal education funds for busing to carry out a plan of school desegregation was accepted with modifications. The Green amendment, prohibiting federal agencies from inducing or requiring local schools to engage in busing for desegregation or to condition the receipt of federal money on the local schools' undertaking

With the busing issue behind them, the mood was transformed to almost light-headed euphoria. A couple of minor issues dealing with desegregation and the Emergency School Aid Program were rapidly disposed of. The institutional aid agreement was dusted off and trotted out. Senator Pell made an offer that institutional aid be based 50 percent on the Senate cost-of-instruction formula and 50 percent on the cost-of-instruction formula included in the House bill. Congressman Brademas proposed a counteroffer, the 45-45-10 formula, which was accepted by his House colleagues on a voice vote and agreed to by the Senate side. Institutional aid was settled in less than five minutes. This final little exchange of offers had been staged to suggest a give-and-take.

Mrs. Green sat through this performance in silence. She probably realized that she had been sandbagged and that the outcome was a foregone conclusion. The rumored proposal that she had dismissed as absurd became a reality. On the important and symbolic issue of institutional aid, Mrs. Green was decisively defeated.

The conference steamed ahead. After rapid flurries of proposals and trades, with no one too anxious to do battle, a cost-of-instruction program related to enrollments of veterans and a very modest version of the emergency bail-out program were adopted. These had been held back pending an agreement on institutional aid.

Mrs. Green icily observed the proceedings. Her purpose in remaining was not evident until almost all the final issues had been settled. After the busing debate, some House conferees had begun drifting away, leaving their colleagues to mop up. The number of House conferees dwindled to eleven, exactly the number needed to constitute a quorum. Then Congressman Reid gathered together his papers and left the room. A few minutes after Reid's departure, Mrs. Green broke her silence and made the point of order that a quorum was not present among the House conferees. She had remained to make one last fight. If a quorum, technically needed to conduct business, was not present, then the conference could not be concluded that night. Delaying the finish of the conference for an additional day might provide Mrs. Green with an opportunity to rally support.

Indeed, a forum would be available later the same day—a caucus of the Democratic Members of the House, where the major item on the agenda was an antibusing resolution sponsored by Congressman Joe Waggonner of Louisiana. Waggonner's resolution instructed the Democrats on the Judiciary and the Education and Labor Committees to report the antibusing legislation and constitutional amendment that were before them. If the conference were not concluded before the caucus, Waggonner's resolution could easily be amended

---

busing for desegregation, was also accepted but again with important modifications. Basically, the comparable and weaker provisions from the Scott-Mansfield amendment were adopted. On other issues, the Senate conferees agreed to drop the requirement for "one quality integrated school" in the Emergency School Aid Program. The Senate accepted a slightly modified version of the House provision to protect the neighborhood school. The Senate provision authorizing parents to intervene in court orders requiring the busing of their children was also retained in a modified form.

to include additional instructions from the caucus to the House Democratic conferees on the higher education bill.

The reason May 16 was selected for ending the conference and for Chairman Perkins driving the conference through the night was precisely to finish before the Democratic caucus, and thus to avoid embroiling the bill further in the busing debate.

When Congressman Reid left the conference, his still-alert staff assistant followed him out into the hall and told him he was needed for a quorum. The Congressman was skeptical and protested that he was dead tried. Finally yielding, Reid agreed to stay and set off down the hall to get a drink of water. A near frantic Education and Labor Committee staffer ran into the hall to try to catch Reid, who he assumed had already left the Capitol. Relieved to find the Congressman, he reported that the absence of a quorum had been noted by Mrs. Green. Before the call of the roll was completed, Reid calmly walked back in and answered to his name, establishing a quorum.[P] Her final strategem having failed, Mrs. Green departed and sadly trekked alone through the darkened Capitol rotunda back to her office.

The remaining business was quickly disposed of, and the conference adjourned at 5:13 a.m. A veteran Senator called it the toughest conference he had ever experienced, and a House member could think of only one other in his eighteen years in Washington, the 1959 conference on the Landrum-Griffin labor bill, that was comparable. Gray with fatigue but nevertheless managing broad smiles, Democrats and Republicans, House Members and Senators shook hands all around congratulating each other on having reached an agreement. There was even a tinge of sadness in their parting. New respect and in some cases even new friendship had grown among many members who had scarcely known each other two months earlier. While it could not be said that they enjoyed the conference, it had become a major part of their lives. They trailed out leaving behind a littered landscape; every surface in the august Chamber was covered with discarded notes, memoranda, draft amendments, paper cups half-filled with stale coffee, food wrappers, and overflowing ashtrays.

The Finishing Touches

Because politics does not follow the conventions of a dramatic script, there was still an anticlimax to be added. Chairman Perkins was concerned that despite the quorum call, the legitimacy of the decision of the conference might be challenged in the House on the grounds that a quorum had not been present.

He called an additional meeting of the conference for May 18. With a

---

[P]In addition to Reid, the other House conferees present for the quorum were Perkins, Green, Brademas, Meeds, Mazzoli, Quie, Bell, Esch, Dellenback and Steiger.

quorum present, a motion approving all actions taken during the conference was approved by the House conferees. Senator Pell eagerly assented on behalf of the Senate conferees. Frank Thompson could not resist a final dig at his foe, Mrs. Green. As the vote was taken among the House conferees, he asked her, "Aren't you going to vote your proxies?" She replied, "That is pure venom." To which Thompson responded, "You're the expert."

One important and generally unnoticed task remained. The conference report, including the text of the law as agreed on in conference and the "Joint Explanatory Statement" describing each difference and the action taken, had to be drafted. Writing the report fell to the staff, with technical assistance from congressional and HEW legislative draftsmen. They faced a massive chore, and to expedite the job, they divided up into two teams, one writing the text of the law and the other the statement. Two aspects of the drafting of the conference report are significant.

First, in many important cases, the staff had to rely on imperfect records and their fatigue-dimmed memories to reconstruct what the conference had done. Two separate teams working with these resources resulted in some inconsistencies between the text of the law and the Statement. This could complicate the task of administrative implementation or judicial interpretation.

Second, during the conference, many of the staff had been partisan advocates for the positions of their Members. It was natural for them to once again push for their particular views when disagreements arose, though it is impossible to tell whether staff bargaining produced any results substantially different from what the conferees had agreed on because there was no authoritative record.

Reflections on the Conference Committee

Decision Making on the Substantive Issues

One basic factor conditioning decisions in the conference was the massive character of this bill. When combined with the idiosyncratic interests of the individual conferees and the variation in who happened to be attending conference sessions, this resulted in an uneven focus on parts of the bill. Issues of equal importance did not receive equal attention. Some large and significant programs like those for graduate education or the Student Loan Marketing Association slid through with relatively little sustained discussion. Others, like a proposed affidavit to be signed by students receiving a guaranteed loan, were the subject of prolonged and intense debate. One whole set of issues, the authorization levels for all the programs, was dealt with in an almost cavalier fashion at the marathon conference of May 16. The conferees worked on the assumption that all programs grow. So they proceeded in rapid order generally to split the difference between the House and Senate authorization figures with the amounts increasing for future fiscal years. There was almost no discussion of how much money the programs actually needed or at what rate they would or should grow in the future.

The fact of important issues escaping the attention of the conference was significantly aggravated by the lack of systematic and sustained input from both the Administration and the higher education associations. They could have served an important function in flagging potential problems. In addition, with the lobbyists and the Administration on the sidelines, when the conferees did focus on an issue, they frequently did not have the information needed to make well-informed decisions. The members were frequently thrown back on their personal experiences and prejudices or the situations in their home state. While Members have a high propensity to assess issues in personal and parochial terms, this tendency was accentuated in the conference. For example, during the discussions of the Guaranteed Loan Program, Congressman Quie cited the case of a student in Minnesota who admitted to the Congressman that he had used his guaranteed loan to buy a red Corvette. Quie's view of the program was shaped by this example, which he recounted several times in the conference, and he was one of the prime movers behind the adoption of a needs test for this program.

The administrative feasibility of doing what the conferees agreed to mandate in the law was usually not a major consideration in conference decisions. This weakness of conference decision making was also increased by the passivity of the lobbyists and the Administration during the conference. Representatives of those who would be running the programs and those who would be participating in them as recipients of their benefits were not looking after their own interests.

The Role of the Administration

The Department of HEW produced comments on some student aid provisions, but for the most part the Administration's role was confined to monitoring the conference rather than any broad effort to influence the outcomes. This minimal role is accounted for by several factors.

First, while important programs before the conference had either been initiated by the Administration or had its support, neither bill could be characterized as the Administration's. The Administration's bill was rejected in committee in both houses, and the bills that emerged were congressional creations molded out of bills sponsored by Senator Pell and Mrs. Green. Thus the low level of Administration activity is in part accounted for by the fact that "their" bill was not before the conference.

Second, because the Congress had Democratic majorities in both Houses, the barrier of partisan distrust inhibited easy access and communication. Third, the restraint in relations introduced by partisan differences was heightened by the generally close-to-the-vest style of the Administration in relating to Congress, even to the Republican Members.

With respect to only one issue, the Cranston educational renewal amendment, was HEW aggressive in attempting to affect the decisions of the conference. Secretary Richardson, however, was unable to satisfy Senator Cranston's concerns, and the amendment was retained. Fundamentally, the issue was legislative versus executive prerogative in making policy. HEW argued that the Cranston Amendment would deny the discretion and flexibility it legitimately needed for effective administration. Congressional proponents of the amendment contended that administrative discretion had been used to frustrate congressional intent and to accomplish objectives not authorized by law. HEW officials drafted compromise language and enlisted the support of Republican conferees to present their case. It was even suggested that Secretary Richardson would be willing to appear personally before the conference. This idea was rejected as an unacceptable intrusion by the executive branch into internal congressional processes. One Congressman remarked that the Secretary would be welcome in the conference when the Congressman could attend the Secretary's policy meetings with his assistant secretaries. This issue was a rare instance where the House Democrats were united, with Mrs. Green and John Brademas taking turns in cataloging HEW's abuses of power. With some minor modifications, the amendment was accepted on almost straight party-line votes on both the House and Senate sides. This was the only important issue that divided the conferees along party lines.

The Role of the Higher Education Associations

Like the Administration, the higher education associations monitored but did not energetically try to influence the conference. Their adbication derived in part from relative inexperience in dealing with Congress. It was also reinforced and rationalized by an apparently widespread belief that conferees would perceive lobbying as inappropriate and that it therefore would be counterproductive. Mrs. Green did, in fact, seem to believe that it was unseemly for lobbyists to gather in the halls outside the conference. Since most of the associations looked to Mrs. Green as their advocate, her attitude encouraged the passivity of the associations.

The picture should not be overdrawn. A few higher education representations and researchers provided valuable data and analyses to the conferees. The Association of American Universities and the American Library Association provided memoranda explaining their preferences and how the differences in the bills on the programs that most interested them should be reconciled.

The activity of Aims McGuinness of Maine on state planning and the data support on institutional aid have been noted. But compared to the need for information, the range of issues before the conference, and the opportunities for influence, the role of the associations was indeed small. Even in monitoring the conference, they failed to sniff out the 45-45-10 agreement on institutional aid.

The Roles of the Conferees

The role of a conferee is inherently paradoxical. On the one hand, a conferee is expected to act as a representative of his house and to defend its version of the bill. On the other hand, he is expected to reach an agreement, which necessarily involves compromise. Thus conferees are almost always vulnerable to the charge that they failed adequately to protect their house's position.

There was a great deal of specialization among the conferees, both on substantive issues and in the functional roles they played within the conference. Two functional roles were most visible—the legislative craftsman and the political facilitator. The legislative craftsmen were in the thick of the debate on the issues, arguing and exploring alternatives. Words of legislative art to take care of a potential problem are their stock in trade. These conferees had the ability to read the original language of the two bills, read the language of a proposed compromise, listen to the compromise being explained by its sponsor, assimilate whispered comments from the staff man at their elbow, lean over and confer with a colleague, draft their own compromise language, and be prepared to present and defend their alternative, all practically simultaneously. This role involves the political skill of formulating, packaging, negotiating and compromising on the issues. Congressmen Brademas and Quie and Senators Javits and Dominick were primarily legislative craftsmen.

Those who specialized as political facilitators were less concerned with substantive content. They were more interested in structuring the process so the legislative craftsmen could operate effectively. Opening lines of communication, getting the right people together, avoiding unproductive personality clashes and fruitless deadlocks, timing the pace of activities and, in general, greasing the wheels were their speciality. Chairman Perkins, of course, preeminently exemplified this role.

The Political Norms and Social Environment of the Conference

The most striking conference norm was egalitarianism. The public prestige and reputations of the conferees were left at the door, and they carried no special weight in the conference. What counted were a Member's knowledge of the issues and legislative skills, not his press clippings. If Senator Kennedy and

Congressman Meeds shared a public platform, the presence of the latter would probably be scarcely noted by the national media. In the conference, however, they met as equals resolving the issue of Indian education.

There was only one significant exception to the egalitarianism that prevailed in the conference. Senator Pell, on behalf of his Senate colleagues, insisted that issues of special interest to individual Senate conferees not be dealt with in their absence. This resulted on several occasions in juggling the agenda to accommodate a Senator, while House Members were only rarely accorded the same privilege.

Failure to modify the conference schedule to suit House Members was noted and resented by the House conferees. On one occasion Senator Javits requested that further consideration of the Emergency School Aid Program be suspended because he had to leave to host a dinner party. Congressman Bell said he expected to be accorded the same privilege when he had to leave early the next day. Senator Dominick responded that Bell could leave his proxy with someone else when he left. Bell replied that Javits could do the same. But Javits was particularly interested in and knowledgeable about the program, said Dominick. Bell observed that the same was true for him. The dispute was resolved by an agreement that the consideration of the Emergency School Aid Program would be arranged to accommodate both Javits and Bell.[q] Following this interchange, Mrs. Green remarked that House Members should stop allowing themselves to be treated like second-class citizens. On a note of resignation, Chairman Perkins observed that adapting the conference to the Senators' schedules was the only way to get something done.

Other differences between the House and Senate conferees were also apparent. The average House conferee was more expert and informed on the substantive issues than his Senate counterparts because House Members serve on fewer committees and subcommittees and can specialize more intensely.

The Senators also dealt with each other in a courtly and respectful manner compared to the more rough and tumble attitude of the House Members. For example, at an informal caucus, a Senator hurried in following an important and close Senate vote on the space shuttle, casually remarking to a fellow-Democrat from the House that a Senator from the House Member's state had voted the wrong way. The Congressman observed that the Senator in question was like a pigeon: if you kicked him, all you got was "shit and feathers." Pained looks appeared on the faces of the Senators present, and they lapsed into an embarrassed silence. The Senators found this remark, not especially unusual in House Members' conversations about each other, most inappropriate as a reference to a fellow Senator, even one who had voted wrong.

---

[q]It is noteworthy that this interchange among Bell, Javits and Dominick was between three Republicans. Institutional loyalties and prerogatives can divide members independent of any effects of partisanship.

The banter among the legislators should be mentioned to provide the full flavor of the conference. While one could scarcely characterize the conference as light-hearted, it was neither as entirely serious as the analysis of the negotiations and decision-making process may make it appear. Jesting references to Congressman Pucinski, who was running for the Senate, as "Senator" Pucinski were frequent. A volley of ribbing followed when Pucinski arrived late at one session and mistakenly took a seat reserved for a Senator. During the consideration of the Emergency School Aid Program, a question was raised concerning the inclusion of the Portuguese in the definition of the minority groups who would receive the benefits of the program. Senator Javits observed, "Let's remember that the Chairman on this side [Senator Pell] comes from Rhode Island. This is the least we can do for him." Rhode Island, where Pell was fighting for re-election, has a large Portuguese minority. The banter reflected the personal relations that developed among the conferees as well as the general spirit of egalitarianism. It also served occasionally to relieve the tension.

The Conference Decisions and Prior Expectations

Many important decisions of the conference, like the Basic Grant, NIE, community colleges, occupational education and state planning, came out about as had been expected. For the pessimists, the fact that the conference reached agreement at all was a surprise.

Acceptance of a scaled down version of the Administration's National Foundation for Postsecondary Education was unexpected. Its survival is accounted for by the diligent efforts of Senator Javits and his staff aide, Roy Millenson. There was also a feeling among the conferees that they should respond to the demands for federal action encouraging innovation and reform in postsecondary education. Finally, some Democrats felt that the prospects of passing the conference report in both houses and of convincing the President to sign the bill would be improved if major programs supported by the Administration were included. The Basic Grant, cost-of-instruction institutional aid and the NIE were such programs. The modified Foundation was another.[1] It was, in the words of two Democratic conferees, "a pelt on the wall" or "a conspicuous jewel for their crown."

Perhaps most surprising was that Mrs. Green did not dominate the conference. In large part, the surprise was a function of an initial overestimation of Mrs. Green's potential strength. A dispassionate analysis of the divisions within the House Education and Labor Committee and of the composition of the conference should have led to a more modest view of Mrs. Green's power.

---

[1] The Foundation proposal was recast into an authorization that led to the establishment of the Fund for the Improvement of Postsecondary Education in HEW.

Mrs. Green had qualitatively weaker supporters than her opponents. Many of her allies went along in part out of the habit of following the legislative norm of backing one's subcommittee chairman. Her supporters were also in many ways mercenaries whose proxies had been purchased by the inclusion of their specific pet programs in the House bill. Lacking in commitment, her allies were frequently absent and not generally very knowledgeable about the issues. They supplied votes but could not help much in arguing substance. Mrs. Green also seemed to be understaffed during the conference, her veteran and knowledgeable higher education aide having recently resigned.

In addition, the bitterness of the rift, both personal and substantive, between Mrs. Green and her opponents, especially Congressmen Brademas and Thompson, transformed the usual politics of compromise into the politics of annihilation. Neither side saw accommodation as possible, and the winning side pushed for almost total victory rather than a predominant share in settling the issues, particularly institutional aid. Fighting Mrs. Green brought out a special fervor in many of her opponents.

Mrs. Green's support outside the Congress among the higher education associations and institutions was never effectively mobilized. This was due both to their approach to lobbying, which dictated refraining from aggressive and visible action, and to the cues they perceived from Mrs. Green. In one respect the support of the higher education associations was even a liability to Mrs. Green. Senator Pell and his staff felt that the higher education associations had ignored them during the formulation of the bill, banking instead almost exclusively on Mrs. Green. Thus Pell derived an extra measure of enthusiasm in defending the Senate's cost-of-instruction formula from the fact that its adoption and the defeat of Mrs. Green would demonstrate to the associations the error of their ways.

The single most important cause of Mrs. Green's defeat was the basic political dynamic of the conference. With the Senate conferees unanimous on institutional aid as well as most other issues and the House conferees evenly divided, especially on institutional aid, the most feasible and likely agreement was one favoring the Senate bill. This was particularly the case given that Chairman Perkins, who had supported Mrs. Green earlier, put reaching agreement on a bill as his first priority in the conference. Mrs. Green's defeat was almost guaranteed when Perkins read Mrs. Green's floor statement and concluded that she did not share his commitment to getting a bill out of the conference.

Following every conference, the question is inevitably asked, "Who won?" Insofar as this question refers to whether the conference agreement is closer to the position of the House or the Senate, it is difficult to answer. There are divisions within legislative committees, and divisions on floor votes. There is also a tendency for Members not on the committee to ratify the recommendations of the committee no matter how closely divided the committee was and without much evaluation of the merits of the issues. Thus the definition of each house's "position" is open to some debate and interpretation. It can also be argued that in every successful conference both sides won, in the sense that at least a majority from each house finds the agreements acceptable. Finally, simply counting the number of differences settled by adopting the position of each house and the number that were compromised overlooks the relative importance of the issues.

These caveats noted, it is nevertheless fair to say that on the major higher education issues, student aid and institutional aid, the Senate won. On the hundreds of additional differences between the two bills, both sides won about an equal number, and a large number of issues were settled by compromises that could not be characterized as a victory for either. The busing issue was compromised with a substantial residue of dissatisfaction on both sides. The busing compromise was, however, weighted in favor of the Senate position.

On the House side, Quie and Brademas and their allies, who represented a minority position on the House Committee and in the House, also won. Thus the Senate victory was also their victory. Insofar as the Administration's legislative goals coincided with the Senate bill and the position of Quie and Brademas, they also won. Among major new programs, the Basic Grant, NIE, Sally Mae and the scaled down version of the Foundation could be identified with the Administration. The Administration also considered cost-of-instruction institutional aid a victory. The busing language was the major source of Administration displeasure.

Looking Ahead to the Final Legislative Round

The morning after the final all-night session, the bleary-eyed leaders of those who had prevailed held a press conference. They emphasized the scope and significance of the bill as a higher education measure. Chairman Perkins characterized it as "one of the greatest accomplishments in higher education that has ever taken place in Congress." Nevertheless, in the media, the Administration, the Congress and the nation, the focus was on the busing amendments. The headlines of the lead stories on the conference in three major papers read: "Busing Curb Agreed on By Conferees," "Conferees Agree on Busing Limits," and "Conferees Vote 19-Month Delay on Busing Edicts."[3] Rumblings of discontent were heard almost immediately from both the civil rights forces and the antibusers. Senators Kennedy, Mondale and Javits took the unusual step of refusing to sign the conference report. To them it represented a step backward in civil rights. Among the House conferees, Mrs. Green and Congressmen Daniels, Hawkins and Burton did not sign. Hawkins and Burton withheld their signatures on civil rights' grounds. Mrs. Green was extremely dissatisfied with both the higher education provisions and the busing amendments. Congressman Daniels apparently shared her displeasure with the higher education agreements as well as harboring his own special disappointment over the loss of the Youth Camp Safety title.

While the conference had been the most difficult hurdle faced by the bill, its final enactment was still not a foregone conclusion. Civil rights and antibusing sentiment in both the Senate and the House clearly threatened defeat of the conference report. Discontent with the higher education programs posed an additional problem in the House. Finally, the bill would confront the possibility of a veto by President Nixon who was making antibusing a key issue in his re-election campaign.

Notes

1.   *The Washington Post*, January 8, 1972.

2.   *Congressional Record*, April 12, 1972, pp. 12298-12299.

3.   Eric Wentworth, *The Washington Post*, May 18, 1972, p. 1; John Matthews, *The Washington Star*, May 17, 1972, p. 1; and David E. Rosenbaum, *The New York Times*, May 18, 1972, p. 1.

The Last Lap: Senate, House, and President

The Senate took up the conference report early in the week following the conference. The bill's Senate sponsors anticipated opposition on both sides of the busing issue with the major threat from liberals. Thus the strategy in the Senate was to act quickly before civil rights groups had an opportunity to mobilize.

By the rules, the Senate acted first, and this probably improved the chances of the conference report. Because the conference report was not seriously threatened in the Senate, its passage there provided momentum as it came before the House, where the prospect of defeat was much more serious. Considering the bill first in the Senate also closed off a parliamentary option to its House opponents. When a conference report has passed one house, the conference committee officially ceases to exist. The house that considers the conference report second does not have the option of recommitting the report to the conference committee.

The Senate Acts with Dispatch

On May 23, the Minority Whip, Senator Robert Griffin, opened consideration of the conference report by offering a motion to recommit with the instruction that the Senate conferees accept the original House busing amendments.

In the debate, Senator Pell compared the bill to an iceberg: only the tip—busing—was visible while its great bulk—the education provisions—was obscured. Pell also predicted that if the Griffin motion were adopted, it might be impossible to reach agreement in conference. Senator Dominick, the ranking minority member of Pell's subcommittee, similarly counseled the Senators to see the bill in broader terms than just busing. He said, "Assuming that one can still remain practical in the barrage of emotional rhetoric swirling around the busing issue, no Senator should allow busing alone to dictate his vote on this report."[1] Senator Javits and other liberals also opposed the Griffin motion because they already found the busing language in the conference report unacceptable and certainly did not want to provide the opportunity for it to be made even worse. A motion to table the Griffin motion was adopted, 44-26. Most "nay" votes came from southern Senators and conservative antibusing Republicans.

The next day it was the same dance but with different partners. With no opportunity to strengthen the busing amendments, most of the antibusers praised the bill for its education programs, criticized the inadequacy of its busing language, but conceded that these amendments were the best available at the moment. The busing language was stronger than that contained in the Senate bill sent to conference in February. The "anti-antibusers" praised the conference bill as an education measure, in some cases noting their own contributions to it, but sadly concluded that the setback for civil rights that the busing amendments represented was too high a price to pay. Calling again on his iceberg analogy, Senator Pell urged approval of the conference report, speaking for those liberals who were sympathetic to the civil rights cause but who saw the educational significance of the bill outweighing its costs to civil rights.

With the ritualistic debate concluded, the Senate adopted the conference report, 63-15. With few exceptions all of the votes against it seemed to be votes of conscience by the anti-antibusers who were not unhappy to see the bill pass but who felt that they could not be true to their principles and vote for it. Senator Nelson of Wisconsin remarked shortly before voting against the conference report, "If my vote is needed, I will support it. If not, I will vote 'no' as a protest against the conference modification of the Senate busing amendment."[2]

There was even a suspicion that some of the negative votes were motivated by strategic considerations looking toward House action. Because most of the opposition to the conference report in the House would come from antibusers upset at the weakening of the House amendments, votes against the conference report by procivil rights Senators would lend credibility to the argument that what was left of the House amendments was still a meaningful curb on busing.

The House Delays

In the House, the conference report was attacked from three sides. The higher education provisions, especially student aid and institutional aid, were characterized as a fraud and a repudiation of the views expressed by the House. This criticism did not appear to carry much weight and, had it been the only grounds for opposing the conference report, the report would have been accepted overwhelmingly. Second, a group of civil rights advocates were opposed because, despite the weakening of the House antibusing amendments, they still found them unacceptable. Again, if this had been the only opposition, the conference report would have easily won approval. Third, the largest group opposing the conference report were House antibusers unhappy with the weakened busing amendments.

Where the Senate had moved expeditiously to take up the conference report, Chairman Perkins, the House manager, sought to delay consideration to give the higher education constituency time to be heard in support of the bill. Delay would also push the House vote closer to the deadline of June 30 when the authorizations for most higher education programs would expire; thus killing the conference report would leave almost no time to take some alternative legislative action.[a]

In one respect Perkins' decision on timing backfired. On May 31, a federal appeals court upheld a district court order requiring busing to achieve desegregation in the Nashville, Tennessee schools. This gave fresh impetus to the anti-busers during the period of delay.

The conclusion of the conference left the higher education associations in an awkward position. Their primary objective, capitation institutional aid, had been rejected, and their champion Mrs. Green had been defeated. Yet the conference bill authorized $21 billion dollars, mostly for higher education, and it included a large array of new and old programs that were either highly valued or at least acceptable to the higher education community.

The day after the conference ended, Mrs. Green called to her office the Washington representatives of the major higher education associations. Her message was simple and direct; she wanted their assistance in killing the conference report in the House. According to one of the higher education representatives, "She was, in effect, saying, 'I carried the ball for you guys, and now it is up to you to help me.' " The higher education spokesmen demurred, asking for time to consult their college and university constituency.

Their soundings among the institutions indicated a wide divergence of opinion. Some college officials were opposed to the institutional aid formula. Another group was horrified by the idea of supporting a bill with antibusing amendments attached. But there was a consensus by a fair margin that higher education had no choice but to support the conference report. The association representatives were still personally troubled by the prospect of deserting their long-time friend, Mrs. Green. One explained that

. . . we were tormented by the choice she presented to us. We felt she had done our bidding and now we had some obligation to help her and stick by her. However, the question really becomes, does one have an obligation to commit suicide.

So the higher education associations reluctantly came to the conclusion that they had to back the bill that had come out of conference.

Early the next week Roger Heyns, the recently appointed president of the American Council on Education, sent a letter to the association's membership cataloging the bill's departures from the positions that had been supported by

---

[a]Bibby and Davidson note that the strategy of delay to let public support build was also used by Perkins in the consideration of the Office of Economic Opportunity Bill in 1969 and that it is a common legislative strategy. John Bibby and Robert Davidson, *On Capitol Hill*, 2d ed., The Dryden Press, Hinsdale, Illinois, 1972, pp. 166-167.

the Council, especially institutional aid; briefly noting its "major new thrusts" and commenting that if the conference report were defeated, the busing amendments would reappear in perhaps an even less acceptable form. The letter concluded with a lukewarm endorsement of the conference report: "On balance, it is the advice of those whom we have consulted that we should support the conference report. I concur. If you agree, I hope you will so inform your own Senators and Representatives. . . ." All of the other major higher education associations, with one exception, also expressed their support. The Association of Jesuit Colleges and Universities, after tentatively supporting the conference report, backed away and "reluctantly decided that it cannot endorse the Conference Report. . . ."[b]

Chairman Perkins likewise called the association representatives together for a meeting in his office. Perkins and the other Members present cracked the whip. To pass the conference report in the House, they said, would require enthusiastic support from the associations—not just passive assent. They warned that if the conference report were defeated, nothing better could be achieved for a long time to come and also that worse busing legislation would result. One Member remarked, "If higher education fails to back this now, cries of fiscal crisis in higher education will fall on deaf ears in the future." The brusque treatment received by the association representatives coated with acid the bitter pill they had swallowed in deserting Mrs. Green.

Endorsement of the conference report by the higher education associations was an important resource the House supporters could point to as proof of higher education's acceptance of the bill and the need to have the legislation enacted.

Probably the most effective form of lobbying is Members of Congress lobbying other Members. Chairman Perkins was the most diligent and tireless in support of the conference report. He had the Education and Labor Committee staff prepare two mass mailings to the higher education community throughout the country. The first outlined in seven single-spaced pages the provisions and benefits provided in the bill. The second was a bulky document containing another brief summary of the bill, a fact sheet, and twenty-eight pages of excerpts from letters from higher educators and state officials supporting the bill. A cover letter cosigned by Perkins and ranking minority member Quie stressed the bipartisan nature of the bill, "the strong support" of the national associations, and the special treatment under the institutional aid formula of private colleges and universities. One of the staff described Perkins' efforts:

After the conference concluded, we at the full committee level were working the colleges and universities and every interest in the nation. We were sending

---

[b]See *Congressional Record*, daily edition, June 5, 1972, pp. H5262–H5263.

out poop sheets and summaries and analyses and countersummaries, and we were on the telephone with everyone we could think of. Perkins was talking to every Member on the floor and particularly cornering the southerners. He would call them up at home in the evening. He has a great knowledge of each of them as persons and knows their districts as well. So he could dwell on whatever piece of the bill was most of interest to them. We worked to match up the colleges and the congressional districts where they were and who knew the Members at that college in that district. . . . We were all over the country.

The opponents of the conference report were also active. Mrs. Green sent out two mass mailings to the higher education community, noting that only a few short months before, the higher education associations had opposed major provisions now contained in the conference report. "If these provisions were opposed in November because they were not based on sound educational policy, then surely they're not sound educational policy in May," she argued. A boost to Mrs. Green's case against the conference report on educational grounds came from Terry Sanford, the president of Duke University, and a Democratic presidential candidate, who characterized the bill as "full of empty promises."

In her second mailing, Mrs. Green sent out a compendium of statements by those opposed to the conference report comparable to the collection of statements of supporters sent out by Chairman Perkins and Quie. Mrs. Green's efforts were limited because she could not call on staff resources like those available to Perkins and Quie. One story pictured Mrs. Green in her office late at night as the House vote approached, personally stuffing envelopes and licking stamps.

Congressman Joe Waggonner of Louisiana worked diligently to mobilize antibusing sentiment among southerners and coordinated his efforts with those of Mrs. Green.

Meanwhile civil rights groups also organized opposition. Shortly after the Senate vote, the Leadership Conference on Civil Rights, a coalition of Black professional and church groups and organized labor, announced a campaign against the conference report. Members of the House received a "Dear Colleague" letter cosigned by three members of the Black Caucus and a liberal Democrat from California urging its defeat. The letter argued,

The price we must pay at the moment for refusing to equivocate on civil rights is the higher education bill. Although it can be argued that it is a large price to pay, it is not comparable to the invaluable cost of sacrificing constitutional guarantees.

The Administration Equivocates

During this pulling and hauling in Congress, the public position of the Administration was one of studied ambiguity. John Ehrlichman, the President's chief assistant for domestic policy, would neither predict nor rule out a presidential veto. However, he made it clear that the President was dissatisfied with the busing amendments. Ehrlichman remarked, "It is the President's position that what the conference has done here is no substitute for the necessary busing legislation."[3] Secretary of HEW Richardson also noted the serious "omissions" in the bill and his "personal reservations" with respect to busing. But the thrust of Richardson's remarks were praise of the higher education programs as "a major achievement" and "the heart of President Nixon's higher education initiatives."[4]

The Administration's strategy was apparently to try to get the best of both worlds, the higher education legislation and better antibusing legislation. Acting on behalf of the Administration, House Republican Leader Gerald Ford approached Chairman Perkins and warned that the conference report could be defeated in the House if the Administration were either neutral or actively opposed. He mentioned the possibility of a presidential veto, but also dangled the prospect of a softer Administration line if Perkins would set a date for action on the Administration's antibusing legislation, which had been bottled up in the Education and Labor Committee since March. Perkins pledged to "consider" such action, but he would not commit himself to a date. Ford's offer crossed Perkins' personal line between expediency and principle.

Having failed in its attempt to use the threat of opposition or a presidential veto as a lever to get action by Perkins on busing legislation, the Administration refrained from an official position on the House vote on the conference report.

House Passage

Perkins and the House Democratic leadership scheduled consideration of the conference report for June 8. As the day approached, the chairman and others mapped out a floor strategy. Decisions were reached on who should speak on the floor and how speakers in support should be paired with the speakers in opposition to maximize the impact of the former and minimize the impact of the latter. One pairing was suggested on the grounds, "Let's match our best demagogue against their best demagogue."

The most difficult problem was how to respond to a request for more time for consideration of the conference report. Under the rules of the House, debate on all conference reports is limited to one hour and can be extended only by unanimous consent on the floor. Congressman Waggonner and Mrs. Green approached Perkins and Quie, having first gotten a sympathetic hearing from the Speaker, with a proposal for two hours of debate. Waggonner and Mrs. Green argued that this was an unusually complex bill requiring more time for adequate consideration and for all who were interested to have a fair opportunity to be heard.

Perkins agreed not to object and was supported by Quie and Dellenback who maintained that objecting to the request for an additional hour would look like an attempt to muzzle the opposition. They suggested that such an impression could cost the bill a crucial margin of support, especially among moderate Republicans.

As a strategy meeting in Perkins' office was about to reach a consensus to go along with the chairman, Congressman Thompson arrived. Told of the earlier discussion and the apparent consensus to agree to an additional hour of debate, Thompson exploded: "They'll demagogue us to death! It is only to our disadvantage to allow the opposition time to rabble-rouse the emotional busing issue. That's crazy! I'll object! Whose idea is that?" Only slightly abashed to learn the idea was being advanced by the chairman, Thompson continued to "respectfully" insist that he would object to a request for two hours of debate. He finally agreed that he would object to two hours of debate but not to an additional half hour.

It was later argued, however, that if Thompson objected it might look like collusion between him and Chairman Perkins. It was widely known that Thompson and Perkins were allies in their support of the conference report, and the chairman might appear to be weaseling out of his agreement by getting Thompson to object. Seeing the point, Thompson agreed to recruit another Member to offer the objection and enlisted Congressman Bill Clay of Missouri, a member of the Black Caucus and Thompson's labor subcommittee.

Floor consideration began with Chairman Perkins requesting unanimous consent for one additional hour of debate on the conference report. Congressman Clay asked Perkins for control of a half hour of the time on behalf of thirty members "who are opposed to the legislation" and who "have a unique position that perhaps might differ from the position of others who are opposed."[5] Clay was referring to the pro-civil rights opponents of the conference report. When Perkins indicated that he could not give Clay control of a half hour, Clay then objected. Perkins modified his request and asked for an additional half hour. Clay did not object. A note of comic relief was injected when Congressman H.R. Gross, the conservative gadfly of the House, asked Clay to explain who was this group that Clay claimed to represent. Clay replied, "For your information, they are the good guys who wear the white hats."[6]

Thus far everything had proceeded according to plan. The unexpected then intruded. Congressman Fletcher Thompson of Georgia, one of the most fervent antibusers, said angrily, "I intend to object to anything less than two hours. I think we should have three hours, and if we are not going to have at least two, I object to an hour and a half."[7] Waggonner argued in vain with Thompson of Georgia that the effect of his objection was to limit the debate to one hour and that one and a half hours was still better than one hour. Thompson of Georgia was impervious to Waggonner's logic, and the time for debate was set at one hour, much to the happy surprise of Frank Thompson of New Jersey. The objection by Thompson of Georgia to the request for an hour and a half also vitiated any argument that the supporters of the conference report were gagging the opposition.[c]

The issue of the time for debating the conference report is another example of unusual manipulation of the procedural rules to gain a political advantage that characterizes the entire story of the bill. The objection by Fletcher Thompson illustrates the impact of unplanned and unexpected events. While actions in politics are probably more planned and calculated than is generally assumed, events are only rarely controlled to the degree intended.

The opponents of the conference report next tried to use another set of House procedures. Waggonner raised three points of order against the conference report alleging that the House conferees had exceeded their authority and violated the rules of the House by agreements reached in conference. Sustaining any of the points of order would have negated the action of the conference and returned the legislation to its parliamentary status before the conference occurred.[d]

The Speaker overruled all the points of order, remarking in his first ruling:

> Several of the managers on the part of the House conferred with the Chair during the conference deliberations and stressed to the Chair that at every stage of their negotiations particular attention was being given to the rules governing conference procedure and the authority of the conferees. . . .
>
> When a possible compromise infringed or even raised a question of the infringement of the rules of the House, the Chair was informed that the managers on the part of the House resolved that matter so there was no conflict with the provisions of [the] rules. . . .
>
> The Chair is satisfied that the managers have conformed to the rules of the House, and therefore overrules the point of order.[8]

Thus Perkins' practice during the conference of religiously consulting with the Parliamentarian and the Speaker on possible infringements of the House rules seemed to pay off, as he had hoped, in sympathetic understanding.

In the normal pattern, the debate time was divided equally between the majority and minority parties, and Perkins and Quie each controlled a half hour. Because they were both strong backers of the bill and had jointly arrived at a floor strategy, they could arrange the order of speakers and allocate time to present the best case in support of the conference report. Perkins and Quie

---

[c]Later in the proceedings, Quie renewed the unanimous consent request for one and a half hours of debate. Clay objected. *Congressional Record*, daily ed., June 8, 1972, p. H5398. Why clay objected to one and a half hours at this later point is not known.

[d]Among the points of order that the Speaker overruled was one that charged the conferees with transgressing the rules by violating the instructions that were twice voted by the House. In overruling this point of order, the Speaker remarked, "[A]lthough conferees disregard the instructions of the House, the Speaker cannot for that reason rule the conference report out of order." Ibid., p. H5397.

yielded 23.5 minutes to the opponents of the conference report and 36.5 minutes to the supporters.[e] They allocated time to nineteen different Members, and a few of these yielded to colleagues. In all, twenty-two Members made substantive statements in the debate. Of these six spoke in opposition to the conference report and sixteen in support. Working on the theory that people tend to be more persuaded by the final arguments they hear, Perkins and Quie yielded time to the most effective opponents of the conference report at the beginning of the debate and saved their most effective advocates for the end.

Mrs. Green presented the most extensive attack on the conference report for its deficiencies as both a higher education and antibusing measure. She argued that the higher education community was divided over the bill, citing the statement by Terry Sanford, and laid heavy stress on busing saying, "a vote for this bill is a vote for busing . . . This is a probusing bill."[9] She also indicated that if the conference report were defeated, a preferential motion would be in order to pass a new higher education bill that she already had prepared. This new bill, as she described it, would continue all existing higher education programs, would add the occupational education and community college section of the conference bill and would include the original three House busing amendments.

Congressman Earl Ruth (R-North Carolina) echoed the sentiments expressed by Mrs. Green, demonstrating Quie's wisdom in keeping Ruth off the conference committee. Minority Leader Ford also spoke in opposition to the conference report expressing dissatisfaction with the busing amendments. He noted his unsuccessful negotiations with Perkins but significantly did not state that he opposed the conference report either as a representative of the Administration or as a leader of the Republican party in the House. Gus Hawkins, a member of the Black Caucus and a Democratic conferee, presented the case against the conference report on civil rights grounds.

The supporters emphasized the education merits of the measure. In addition, they argued that the busing amendments constituted meaningful and effective action against busing. Chairman Perkins reviewed the arduous legislative history of the bill and challenged the view that a new and better higher education bill could be obtained if the conference report were defeated: "The conference report before us represents the only compromise possible between the divergent views of this House and the Senate on any number of issues."[10]

Congressman Steiger captured the essence of the argument by the supporters of the bill with an adage, "Keep your eye on the doughnut and not the hole."[11]

During the debate and as the clerk began to call the roll, many members were genuinely torn: "the vote I cast today. . . .is the most difficult and personally

---

[e]Actually, Quie gave 14 of his 30 minutes to the opponents of the conference report, while Perkins gave the opponents only 9.5 minutes of his 30 minutes.

painful vote I have ever cast in the Congress;" "today I must decide on a vote which is one of the hardest decisions I have had to make since my election to Congress." The final vote was 214-180, and the conference report was agreed to.

The Elements of Success in the House

The outcome was largely the product of political efforts by political men. First, the situation was structured to favor passage of the conference report. Perkins delayed bringing the bill to the House floor until the June 30 deadline was near. He also conducted the conference committee to make adoption of Mrs. Green's alternative bill look highly improbable. It was argued, particularly on busing, that the Senate would simply not give any further. The care that Perkins had taken during the conference to consult with the Speaker and the Parliamentarian seemed to produce a tilt toward giving the conference report the benefit of the doubt. Finally, Perkins and Quie managed the floor debate to the advantage of the supporters.

The situation in which the conference report was considered was also fortuitously and inherently biased in favor of adoption. It was largely a matter of chance that the conference report was considered first in the Senate. In addition, there is in both houses a strong presumption in favor of approving conference reports. The general feeling seems to be that bills that have advanced this far in the legislative process ought to be killed only for the most compelling and extraordinary reasons.

Second, the conferees brought to the House a conference report with broad appeal and with provisions especially attractive for crucial blocs of potential supporters. The higher education programs served schools and students in every congressional district in the country. Several provisions could also be characterized as initiatives from the Republican Administration. And there were particular programs in which individual Members or small groups had strong vested interests. Youth Camp Safety (the "seven Texas votes") is one example.

Third, the supporters did an effective job of selling the bill. Congressmen Quie and Dellenback seemed successful in persuading their moderate Republican colleagues that the bill was in many of its essential features a good "Republican" measure. House Republicans voted 89-76 in favor. Compared to the November vote on final passage of the House bill, thirty-nine fewer Republicans voted for the conference report. The busing issue was key in the erosion of Republican support with about half of the defections by southern Republicans. When the Republican Minority Leader and the Administration did not make opposition to the conference report a Republican party position, moderate Republicans could support it.

The major reason for the change from almost overwhelming support of the House bill in November to the close vote on the conference report in June was dissatisfaction with the busing amendments. Support for the bill among both Democratic and Republican Congressmen from the South almost evaporated. Most spectacularly, the Virginia delegation switched from a November vote of 9-0 (with one Member not voting) to a 0-10 vote against the conference report. However, Perkins worked assiduously among the "Dixies," aided by Majority Leader Boggs, and twenty southern Congressmen voted for the conference report, fifteen Democrats and five Republicans. Outside the southern delegations, the Broomfield amendment gave the conference report enough antibusing credibility to gain the support of some northern antibusers. The vote of the busing-preoccupied Michigan delegation was 13-4 for the conference report.[f]

A group of about twenty-five pro-civil rights liberals also switched from support of the House bill in November to opposition to the conference report. The size of this group was minimized by the absence of an effective all-out effort by the civil rights forces. Both the *Washington Post* and the *New York Times* editorially advocated passage of the conference report on its education merits. They decried the antibusing amendments but characterized them as an "addenda" and a "sideshow."[12] This support from the "liberal establishment" press may have helped to defuse some of the pro-civil rights opposition to the conference report.

The avid supporters of the conference report among the former House conferees appeared to be successful in convincing their state congressional delegations to vote for the conference report. For example, Pennsylvania, the home state of conferees Dent and Gaydos, voted 20-4 for the conference report and the ayes carried in Frank Thompson's New Jersey 12-2.

With the bill on its way to the White House, Chairman Perkins' prodigious efforts finally took their toll. A few days after the conference report was passed, Perkins collapsed and was hospitalized. One of his staff remarked, "This bill practically killed the Chairman." In addition to chairing the conference, overseeing the Education and Labor Committee staff efforts to build support for the conference report, and lobbying his House colleagues, Perkins had simultaneously chaired two other conferences on black lung and manpower bills. He also commuted by car almost every weekend to his Kentucky district where he faced primary challengers and the prospect of a formidable Republican opponent in November. Even his favorite form of relaxation, horseback riding, did not provide such solace. During the conference, he was kicked in the head by one of his horses.

Decision in the White House

From the White House point of view, the bill was "a mixed bag." Many of its central provisions either were Administration initiatives or were supported

---

[f]In November, the Michigan delegation had voted for the House bill 15-1.

by the Administration. There was some dissatisfaction with the total cost of the programs, with the Cranston amendment limiting administrative discretion in HEW and with the requirement that the existing student aid programs be funded before money could be spent on the Basic Grant. But these were relatively minor reservations. On the other hand, one White House aide characterized the busing amendments as "a meaningless charade" and "a cop-out by the Congress."

A press report shortly after House action on the conference report indicated that the President was leaning toward signing the bill. But again busing and the Courts intervened. On June 14, federal district court Judge Stephen Roth ordered preparation of a school desegregation plan encompassing not only the city of Detroit but also school districts in fifty-three surrounding suburban communities. Roth's order brought antibusing sentiment to a new crescendo. Two days later, John Ehrlichman announced that the President's decision on signing the bill was being postponed pending a study of the applicability of the busing amendments to the Detroit case.[13]

Vetoing the bill on busing grounds would, of course, have no impact on deterring the implementation of court-ordered desegregation plans in Detroit or anywhere else. But a veto might stimulate the Congress to pass more effective busing legislation. It would also allow the President to portray the Democratically controlled Congress as the barrier to action on this issue. A veto of the education bill would also mean in all likelihood that the President's higher education initiatives would be lost.

With the deadline approaching when the bill would become law without the President's signature, the President revealed his own thinking in a press conference on June 22, 1972. After his now-infamous statement, ". . .the White House has had no involvement whatever in this particular incident [Watergate]," the President answered questions related to busing and the education bill.[g] Asked whether he intended to sign the bill, the President responded:

> I have to make the decision tomorrow. I will be very candid with you to tell you that it is one of the closest calls that I have had since being in this office. . . .[S]ome of the members of my staff and Members of the Congress are enthusiastic for signing it, and others are just as enthusiastic for vetoing it.
>
> I have mixed emotions about it. First, as far as many of the education provisions, strictly education provisions, they are recommendations of this Administration. I think they are very much in the public interest. If they could

[g]One of the transcripts of the tapes of presidential conversations on June 23, 1972, contains a fragmentary record of a discussion between the President and H.R. Haldeman concerning the higher education bill. The remarks are too brief and incomplete to permit a full view of the thinking in the White House; however, two things seem clear from this transcript. First, the politics of busing, particularly with respect to the Detroit case, was the dominant consideration in the decision on whether to veto the bill. Second, the decision was a "close call." This segment of the transcript is reprinted in *Education Daily*, Volume 7, August 7, 1974, pp. 1-2.

be separated from the rest of the bill, and stand on their own, there would not be any question about signing the bill. On the other hand, the Congress, as you know, did add a provision, section 803 [the Broomfield Amendment], with regard to busing. It was certainly a well-intentioned position, but from a legal standpoint it is so vague and so ambiguous that it totally fails to deal with this highly volatile issue.

What brought that home to me was when I asked the Attorney General for an opinion as to whether or not it could deal with the problem of the busing order that has been handed down in Detroit. The answer is that it is highly doubtful that section 803 of the Higher Education Act, in the event that it is signed into law, will deal with that problem. . . .[14]

Perhaps calculating that the Democratic Congress could be blasted on the busing issue just as effectively whether he signed the bill or vetoed it, the President signed S. 659 into law the next day.[h] In his statement the President fired a broadside at Congress:

Confronted with one of the burning social issues of the past decade, and an unequivocal call for action from the vast majority of the American people, the 92nd Congress has apparently determined that the better part of valor is to dump the matter into the lap of the 93rd. Not in the course of this Administration has there been a more manifest Congressional retreat from an urgent call for responsibility.[15]

So, bedeviled by busing to the very end, the higher education bill became Public Law 92-318. Aspirations and ideas articulated over a period of years and the efforts to transform them into a legal reality finally resulted in the Education Amendments of 1972.

Notes

1. *Congressional Record*, daily ed., May 23, 1972, p. S8289.

2. Ibid., daily ed., May 24, 1972, p. S8403.

3. Eric Wentworth, "Busing Bill Displeases Nixon," *The Washington Post*, May 20, 1972, p. 1.

4. "Remarks by the Honorable Elliot L. Richardson, Secretary of Health, Education, and Welfare before Independent Colleges of Southern California, Los Angeles, California, June 2, 1972," press release, Department of Health, Education, and Welfare, June 2, 1972.

5. *Congressional Record*, daily ed., June 8, 1972, p. H5394.

[h]In line with technical parliamentary procedure in Congress, the bill signed by the President carried the number of the Senate bill, S.659, rather than the number of the original House bill, H.R. 7248, because the Senate was the first to act.

6. Ibid.

7. Ibid., p. H5395.

8. Ibid., pp. H5396-H5397.

9. Ibid., pp. H5401-H5402.

10. Ibid., p. H5422.

11. Ibid., p. H5420.

12. "The Busing Sideshow. . .and the College Crisis," *The New York Times*, May 19, 1972, p. 36; "A Breakthrough for Higher Education," *The Washington Post*, May 21, 1972, p. B6; and "Higher Education: The Busing Addenda," *The Washington Post*, May 30, 1972, p. A18.

13. "Nixon Holds up Bill on Busing Pending Study," *The Washington Post*, June 17, 1972, p. A4.

14. "The President's News Conference of June 22, 1972," *Weekly Compilation of Presidential Documents*, June 26, 1972, p. 1078.

15. "Education Amendments of 1972: Statement by the President upon Signing the Bill into Law," *Weekly Compilation of Presidential Documents*, June 26, 1972, pp. 1084-1085.

Part III
Impact and Process

Legislation unquestionably generates legislation. Every statute may be said to have a long lineage of statutes behind it. . . . Every statute in its turn has a numerous progeny, and only time and opportunity can decide whether its offspring will bring it honor or shame.

Woodrow Wilson
Congressional Government (1885)

10 Policy Outcomes

The enactment of enabling legislation culminates one phase in the evolution of public policy and marks the beginning of another. When President Nixon crossed the "x" on his signature of S.659, the Education Amendments of 1972, a set of authoritative Congressional decisions became law. While these decisions in themselves carried symbolic weight, their operational meaning and impact would necessarily depend on other decisions involving administrative guidelines and regulations, budgets and appropriations. Congress had acted, but it remained to translate legal language into concrete effects on the lives of people and institutions.

Legislation is a moving target. Once enacted, it continues to change as the skill and imagination of administrators are applied to its provisions, as the intent of Congress is interpreted, as funds are appropriated and spent, as social and political conditions change, and as Congress exercises oversight of the law's implementation and considers its amendment and extension.

The process of implementing a law is as fundamentally political as the process of its formulation and enactment. The struggle over policy continues, only in different forums with different ground rules. The President's signature on a bill punctuates but does not end the policy-making process.

This chapter sketches the dynamics of policy development since the signing of the 1972 legislation and indicates the directions of policy change. It serves as but an epilogue to the main study we have undertaken, for the events and debates since June 23, 1972 have been as complex and contentious as those leading to the bill's passage and could fill another book. First, we will summarize the policy judgments and aspirations expressed in the Education Amendments of 1972.

A Basic Charter

To describe a law in any but process terms is to arbitrarily freeze it, to substitute a taxidermist's specimen for the living organism. Nonetheless, a basic charter for federal higher education policy was established in 1972, one that would have enduring significance. The broad themes of the 1972 Act are the starting point for understanding subsequent developments.

Some of the policy themes were largely unarticulated during passage of the law and are only implicit in it. Others were voiced again and again but

223

only in catch phrases that were more frequently incanted than analyzed—"equal educational opportunity," "postsecondary education," "innovation" and "accountability." Most of the themes are interrelated. Some are at odds with others. Not all were unanimously espoused or understood in the same way by the principal legislators. In short, one does not find a systematic, fully coherent philosophy, for the legislation amalgamated a variety of purposes, values and ideas. Yet we suggest the following eight policy themes as most salient.

Equal Opportunity

One theme above all dominates the law and the legislative history. The equalization of opportunities for higher education, a goal historically more incidental than integral to federal involvement in this field, clearly became the central commitment of federal higher education policy with the passage of the Education Amendments of 1972.

As an abstraction, equal opportunity is implicit throughout the bill—in the provisions for community colleges and occupational education, in the state planning provisions, in the institutional aid formula. But operationally, its principal meaning was that lack of money should not be a barrier to an individual's pursuit of education or training beyond high school. Thus the equal opportunity theme is most directly expressed in the student aid provisions, which form the centerpiece of the legislation. Removing the financial barriers facing students was the overriding concern of the legislators, as it had been of the Carnegie Commission and the Rivlin Report.

The law embraces a set of new and old student assistance programs designed to ensure equal *access* to the postsecondary system and to go far toward ensuring equality of *choice* among institutions. Basic Educational Opportunity Grants (BEOG) were envisioned as the foundation, enabling every student to start out with at least $1,400 from a combination of family resources and federal grant aid, though this commitment was hedged by the limitation of the BEOG to one-half the student's cost of attendance. The BEOG was intended to provide an assurance of a minimum amount of aid—and early knowledge of it during the high school years—for low- and moderate-income students. To finance additional costs, the law continues the earlier student aid programs— Supplemental Educational Opportunity Grants (SEOG), College Work-Study, National Direct Student Loans (NDSL)—and creates a new incentive program for need-based state scholarships. The legislative intent was that these programs would supplement the BEOG floor.

Equal educational opportunity has dimensions in the law other than removing financial barriers—for example, motivating and counseling disadvantaged students to make use of postsecondary opportunities. The 1972 Act also takes a new stride in the direction of realizing the oldest meaning of equal educational opportunity, removing arbitrarily discriminatory barriers. Title IX, "Prohibition of Sex Discrimination," focuses not only on the ability of women to get into the postsecondary education system but also on their right to reap the full benefits once they have entered and after they have completed their education.

Student Needs Before Institutional Needs

Corollary to the equal opportunity theme, the law enunciates the basic policy choice that students, not institutions, are the first priority in federal support for higher education. The legislators were concerned about institutional well-being and survival, particularly of private schools, but they determined that these concerns should not be the basis of federal policy. Better, they decided, to put purchasing power in the hands of needy students and let the students make their own choices in the marketplace of postsecondary education. This strategy would have the effect of concentrating available federal resources on students who might otherwise be barred from postsecondary opportunities; it would also, so the reasoning went, serve to make institutions more responsive to the needs and interests of such students.

While it might be inferred from the student orientation of the bill that the views of economists prevailed in the process, the legislation did not by any means embrace the "full-cost pricing" model advanced in much of the economic analysis of higher education. The bill puts the emphasis on targeted student aid, a strategy favored by most economists writing on the subject, but it does not contain a suggestion of support for raising tuition levels to more nearly approximate full instructional costs, the other prong of the economists' prescription. If anything, some of the key legislators might have legislated lower tuition levels if it had been in their power. The bill's focus on students derived not from a sophisticated economic philosophy of higher education finance but from the simple conviction that the principal objects of federal policy should be the consumers rather than the suppliers of higher education.

The 1972 Act did authorize for the first time a federal program of institutional aid through which unrestricted grants could be made to all accredited institutions, profit-making schools excepted. But the formula adopted for distributing such institutional grants, or "cost-of-education allowances," once again asserted the student-assistance priority and was even designed indirectly to harness the institutions to the realization of this priority. Of the funds 90 percent would be linked to the institution's enrollment of federally aided students. Moreover, a major part of the formula would not become effective until appropriations for the BEOG program reached at least 50 percent of full entitlements—theoretically an incentive for institutions to lobby for BEOG funding.

The Division of Federal-State Roles

The 1972 Act reaffirms the traditional boundary between federal and state roles in the support of higher education. The basic responsibility resides with the states while the federal government provides funds to fill specified national needs.

Thus Congress pulled up short of a plan that amounted to federal revenue sharing with institutions of higher education—across-the-board general operating support distributed on the basis of enrollments. It was unwilling to underwrite the entire system without reference to any national objective other than preserving and strengthening educational institutions. Instead, Congress decided on a program that would help institutions only in such a way as to advance the purpose identified above as the hallmark of the Act, equal opportunity for higher education. The responsibility for general support of institutions, it was decided, should continue to rest with the states.

Federal-State Partnership

On the one hand, the Act reaffirms the historical division between federal and state roles. At the same time, the Education Amendments of 1972 build on a tradition of federal-state partnership and interaction in this field that dates most visibly from the Morrill Land-Grant College Act of 1862. The 1972 law adds two new threads to the fabric of this tradition: (1) Section 1202, which calls for comprehensive postsecondary education commissions in the states, authorizes federal grants to such commissions to conduct statewide planning and encourages the unification of all responsibility for the administration of federal higher education programs requiring the use of a state agency; and (2) the new State Student Incentive Grant program, which creates a federal-state matching arrangement to increase funding of scholarships for needy students, thus enlisting the states in helping to achieve the federal objective of equalizing opportunity for higher education.

Broadening the Educational Mainstream

The Education Admendments of 1972 encourage and in some ways mandate a broadening of the educational mainstream to include types of students and institutions that have generally been excluded or given second-class status in the past. The new term is "postsecondary education." The intent is to break the stereotype that education beyond high school means a four-year academic program leading to a baccalaureate degree. Explicit federal recognition and legitimacy are accorded to programs of career preparation and occupational education, to proprietary institutions and community colleges, and to students who attend less than full-time.

The broad significance of these changes is that Congress now conceptualizes education beyond high school as a range of options that are equally appropriate depending on an individual student's needs and interests. As a spokesman for the proprietary schools noted, the Education Amendments of 1972 finally "illuminated the whole horizon."[1] The legislation recognizes that sound policy must address all segments of the system.

Reform and Innovation

The Education Amendments of 1972 seek not only to widen the pale of respectability in postsecondary schooling; they also reflect a desire for revitalization and reform of the traditional system. The legislators were fairly confident that something was wrong in higher education, that too much of the academic enterprise was hidebound and poorly managed. They did not feel nearly as confident, however, in selecting or creating what was right to give it special support. They felt constrained not only by their lack of expertise in pedagogy, curriculum and the other professional concerns of educators, but also by the traditional doctrine of academic freedom that places these subjects beyond the reach of government decision-makers. Therefore, the law establishes certain mechanisms through which the federal government can encourage but not dictate innovation and change in higher education.

The BEOG program and the cost-of-education approach to institutional aid embody elements of reform thinking. Student choices were selected as the surrogate for federal choices, and the mechanism through which student choices are to operate is the free market. If students are entitled to federal aid prior to their enrollment at any postsecondary institution and independent of which institution they choose and if, in addition, such federally aided students carry with them additional federal dollars (cost-of-education allowances) to the institutions, then those institutions that are most responsive to student needs and interests will flourish and those that are not will wither. The students, "voting with their feet," will carry federal funds into the schools they decide to attend. Moreover, the adoption of the concept of postsecondary education gave federal recognition to a broader range of options—a bigger marketplace—within which student choices could be exercised, thus helping to assure that the basic dynamic of the market, competition, would work more effectively. An enrollments formula for distributing institutional aid was rejected in part because it was feared that such an approach would inflate the standard of living of institutions without providing any leverage or incentive for change.

This is not to suggest that there was a naive faith in the "unseen hand" of the free market. Maximizing the perceived educational satisfaction of those students who are identified as having high priority in federal policy, financially needy students, was simply adopted as the best *available* way to attain educational change and innovation.

The legislation also authorized an instrument to encourage change by direct means: the Fund for the Improvement of Postsecondary Education. Watered down from the Administration's original proposal of an independent national foundation for higher education, the Fund nevertheless has a broad mandate to provide "seed money" for experimental and creative ideas. The law mentions support of alternative types of career training, cost-effective methods of instruction, more flexible patterns of entering and re-entering institutions, reform of the structure of academic professions, and the creation of new institutions for awarding educational credentials—all concepts reminiscent of the Newman Report.

Information and Accountability

Closely related to the theme of innovation and reform is the quest by federal policy-makers for more information about and greater accountability from higher education. There is throughout the law a sense of tentativeness born of inadequate information. At one point the legislators threw up their hands in the admission that

insufficient information is available on the basis of which the Congress can determine with any degree of certainty, the nature and causes of such financial distress [in institutions of higher education] or the most appropriate means with which present and future conditions of financial distress may be dealt.[2]

The legislators did more than throw up their hands. The law mandates about a dozen studies and reports through which the policy-makers hope to gain a better view of the lay of the land in postsecondary education, a cognitive map of the system they are trying to deal with. The objective is to be able to make more informed decisions in the future, particularly in the areas of institutional aid and student aid. The most important inquiry was to be conducted by a new National Commission on the Financing of Postsecondary Education.

One aspect of this desire for policy-relevant information is a feeling that everyone, including educators, needs to understand more about learning and education. Thus the law creates the National Institute of Education to provide federal "leadership in the conduct and support of scientific inquiry into the educational process."[3]

In addition to promoting more informed decision making in the future and a better understanding of what education and learning are, good information is the precondition for systematic evaluation. The quest for information is therefore an integral part of an attempt in the law to ensure greater accountability.

In terms of the evaluation of government activities, "accountability" has several meanings, all touched upon in the Act. Sometimes it means simply the legality of expenditures: Is money being spent in a manner and for purposes authorized by law? Thus the 1972 Act reinforces the mandate of the General Accounting Office, the investigating agency of the Congress, to audit federal education programs and to review the contracting practices of federal education agencies. It sometimes means faithfulness to legislative intent: Is administrative discretion being used not only within the letter of the law but in a way that complies with its spirit and the intent of Congress? In an attempt to get at this question, the legislation requires the Commissioner of Education to conduct a study and make a report to Congress on all administrative guidelines and regulations related to education programs, including an explanation of the legal justification for each exercise of administrative rule-making power. Accountability also means program performance: Are programs achieving the objectives for which they were established? Thus the GAO is also directed to "evaluate" federal education programs and projects.

Finally, the law incorporates provisions that seem to move federal policy in the direction of cost accounting standards for institutions of higher education. The possibility of such direct accountability of colleges and universities to the federal government is suggested in the little-noticed section of the law authorizing the Commissioner to require from institutions, as a condition of receiving federal institutional or student aid, data on how much it costs them to educate students.

Continuity: Reauthorization of Existing Programs

The seven themes described above all deal with policy directions established by new programs and initiatives. A final theme is the extension of old programs. The policy-makers clearly were not fully satisfied with what existed, but they did not want to abandon it wholesale. Much of the Act is concerned with reauthorizing existing programs in areas like college libraries, developing institutions, academic facilities construction, graduate education, foreign language and area studies and education professions development.

Some legacies of the Great Society, most notably the Office of Economic Opportunity (War on Poverty), have had to struggle to stay alive politically. This was not the case in 1972 when it came to higher education programs which had their origins in the 1960s. There was an easy assumption, at a minimum, that the enabling authority for such ongoing measures would be renewed. Not only are old programs reauthorized, but the Act includes several "hold-harmless" and "grandfather" clauses to protect the existing programs and their beneficiaries from retrenchment as new programs are added. The most important example of grandfathering is the requirement that three of the existing student aid programs, SEOG, College Work-Study and NDSL, be funded at their fiscal year 1972 level before any BEOG payments are released.

The law extends the Guaranteed Student Loan Program and also creates the Student Loan Marketing Association, a government-sponsored private corporation designed to help banks and other lenders generate more loans under the program. Sallie Mae and the grandfathering of the student aid programs are steps that the legislators felt would serve the interest of middle-income students.

These are the major outlines of federal higher education policy established by the Education Amendments of 1972, a distillation of the 146-page law and its legislative history. The measure also reorganized the basic higher education statutes under one code and combined many disparate slices of federal policy making, not all related to higher education.[a] In the area of elementary and secondary education, the Act included the antibusing amendments—which politically overshadowed the rest of the bill—as well as an Indian education title and the Emergency School Aid Program to assist schools in the process of desegregating. Ethnic heritage studies, a reauthorization of vocational education programs, and a study of youth camp safety also found their way into the Education Amendments of 1972. And the law includes a number of odd bits and pieces of higher education policy, such as granting land-grant status to the College of the Virgin Islands and the University of Guam and a statement by the Congress that college and university boards of trustees should consider incorporating student members.

Finally, the legislation mandates administrative changes designed to elevate the status and visibility of education in the executive branch. A new Division of Education is created within HEW, composed of OE and the new National Institute of Education and headed by a new Assistant Secretary for Education. Some of the legislators envisioned this restructuring within HEW as a step along the road to a separate Department of Education of the Cabinet level.

Public Law 92-318 was indeed a measure of staggering comprehensiveness, easily the longest federal education statute in history. Senator Pell called it a "magnificent edifice."[4] A Christmas tree, a bonanza, a smorgasbord, a garbage dump—these descriptions have also been applied to P.L. 92-318. Assessments of the measure's soundness and significance in terms of higher education varied widely in the aftermath of passage by Congress. Among the congressional contestants, the division of opinion fell along lines one would expect. Mrs. Green was the principal detractor, charging that the bill does "not offer substance but false promises" and warning that "our institutions and our students would be sadly advised to chart their. . .course on the basis of its provisions."[5] The bill's proponents, on the other hand, claimed an historic achievement, Congressman Brademas calling it "the most significant piece of legislation on higher education since Congress created the national system of land-grant colleges in 1862."[6]

The potential of the legislation would be determined not by rhetorical claims and counterclaims but by time and experience. The task of implementation would generate a new debate and new political dynamics centering on the bureaucracy and the budgetary process—and engaging the legislative and executive branches of government in a nearly constant tilt over prerogatives and priorities.

---

[a]The "recodification" was a product of technical draftsmanship. The Senate bill had integrated all the basic authority for higher education programs under the Higher Education Act of 1965, and this format was accepted by the conference committee.

The Administration: Control by Budget and Rule Making

If Congressman Brademas, Mrs. Green, and the other protagonists of the Education Amendments of 1972 agreed on one thing, it was basic distrust of the Administration's competence and readiness to carry out the will of Congress in the field of education. Not only were Hill Democrats generally suspicious of the Nixon Administration's good faith in executing the laws, but congressional dissatisfaction with the past performance of the Office of Education predated the Nixon Administration and ran deep. Mrs. Green warned that OE was becoming "a diverse, overlapping, unplanned, confusing array of governmental efforts whose faults are beyond remedy and whose abuses are beyond belief."[7]

Both the House and Senate committee reports on the respective higher education bills in 1971 admonished the Office of Education on a number of points of administrative judgment and policy, and the final legislation in 1972 contained specific provisions designed to put a congressional leash on the agency by modifying its administrative structure and authority. For example, the controversy over OE's educational renewal strategy resulted in the Cranston amendment, explicitly prohibiting OE from consolidating or limiting education programs except as specifically authorized by law. By forcing the establishment of a new Bureau of Occupational and Adult Education and a Community College Unit in OE, the Act seeks to give bureaucratic stature to these sectors of education, which the Congress felt OE had too long neglected in favor of traditional four-year academic programs and institutions. Congressional unhappiness with the quality, utility and dissemination of OE-sponsored research is starkly expressed by the creation of NIE; the research function, a major concern of OE since its inception in 1867, is almost entirely transferred to a new agency. The requirement that OE prepare an exhaustive report on all extant regulations and guidelines is a unique, albeit cumbersome, device for trying to get a handle on what OE is doing across the board.

Parts of the law were thus aimed at hedging the discretionary power of the bureaucracy. But the new legislation also carried with it a large grant of administrative authority. By its nature legislation expands rather than contracts the domain and influence of executive agencies. With the passage of the Education Amendments of 1972, major new programs were placed on the books and major new responsibilities fell to HEW and the Office of Education.

It has been said that legislation is like rough carpentry rather than fine cabinet making. The edges must be smoothed out—ambiguities of language resolved, specific cases addressed, operational details and logistics pinned down—by the executive arms of government. There is, of course, no simple demarcation between legislative and executive activity. The proclamation of ends and the devising of means are functions that merge in the real world. But the character and focus of policy making change as the formal stages of government proceed. Once a bill becomes law, attention shifts to matters of funding and operations. However little confidence the education committees of Congress may have had in HEW/OE, it is in these agencies—and at the White House/OMB level—that many key decisions would be made on the future of Public Law 92-318.

Even before the bill was signed, OE and HEW had established a series of primarily in-house task forces to map plans for implementation. The sections of the law authorizing new initiatives were parceled out for detailed staff analysis and legal interpretation. "Issue papers" were to be developed, followed by the drafting and publication of regulations. It soon became clear that most provisions, particularly the big new programs like BEOG, would not become operational in the school year beginning in the fall of 1972. Time was too short to gear up administratively, and the Administration was not prepared to make the necessary budgetary commitments at this stage, nor was Congress likely to vote appropriations in time. But the task forces pressed ahead with the aim of implementation during academic year 1973-1974. In the early summer of 1972, HEW and OE representatives began meeting with Members and staff of Congress to discuss issues of Congressional intent and with representatives of the higher education community to get their input.

Commissioner of Education Sidney Marland hailed the positive potential of the Act—the "most significant educational legislation of our time," he called it—but also noted problems of complexity and imprecision. "There are hundreds and hundreds of pieces in this mosaic of law, literally hundreds. . .suggesting a number of options as to precisely what Congress meant," Marland said. And consultation with Congressional representatives, he indicated, does not necessarily help to iron out things that seem unclear because "it depends on whom you talk to as to what Congress meant."[8]

One issue of statutory interpretation was joined only weeks after the law's enactment. In contrast to the newly authorized initiatives under the legislation, amendments to ongoing programs became operational directly on July 1, 1972. Thus changes in the Guaranteed Student Loan Program, including new eligibility rules, took effect almost immediately—at the peak of the loan processing season. In mid-July OE issued interim regulations requiring a needs test from all applicants seeking a subsidized Guaranteed Loan, whatever their income level. Students who had previously qualified automatically because their families earned less than $15,000 a year now found themselves having to prove their need. Administrative confusion followed as lending and educational institutions as well as the students tried to figure out how to proceed under the new rules.

HEW and OE officials insisted that the uniform requirement of a needs test was the only way to read the new law, and this reading seemed to be in line with the views of Representative Quie, who had been instrumental in writing the Guaranteed Loan provisions in the conference committee. But other key sponsors of the legislation, like Senator Pell, argued there was no such intent, that the law extended eligibility for the first time to students from families over the $15,000 level if they could meet a needs test but did not impose such a test on students below the $15,000 level. Some Congressional spokesmen charged the Administration was deliberately tightening eligibility for the program to hold down budgetary outlays when the intent of Congress was to broaden access to the loans.

The debate was murky at best, a case of unclear legislative purpose combined with strict construction of the law by the administering agency.[b] The result was a near breakdown of the huge Guaranteed Loan Program, with several hundred thousand students finding their applications denied or seriously delayed as the fall semester approached. The Administration finally asked Congress in mid-August to defer implementation of the new law's Guaranteed Loan provisions, permitting the backlog of loans to be processed under the old rules and allowing time to clarify the issue. Three days later Congress passed an emergency resolution to this effect.[c]

Meanwhile OE's greatest challenge was to launch the BEOG program. Some of the initial thinking in OE favored grafting this program on to the established administrative apparatus of previous federal student aid—SEOG, Work-Study, and NDSL. These so-called campus-based programs operated by way of state and institutional allocations, with colleges and universities making the individual need determinations and awards to students at the campus level. But congressional representatives quickly made clear that BEOG was supposed to be something different: a national entitlement program, aiding eligible students wherever they live or attend college. Its Senate framers intended the program to operate as automatically and directly with students as possible and to treat students consistently on the basis of national eligibility standards.

Thus a new delivery system had to be devised for BEOG's, one that might utilize educational institutions as disbursement agents but not for discretionary administration of the program. The most complicated task would be to develop the eligibility criteria, or "schedule of expected family contributions" mandated in the law. In drawing up the schedule, OE had only the broadest guidance from the Congress. The law directed OE to consider basic factors like the family's (and the student's) income and assets, number of dependents, number of dependents in college, and unusual medical and catastrophic expenses, but did not specify the weighting of such factors. The legislative history generally suggested that Congress wanted to aid both low- and moderate-income students who were needy, rather than targeting the program strictly to the lowest-income groups

---

[b]For an extended analysis of this episode, see "Legislative-Executive Disagreement: Interpreting the 1972 Amendment to the Guaranteed Student Loan Program," *Harvard Journal on Legislation*, Volume 10, April, 1973, pp. 467-485.

[c]Seven months later Congress amended the law essentially to restore the Guaranteed Loan interest subsidy provisions to their pre-1972 status, with the exception that students from families with over $15,000 annual income could qualify on the basis of a need analysis. Students below this cut-off, as before 1972, became automatically eligible for subsidized Guaranteed Loans (as long as the loan did not exceed $2,000).

(which some in Congress suspected might be the Administration's tendency). But the detailed and delicate decisions about what families from differing economic circumstances would be expected to contribute to postsecondary costs, and therefore which students get how much aid under BEOG, were left in OE's hands—though under the law either house of Congress could disapprove the schedule finally drawn up by the Commissioner.

Section 1202, a sleeper among the Education Amendments, posed another set of issues. A welter of pressures came into play as OE set about to develop regulations for the potentially powerful 1202 state commissions. The final compromise language of 1202 adopted by the House-Senate conferees had left much room for argument on just how actively the federal government, through the Office of Education, was supposed to mold the state role in postsecondary planning. Representatives of the Education Commission of the States and many state policy-makers pressed for an expansive interpretation to vest the commissions with broad authority for both planning and coordination of all postsecondary education in each state. Others, including some state governors, argued that the law's intent was not to restructure state bureaucracies but simply, and more narrowly, to facilitate statewide planning in relation to the new federal programs of support for occupational education and community colleges. Many institutions of higher education, both public and private, were alarmed at a federal initiative that might strengthen the state's hand in dealing with colleges and universities. Some viewed 1202 as a dangerous first step toward a state superboard that would threaten institutional autonomy.

Debate mounted on the proper scope of the 1202 commissions, how they should be appointed (governor or legislature), how they should relate to pre-existing state commissions responsible for administering construction and other federal funds for higher education, and how to define the statutory requirement of "broadly and equitably representative" membership. Again, key decisions rested with OE.

Task forces were also at work dissecting the complicated institutional aid formula in the law and sorting out the new authorizations for state scholarship incentives, ethnic studies, community colleges and occupational education. And plans were underway for the organization and staffing of NIE, Sally Mae, and the Fund for the Improvement of Postsecondary Education.

Most of this early planning at the operational level of the bureaucracy had a tentative quality because a great deal would ultimately depend on budgetary decisions by the White House, OMB and Congress. There was little doubt the Administration would try to hold down new spending. White House aides warned of a "tough budget year." In fact, while OE continued its staff work on implementation, word began to filter down of a tight-fisted budget policy that might exclude all but a few initiatives under the new education bill.

Though it applauded the overarching philosophy of the bill, particularly the emphasis on aid to students, and with more or less justification claimed the NIE and BEOG as its own ideas, the Administration clearly wanted to ignore much of what it found in the Education Amendments of 1972. Politically, the Administration had played a minimum-loss game prior to enactment, trying to avoid the worst outcomes from its point of view (such as the Green formula for institutional aid) but not aggressively lobbying to put across its own program. After the Nixon higher education messages fell flat in both 1970 and 1971, the Administration had remained largely on the sidelines. Administration strategists in effect gave up on controlling the legislative process and banked instead on controlling the impact of the bill once it was signed by the President. Through budgetary and regulatory authority, the Administration would seek to bend the legislative outcomes to its own objectives.

This task was part of a new strategy that evolved toward the end of the first Nixon Administration by which the White House hoped to get a rein on domestic policy. During Nixon's first twelve to eighteen months in office, considerable energy was devoted to the development and submission of domestic legislative proposals. The welfare reform and revenue sharing plans as well as the education messages in 1970 were all devised and sent to Congress during this phase. But when few legislative successes resulted, the White House began losing interest. The Administration continued to forward messages to the Congress but in a perfunctory manner, with a take-it-or-leave-it attitude. A former Nixon official, Richard Nathan, has described the new approach that emerged when the legislative route proved frustrating. Sometime in 1971 Nixon and Domestic Council head John Ehrlichman reached the conclusion

that in many areas of domestic affairs, *operations is policy*. Much of the day-to-day management of domestic programs—regulation-writing, grant approval, and budget apportionment—actually involves policy-making. Getting control over these procedures was the aim of the President's strategy for domestic government in his second term.[9]

Flushed by his landslide victory at the polls in 1972, Nixon began immediately and vigorously to push ahead with his new domestic strategy. Hand-picked White House loyalists were deployed to fill key positions in the executive departments. A Cabinet shake-up sent OMB Director Casper ("Cap the Knife") Weinberger, a strong fiscal conservative, to succeed Secretary of HEW Elliot Richardson and presumably to preside over a campaign to contract the commitments of this department. Statements by the President and his spokesmen expressed an increasingly hard-line determination to narrow the role of the federal government in domestic affairs, cut federal spending deficits, discard "outmoded" social programs, and bring the "bloated" federal bureaucracy under control. The old, Democratic psychology of "throwing dollars at problems" would be abandoned once and for all, the President warned. It also became clear that the President was prepared to use an arsenal of weapons in his drive to retrench, including the impoundment of congressional appropriations on an unprecedented scale.

The President's fiscal year 1974 budget proposals, released in January 1973, embodied these themes and launched what came to be known in newspaper headlines as the "Battle of the Budget." The Administration and Congress locked horns in 1973 in a developing confrontation over fiscal policies and the power of the purse. The President threatened "multiple vetoes" of appropriation bills exceeding his budget, and the congressional leadership assessed the override prospects. Basic constitutional questions arose as the President proceeded to impound funds, touching off a long series of court suits.

Before Watergate erupted in mid-April, 1973, the President appeared likely to get his way, indeed, to dominate both the bureaucracy and the Congress as possibly no American President had before. Liberal commentators warned of a dangerous shift toward "executive government" in Washington. The President's proposed budget cuts and radical restructuring of federal programs in education, health, housing and a host of other domestic areas seemed likely to stick. The President appeared to be riding a crest of power that would enable him to defy Congress and the lobbies that sharply protested these changes. There was the feeling in Washington of an era coming to an end. The social programs and liberal traditions of the New Deal and the Great Society seemed to be on the chopping block.

This atmosphere at the beginning of the second Nixon term clouded the prospects for the newly enacted education bill. As expected, the President's budget disregarded most of the new authorizations and called for the termination or phase-out of a string of ongoing higher education programs. It did, however, follow through on BEOG, calling for appropriations approaching $1 billion. In combination with funds requested for Work-Study, this represented a commitment to student aid that far exceeded previous spending levels. In fact, the Administration's willingness to commit substantial resources to this priority was a notable exception to the new hard-line laid down by the White House. Unlike certain other domestic goals of Nixon's first term, like welfare reform, that were abruptly dropped at the beginning of the second term, the commitment to equalizing educational opportunity through student aid was sustained. So also were the commitments to postsecondary innovation and educational research. The budget included a small sum for the Fund for the Improvement of Postsecondary Education and a sizeable request for the NIE.

Thus the Nixon budget proposals were a mixed bag for higher education. The proposed investment in student assistance was unprecedented, but it was supposed to be at the expense of existing categorical aid programs, and it was not balanced by even a token commitment to institutional aid. Outgoing Secretary Richardson had appealed to OMB and the White House for modest funding of the newly authorized cost-of-instruction allowance program, arguing that the Administration had endorsed it in Congress and that it was in line with the Administration's objective of equalizing opportunity – but to no avail. Moreover, the make-up of the student aid package in the President's new budget ran directly counter to the congressionally stated requirement that the existing programs be continued at specified minimum levels. The budget called for phasing out the old EOG and NDSL programs to help finance the new commitment to BEOG's.

The exposure of Watergate, of course, gradually dissipated the plans and hopes of the Nixon Administration for achieving an iron grip on domestic policy. The White House operated from a position of less and less strength in the remaining months of the ill-fated Nixon regime. Yet the Administration's formal posture on most issues remained unchanged. The President was obviously distracted by other problems but did not back down from his new domestic strategy. The budget battles continued, as did the struggle over the interpretation and implementation of the Education Amendments of 1972.

Congress: Appropriations and Administrative Oversight

The President's education budget did not sit well with members of the Senate and House authorizing committees. The framers of the Education Amendments were naturally displeased to see so much of their handiwork brushed aside by the Administration, and they were particularly incensed by the proposal to sidestep the legal provision governing the funding of student aid programs. "It's going to be a mean, divisive, disagreeable two years," Congressman Brademas said, anticipating the inevitable clashes with the President.[10]

But it was not the authorizing panels that had the power to deal with the President's budget. The arena of decision now shifted to the appropriations process and an entirely different committee sturcture of the Congress.

The shift was dramatized by an unexpected development at the beginning of the 93rd Congress. In January, 1973, Mrs. Green gave up her subcommittee post and eighteen years of seniority on the Education and Labor Committee to take a low-ranking seat on House Appropriations—an unorthodox move that stunned her colleagues.

No doubt contributing to Mrs. Green's decision was her frustration at having been foiled in the recent round of higher education legislation. In the aftermath of the fight over the 1972 bill, she had few if any stable alliances remaining on her own subcommittee. Moreover, authorizing legislation for higher education would not come up again for several years, during which her subcommittee would be largely confined to administrative oversight. Mrs. Green calculated that less influence would reside in the committees that write legislation than in the committees that control funding. "I have decided that the action this year is going to be on the Ways and Means Committee and on the Appropriations Committee, based on the Presidential vetoes of appropriations bills, the impoundment of so many billions of dollars' worth of funds, and the executive action to terminate programs," she said in a statement explaining her switch.[11]

Not only did Mrs. Green move to Appropriations, but she managed to win a slot on the subcommittee with jurisdiction over the Departments of Labor and HEW, thereby giving her a direct hand in the funding of education programs. As a junior member, she would hardly be in a position to dominate the Labor-HEW panel, which was firmly led by the silver-tongued Daniel Flood of Pennsylvania. But her background and detailed knowledge of the education laws almost insured that she would be listened to and accorded a degree of respect not usually enjoyed by new members, particularly on the tradition-bound Appropriations Committee. Indeed, her old antagonists on Education and Labor feared she might be able to use her influence in this new arena to sidetrack programs she opposed, like the BEOG and the NIE.

The issue of student aid appropriations came to a head in the late spring of 1973. Students, parents and colleges needed to know which federal programs would be funded in the upcoming academic year and in what amounts. A decision had to be made on the Administration's large, but skewed-toward-BEOG student aid request. Testimony before the Flood Subcommittee strongly supported a balance of programs as envisioned in the 1972 bill. A string of witnesses argued for upholding the law and funding all three existing student aid programs at least to the statutory minimum levels, while at the same time giving the Administration its full request for BEOG.

This strategy, however, would have bust the budget by several hundred million dollars, and Representative Flood was unwilling to invite a Presidential veto. The question, then, was how to reorder priorities within the nearly $1 billion total proposed by the President for student aid. Should all the money go to the three traditional programs, or should part of the total be set aside to give the new BEOG program a start?

Mrs. Green criticized the BEOG approach of establishing a simple national standard of need and "running all of the kids through a computer," claiming this ran counter to the Administration's own professed aim of decentralizing federal programs. She extolled the virtues of the older programs administered at the campus level where the financial aid officer can "sit across the table from the student" and take into account all the circumstances of each individual case. Mrs. Green intimated in the hearings and in private conversation that she might vote for letting some money go into the new BEOG just to demonstrate its administrative infeasibility.

Administration representatives did their best to counter Mrs. Green's strong views and barbed criticism, arguing that previous programs put the student at the mercy of the institution while BEOG would be more equitable because of its standardization. They insisted, moreover, that a "cadre of trained administrators" was ready to put the program into operation. Republican members of the Flood Subcommittee wanted to give the benefit of the doubt to the Administration, though they too were skeptical and wondered aloud whether the slow-moving Office of Education could really get the program off the ground in time for the fall semester, without an administrative debacle.

Amidst such skepticism, the Administration was fortunate to win even token funding for its top priority in higher education. The Flood Subcommittee and subsequently the House finally voted to put the bulk of funds into the tested, familiar programs, well exceeding the statutory minimums for SEOG, Work-Study and NDSL, and reserving only $122 million for BEOG. Senators Pell and Dominick later successfully amended the measure on the Senate floor to reshuffle the amounts, giving more emphasis to BEOG, but the House position was ultimately sustained in conference. The BEOG would have to be inaugurated in 1973-1974 on a budget of $122 million, so small an amount that a separate resolution was quickly approved restricting eligibility for the program in its first year to full-time freshmen. Even with this limitation, it was estimated that the appropriation would fall well short of meeting full entitlements and individual awards would have to be reduced according to the reduction schedule provided in the law.

When it later turned to other areas of higher education funding, Congress restored nearly all the categorical programs the Administration had proposed to cut back or cut out, like college library resources, undergraduate instructional equipment, and language and area studies. Appropriations were also voted for several of the new programs authorized in 1972 that the Administration had not wanted to fund—state scholarship incentives, special payments to colleges enrolling veterans, and planning grants for the 1202 commissions.

On the other hand, the Administration's $162 million request for NIE was reduced by more than half. The fledgling agency that was supposed to become the cutting edge of educational progress through research and development had fallen victim to a series of problems, chief among them fuzzy educational jargon and an inability of the agency's leaders to articulate a concrete set of objectives to the satisfaction of the Appropriations Committees. A long delay by the White House in appointing NIE's policy-making council also contributed, making it difficult for the agency staff to sort out priorities and strategies before having to defend the budget request on Capitol Hill.

The powerful Senator Warren Magnuson, liberal and traditionally sympathetic to education programs as chairman of the Senate Labor-HEW Appropriations Subcommittee, was particularly rankled by the Administration's testimony on behalf of NIE. Magnuson terms it the most "miserable" performance he had heard in his congressional career and quickly became an implacable foe of the agency. NIE also had its critics on the House subcommittee, particularly Mrs. Green, who heaped skepticism on the idea that such a new organization would be any less wasteful or incompetent than the Office of Education had been in administering educational research. Faced with an Administration budget that proposed to slash scores of popular HEW programs, the Appropriations Committees found in NIE a convenient target for some budget-cutting of their own.

Members of authorizing committees sometimes lobby their colleagues on Appropriations when it comes to funding legislation about which they have particularly strong views. John Brademas, for example, did his best to intercede in the NIE situation, trying to save the agency he helped create from an early disaster. Carl Perkins, John Dellenback and James O'Hara, Mrs. Green's successor as chairman of the postsecondary education subcommittee, all appeared before the Flood panel to urge compliance with the law through balanced funding of the student aid programs. Senator Pell pleaded with the Senate Appropriations Committee to keep a "solemn commitment" to the nation's young people by adequately funding the BEOG and other programs under the Education Amendments.

The principal role of the authorizing committees with respect to the 1972 bill, however, now resided in the area of administrative oversight. Congress had built into the legislation itself a number of administrative safeguards and levers. But the job of tracking a statute's implementation and finding out whether bureaucratic rules and regulations comply with the letter and intent of the law, whether statutory deadlines are being met, whether funds are being spent efficiently, how well programs are meeting the objectives they were supposed to meet—these are ongoing responsibilities requiring constant vigilance and study. Students of the Congress have long identified administrative oversight as a vital yet much neglected legislative function, one that Congress usually discharges in sporadic, desultory fashion at best. Staff limitations, the ceaseless flow of new legislation and new issues, and the general lack of political glamor in such activity all work against Congress probing as deeply and systematically as it should in many areas of administration.

As the single education panel in the Senate, the Pell Subcommittee would have less time to monitor the implementation of the new law than the House Committee. The Senate Subcommittee would soon have to devote nearly full time to new elementary and secondary legislation. Pell, however, had a personal investment in the 1972 bill and was especially concerned about the progress of the BEOG program. His staff also kept a watchful eye on the establishment of the Education Division and the new Assistant Secretary slot in HEW to guard against a concentration of bureaucratic authority not intended by the law. Pell distrusted HEW, particularly in the wake of the Guaranteed Loan crisis over the summer of 1972:

We have quite often had problems with the Department's tendency to rewrite the law. . .frequently to the point that we do not recognize it. However, the situation on the present law is more extreme than has ever, to my knowledge, been the case.[12]

On the House side, the Brademas subcommittee did what it could to move NIE off dead center, hounding the Administration to establish the NIE advisory council and prodding the agency's leadership to chart some clear directions. With no new legislation of consequence on the docket, Mrs. Green's former subcommittee had virtually an open field to conduct administrative oversight, and its new chairman was inclined to take the responsibility very seriously.

Jim O'Hara, a seasoned and respected Michigan Democrat with strong labor ties, had not been active on higher education legislation in recent years. But he had the reputation of being a "quick study," and when he took over the Green subcommittee based on seniority in the full committee, there was little doubt he would be active and outspoken in his new position. O'Hara also had deep convictions about the sanctity of the constitutional system. In a statement outlining the philosophy that would guide his chairmanship of the subcommittee, O'Hara spoke of a worsening constitutional crisis brought on by executive usurpation of legislative powers and dedicated himself "to work for a return to the concept that, in the field of education as in all others, this must be a government of law—not a government of men, not of administrative regulations, nor of bureaucratic guidelines."[13]

The new chairman immediately launched oversight hearings—on the BEOG family contribution formula, on the implementation of Section 1202, then on the philosophy, delivery and interrelationship of the gamut of student aid programs. He challenged and grilled Administration officials and searched for ideas among scores of expert witnesses. O'Hara also directed GAO to undertake investigations of the way federal student aid was being administered.

The Higher Education Lobby: Mending Fences, Reorienting

Although on the last lap the major higher education associations supported the Education Amendments of 1972 and helped clear the conference report in the House, it was not their bill, and they had not been instrumental in formulating many of its provisions. Passage of the act was at best a bittersweet victory for the associations. Subsequent criticism of the role they had played led to a period of reassessment and change in the higher education lobby.

On a political level, the benefit of hindsight made it easy to criticize the associations' fateful decision to rely so heavily on Mrs. Green. This had been a miscalculation, though in the spring of 1971 it did not seem unreasonable to make the alliance with the gentlelady from Oregon. She headed the right subcommittee, was willing to support the associations' preferred form of institutional aid, and had a long record of legislative success. The associations' greater mistake may have been their failure to give Mrs. Green more help by lobbying other Members to support the cause. One senior association representative admitted, "We really didn't follow up once we put our chips on Mrs. Green. We are absolutely vulnerable on that score."

Moreover, the associations' single-mindedness about institutional aid had blinded them to other important dimensions of the emerging legislation, and their nearly exclusive dealing with Mrs. Green tended to put off other major participants in the process. If there was an element of backlash against the higher education establishment in the final legislative outcome, it was partly generated by the aloofness of the Washington representatives of higher education.

The association also met a wave of criticism on another level, the quality of research and documentation they offered. Many of the legislators complained that the associations were unable to supply basic information needed to formulate intelligent policy, that they simply enunciated their position on institutional aid without adequate research and data to back it up. The toughest congressional critic was John Brademas, who charged a failure of analysis by the higher education community: "We turned to the citadels of reason. We said, 'Tell us what you need,' and they answered 'We need $150 per student because that's what we've been able to agree on.' "[14] One post-mortem on the role of the American Council on Education, higher education's leading voice in Washington, criticized its tendency "to rely on vague statements of opinion from an elite group of distinguished educators rather than hard-headed sophisticated analyses and data."[15]

Deeply ingrained apolitical and antipolitical attitudes in the academic community, plus the educator's traditional assumption of the self-evident value of education to society, have conditioned the style and performance of the national associations. Their tax-exempt status, which nominally bars lobbying, has also been a factor. But the higher education associations have been changing. Following the 1972 Amendments, the associations made efforts to shore up their congressional relations by creating a more visible and routine presence on Capitol Hill and seeking to provide better data to meet the needs of policymakers. They ran to catch up on issues, like Section 1202, that had slipped their attention prior to enactment. And they began to emphasize policy-related research. Changes were made to enhance both the political savvy and policy research capability of the associations, with the hope that they might be better prepared for the next legislative round in Congress. The associations have been adapting to a more complex political world where the sources of initiative and influence are diffuse, rather than waiting for a return of simpler days.

As for institutional aid, the associations have not abandoned their top priority of the late 60s and early 70s, but it has moved to a back burner. The form of institutional aid that did find its way into the 1972 law—cost-of-instruction allowances—has excited little enthusiasm among the associations or their member institutions. Only limiited, sporadic efforts have been made to lobby for its funding. The associations have adjusted their sights and are focusing more carefully on the center of gravity of federal higher education policy, aid to students, recognizing that students have become the principal channel of federal support for postsecondary education and that the toughest policy issues requiring attention and analysis are student aid issues.

Not only have there been changes within the established associations, but organized representation in behalf of higher education's clientele groups has broadened. The American Council and kindred associations reflect the concerns and positions of top college and university administrators, those who are responsible for the governance and survival of institutions. Ironically, though the legislation in 1972 put the emphasis on the student-consumer, students as a constituency were scarcely heard from in the debates. But since then the fledgling National Student Lobby has established an active presence and voice for students in Washington. Faculty too were largely unrepresented in earlier years, but the American Association of University Professors has recently adopted a more activist role on questions of federal support for higher education. To what degree the views of administrators, students and faculty as represented in Washington will overlap or conflict remains to be seen.

If the big associations ever had the field to themselves, they no longer do. In addition to faculty and student voices, specialized professional groups like the National Association of Student Financial Aid Administrators and the National Association of College and University Business Officers are listened to because of their intimate involvement with the operational phase of federal programs at the campus level. The influence of these groups is growing. Finally, there are prestigious voices outside Washington, like Carnegie, that continue to issue statements on federal policy, and more recently the Consortium on Financing Higher Education, which has advanced recommendations on behalf of a number of Ivy League and other top private institutions.

The Pattern of Implementation

More than three years after passage of the Education Amendments, battles over implementation continue.

Substantial parts of the law remain no more than symbols of congressional intent. The occupational education and community college authorizations are completely dormant and unfunded. Likewise the institutional aid provisions, except for the small program of cost-of-instruction payments related to veterans. In retrospect, the institutional aid decision in 1972 was clearly more significant for what Congress rejected as an alternative than for what Congress positively decided to authorize.

Stop-and-go implementation has characterized other parts of the legislation. After the OE task force on Section 1202 had drafted and redrafted an exhaustive issue paper, the Administration abruptly announced in early 1973 that all activity in this area was being suspended indefinitely because the President's budget did not include funds for any of the federal programs that the state commissions were designed to plan for. Above all, the Administration wanted to avoid spawning fifty state agencies that might exert pressure for funding such programs. HEW policy-makers also decided that encouraging comprehensive state-wide planning was not in line with the Administration's free market philosophy toward higher education. Congressman O'Hara vehemently objected that the Administration had no right to unilaterally undercut the thrust of the legislation.

One year later, the Administration just as suddenly relented and announced it would proceed to implement 1202 under very flexible rules. The congressional Appropriations Committees had explicitly earmarked a small amount of money for setting up the state commissions, and the Administration agreed to distribute the funds.

Administrative blockage and delay have been endemic under the 1972 law, so much so that Congress has subsequently enacted provisions specifying the schedule for publishing education regulations and creating a procedure for congressional review. The complexity of the law, tangled bureaucratic procedures and politics within HEW, hang-ups between HEW and the White House, and legislative-executive deadlock on spending have all been part of the problem. Delay and drift in the case of NIE helped produce its troubled relationship with Congress, which has left NIE having to survive on less funding than the Office of Education previously had to conduct education research. In the case of Title IX, only in July, 1975, did HEW regulations finally go into effect to implement the ban on sex discrimination in postsecondary education—amidst a storm of controversy over their fidelity to the spirit of the law and their potential impact on intercollegiate athletics. New regulations for some of the older programs that were amended in 1972 have even yet to be promulgated.

A litany of problems has accumulated since 1972. Yet what is perhaps more significant is that the central strategy of the legislation, a balanced package of federal aid to students, is slowly being realized. Congress continues to insist on funding the campus-based programs, plus state scholarship incentives, while reducing the Administration's "full funding" requests for BEOG and phasing this program in gradually. Restricted in the school year 1973-1974 to full-time freshmen, BEOG has been extended in each succeeding year to an additional class and is scheduled in 1976-1977 to encompass the entire target population originally conceived in the law, all eligible part-time and full-time undergraduates. The combination of the Administration's enduring commitment to the entitlement concept embodied in BEOG and the congressional commitment to maintaining the other programs simultaneously has produced a burgeoning federal investment in student assistance, doubling and nearly tripling pre-1972 levels.

The BEOG program, however, has had its difficulties operationally, and a sizeable percentage of appropriated funds has gone unexpended in the program's early years. Late issuance of regulations and forms, complicated application procedures, the relatively small size of actual awards and the unfamiliarity of the program to students have contributed to the lack of participation by many of those potentially eligible. As the program becomes more widely known and understood with each passing year and as individual grants reach more meaningful levels with increased appropriations, some of the problems are likely to wash out. Like previously enacted national entitlement programs such as those under the Social Security Act, BEOG may require several years to take firm root. Yet, if the Office of Education proves unable to demonstrate that the BEOG program can deliver benefits expeditiously, the Appropriations Committees—so far willing to give the benefit of the doubt to the Administration—may pull it up short. Nothing more surely endangers continued appropriations for a program than unspent funds.

The BEOG program has also been dogged by controversy over eligibility criteria. The family contribution schedules first proposed by the Commissioner drew strong congressional and public reaction on such points as the treatment of family farm and business assets. Since the first year of the program, under pressure from both the Pell and O'Hara subcommittees, OE has made concessions toward liberalizing the schedules, though they remain generally more stringent than the standards traditionally applied by the colleges in administering student aid.

Some Dilemmas

An appraisal of developments since the 1972 enactment stimulates some basic questions about the evolution of federal education legislation and programs, and perhaps about the federal role in domestic affairs generally—questions without simple answers.

Has, for example, the volume of legislation outstripped the capacity of the bureaucracy to absorb and deal with it effectively? The cumulative product of a long-running congressional obstacle course, the 1972 bill expressed a diversity of political interests and responded to a variety of objective social needs and concerns. The bill is still being sorted out; the administrative agencies are still struggling to come to grips with its implications, or in some areas trying to avoid coming to grips with its implications. It may well be that if all the 1972 programs had been funded, OE/HEW simply would not have had the manpower or expertise to implement them. Does such legislative productivity at some point become counterproductive in the attainment of policy goals?

Moreover, by not exercising greater discipline, are the authorizing committees of Congress in effect abdicating power to the Administration and the Appropriations Committees, which determine which legislation and parts of legislation will be funded and which will not? Alternatively, would not these committees be abdicating their responsibility if they wrote legislation that understated social needs in their respective areas of jurisdiction?

A corollary question is the old dilemma of congressional oversight. Once such legislation has been enacted, how does Congress effectively monitor its execution? Politically and structurally, most committees of Congress are not adequately geared to the function. Even when, as in the case of the O'Hara panel, the circumstances and the chairman favor a strong oversight role, there is the problem of encompassing the sheer breadth of issues involved. When it is on top of an issue, a congressional committee can galvanize an administrative agency. But its impact is likely to be selective and episodic, rather than sustained. Congress is typically outmatched by executive expertise and frequently outmaneuvered by executive control of budgetary and rule-making procedures.

Finally, is it inevitable that federal legislation and programs, as they evolve and expand, become more complex and less comprehensible to their intended beneficiaries? This narrative on the 1972 legislation does not reflect the degree of complexity of the legislation and programs because we have consistently simplified and cut through the technical detail. Much of the complexity inevitably flows from the exigencies of pragmatic compromise in the legislative process and the requirements of responsible stewardship of public funds by executive agencies. But the labyrinthine, frequently cumbersome nature of federal aid, as perceived by the recipient colleges and students, is nonetheless a problem and an issue in itself that yields to no obvious solution. The BEOG program is an example of an originally simple legislative concept that has been transformed into a program involving complex regulatory procedures that get in the way of delivering the intended benefits to individuals.

The Ever Changing Agenda

Continuity and refinement of the charter established in 1972 will probably characterize legislative action on higher education for several years to come.

Many of the principal sponsors of the 1972 bill will be around to preserve their handiwork. Senator Pell, in particular, continues to chair the Senate subcommittee and has no intention of discarding the legislation.

Some new issues have taken form, and some old issues have been redefined or given new urgency by events. But the issues are likely to be dealt with by tinkering and adjustment of the statute in the light of experience, rather than the creation of new programs or major new policy thrusts.

One issue that was relatively unnoticed in 1972, the half-cost limitation in the BEOG program, has since become highly charged. While Congressman O'Hara and others favor its elimination on grounds of equity for low-income students attending low-cost public institutions, many private college spokesmen seek to retain it. These spokesmen view the half-cost restriction as symbolic of federal concern for the protection of private higher education.

Perhaps the most difficult issue that Congress will have to address is the chronic issue of the Guaranteed Student Loan Program, traditionally ridden by crisis and in recent years endangered by the potential of major scandal. The problem of rising student defaults and abuse of the program by educational and lending institutions as well as students will force Congress to reconsider the federal role in student loan financing.

An associated set of issues revolves around the theme of consumer protection in postsecondary education. Pressures have mounted for government action to insure that students are adequately informed before making their educational investment choices and actually receive what they are told they will receive for their investment. This could lead to a reconsideration of the traditional dependence on voluntary accreditating associations in determining institutional eligibility for federal programs. Having broadened the mainstream of "postsecondary" education, Congress may be having second thoughts about the soundness of some of the educational options that were newly legitimized in 1972, as well as some traditionally respectable programs and institutions that may not be serving students honestly or well.

The preservation of the independent sector of higher education *will* be a focus of legislative concern, as it was in 1972. Adjustment of some of the student aid programs, like SEOG, to target them more precisely on the goal of student choice, and thus to aid more students in high-cost private institutions, will be under debate. Direct federal support of private institutions, however, is unlikely.

If new federal money is to be channeled to institutions, it may well take the form of increased administrative allowances to help defray the growing expense of operating and coordinating federal student aid programs at the campus level. But general support for institutions as it was posed in the 1972 debates is no longer a live issue.

Thus the debates of the late 1970s will focus on the problems of management and equity in student aid programs. Efforts to streamline and simplify program requirements and procedures, particularly under BEOG, and the complex question of assessing student need and eligibility under all of the programs, will absorb the attention of the congressional committees.

Notes

1. R. Fulton, "The Future is Now," Volume 37, *The Compass*, June, 1973.

2. Public Law 92-318, Section 122 (a)(1)(C).

3. Section 301(a).

4. Speech by Senator Pell at Conference of Rhode Island Council of Student Governments, December 16, 1972, mimeo, p. 10.

5. *Congressional Record*, daily edition, August 2, 1972, p. H7136.

248

6. *New York Times*, May 18, 1972, p. 1.

7. Edith Green, "Federal Funds in Education: When Does Use Become Abuse," *The Educational Forum*, November, 1971, p. 19.

8. Quoted in Karen DeW. Lewis, "Education Report/Huge Programs in New Education Law Fall Victim to Budgetary Stringency," *National Journal*, September 16, 1972, p. 1472.

9. Richard Nathan, *The Plot that Failed: Nixon and the Administrative Presidency*, John Wiley & Sons, New York, 1975, p. 62.

10. Quoted in *Time*, January 15, 1973, p. 67.

11. Quoted in Cheryl M. Fields, "Rep. Edith Green Gives up Post on Education Panel," *The Chronicle of Higher Education*, January 22, 1973, p. 3.

12. Quoted in Lewis, p. 1466.

13. Statement by James G. O'Hara, February 7, 1973.

14. Quoted in *Higher Education Daily*, July 11, 1975, p. 2.

15. John C. Honey and John Crowley, "The Future of the American Council on Education: A Report on its Governmental and Related Activities," mimeo, September, 1972, p. 3.

11
The Policy Process

As a case study of the policy process, this work has focused on political behavior resulting in authoritative value choices.[a] It is for the most part a traditional case study—a narrative describing a succession of events in a limited period of time from the point of view of detached observers simultaneously watching the major political actors. We have explained events and turning points without pretending to demonstrate causality.[b] We have viewed political behavior as a process where multiple factors interacting over time shaped the output, the Education Amendments of 1972, as well as the outcome, the effects of the law in practice.[c] However, we have also extended the case beyond the formal stages of government decision making by examining the historical, intellectual and social context in which the law was formulated. And we have carried the story forward to assess outcomes following enactment.

As a narrative of federal policy making for higher education, we believe this case stands on its own as a complex and fascinating slice of political life about issues of concern and consequence to a wide spectrum of policy-makers and citizens. However, for it to be of significance for social scientists, it must be linked to the "generalizing activity" of a science.[1] This can be accomplished by using the case study to support, question or modify existing theories of political behavior.[d]

The Higher Education Policy Arena

The first question social scientists ask of every case study is: "Of what is this a case?"[2] The quest has been for a typology of variables on the basis of which

---

[a]See Vernon Van Dyke, "Process and Policy as Focal Concepts in Political Research," and Robert H. Salisbury, "The Analysis of Public Policy: A Search for Theories and Roles," both in *Political Science and Public Policy*, Austin Ranney, ed., Markham, Chicago, 1968.

[b]On the case study method, see James W. Fesler, "The Case Method in Political Science," in *Essays on the Case Method*, Edwin A. Bock, ed., The Inter-University Case Program, Syracuse, New York, 1962.

[c]On "process," see Austin Ranney, "The Study of Policy Content: A Framework for Choice," in Ranney, ed., p. 8.

[d]Lijphart characterizes these respectively as "theory-confirming," "theory-informing," and "hypothesis-generating" case studies, pp. 691-692. See also, Fesler, pp. 77-81 on "the *scientific* usefulness of cases." (Emphasis in original.)

case studies can be aggregated and compared. At the outset, we indicated that ours is a case study of congressional initiative, of domestic politics in the Nixon years, of landmark legislation, and of omnibus legislation. We argued impressionistically that this case may be more typical than the studies of fundamental shifts in the federal role such as the Employment Act of 1946, the Marshall Plan, the Elementary and Secondary Education Act of 1965 or Medicare.[3]

In addition, we would suggest other variables for comparing this case to others—those contained in the concept of a policy arena. In his classic essay, Theodore Lowi maintained that the nature of the issue on which government is acting is the key variable for cumulating and comparing case studies.[4] Other scholars have expanded and refined Lowi's concepts as well as otherwise distinguishing among types of policy issues.[5]

Our concept of a policy arena also starts from the position that the nature of the issue is central to the comparison of case studies of policy making. However, in the search for a unit of analysis, we offer a different approach. From our more inductive perspective, the major shortcoming of the variables offered by Lowi, *et al*, for comparing case studies is that they bear little relation to political reality as experienced and perceived by actors in the policy-making process. Our interest is to define the contexts in which political issues are dealt with in practice in American national politics. We aim at grouping cases in terms of categories that relate to the behavior and perceptions of political actors. Thus we propose a unit of analysis that is both behavioral, related to what political actors actually do, and phenomenological, related to how political actors perceive and define what it is that they do.

One body of literature behaviorally aggregates issues in American national politics by applying factor analysis to roll call votes in Congress.[e] These studies group issues in terms of voting patterns by stable groups of Congressmen. In other words, an issue area is the group of issues to which groups of Congressmen apply common decision rules. The assumption is that the application of the same decision rule to a set of issues implies common perceptions of the issues by the Congressmen in each group. The issue areas or policy dimensions thus defined are behavioral, based on roll call votes, and phenomenological, based on the actors' perceptions of the issues.

This approach to the study of policy making seems both too narrow and too broad. It observes a very narrow category of behavior by only one set of political actors, roll call votes by Congressmen. It also brings under one umbrella issues that at stages other than voting may be dealt with by very different political processes and actors. For example, among the issues grouped by Cimbala

---

[e]For example, Stephen J. Cimbala, "Foreign Policy as an Issue Area: A Roll Call Analysis," *The American Political Science Review*, Volume 63 (March, 1969); the sources cited by Cimbala in note 9; and Aage R. Clausen, *How Congressmen Decide: A Policy Focus*, St. Martin's Press, New York, 1973, especially Chapter 2.

into a single factor are the "Nomination of Gen. Williams" and the "Education and Cultural Exchange Act."[6] These differ at least insofar as the former falls under the jurisdiction of the Department of Defense and the Senate Armed Services Committee and the latter under the Department of State and the Senate Foreign Relations and House International Relations Committees.

Having presented our view of how *not* to define a policy arena, we now offer our own criteria of definition and our argument that federal higher education policy can be analyzed using such criteria.

Substantive Coherence

Political actors usually both perceive their policy-making activity and interact in terms of clusters of issues that are substantively related to each other, for example, housing of petroleum energy.[f] In the case of federal higher education policy, substantive coherence is provided by attention to issues and federal programs that aim at fostering and expanding opportunities for higher education. These are distinguished from other federal programs that significantly support or impinge on higher education but only incident to other federal objectives such as space exploration or the search for a cancer cure. In particular, this policy arena encompasses three types of programs and issues: first, student aid administered by the Office of Education for undergraduate and graduate students; second, institution building programs such as college housing and higher education facilities; and third, categorical programs to improve the quality of instruction in general or for selected higher education clienteles such as librarians. Student aid, intended to make higher education more widely accessible, constitutes the central thrust.

The substantive coherence of this policy arena is far from perfect. A recent study estimated that there are approximately 380 separate federal programs of support for postsecondary education.[7] Many of these are not in the higher education policy arena as we define it here—for example, student aid programs addressed to manpower needs in the health professions as well as major student assistance extended to Social Security beneficiaries and veterans.

The inclusion of federal programs for the support of scientific research and development, which have mushroomed since World War II, is problematical. While federal support for research *on* higher education is clearly within this arena, federally sponsored research conducted *at* higher education institutions in fields like agriculture of atomic energy seem to lie outside. These latter programs fall in a separate, though overlapping arena, that of federal support for research and development.

---

[f]See Harold Wolman, *Politics of Federal Housing*, Dodd, Mead, New York, 1971; and David H. Davis, *Energy Politics*, St. Martin's Press, New York, 1974.

The fuzzy substantive coherence of this policy arena is not unique but rather characteristic of policy making by the national government of a large, pluralistic society. In a few policy arenas, like veterans' affairs, the boundaries are sharp. More typically, however, there is a core of substantive issues and policies, such as student aid. Around this core is an assortment of other issues and policies that are usually considered in the same context. The substantive boundaries of a policy arena are normally fluid.

Statutory Foundations

The substantive coherence of a policy arena is usually reflected in a constellation of statutes which focus attention. For example, in the federal labor-management policy arena, the National Labor Relations Act of 1935, the Taft-Hartley Act of 1946 and the Landrum-Griffin Act of 1959 are the basic foundation. In the case of the higher education policy arena, it is the National Defense Education Act (1958), the Higher Education Facilities Act (1963), the Higher Education Act (1965) and now the Education Amendments of 1972. In concrete terms, the issues involved in extension and modification of these statutes constitute the substance of the higher education policy arena.

A Subgovernment

Policy arenas are also characterized by a stable pattern of interactions among political actors and government institutions. Long-standing and close ties between congressional committees, executive agencies, interest groups and program clienteles in an area of policy making have been identified frequently as a salient characteristic of national politics. Variously called "subgovernments" or "subsystems" examples include "the military-industrial complex," Indian affairs, and the grazing of livestock on the public domain.[g]

As a subgovernment, the higher education policy arena normally encompasses the administrative units dealing with higher education under the Assistant Secretary for Education in the Department of HEW (principally the Office of Education), the House Subcommittee on Postsecondary Education, the Senate Subcommittee on Education, and the Washington representatives of higher education associations.

---

[g]The terms are respectively from Douglass Cater, *Power in Washington*, Vintage Books, New York, 1964; and J. Leiper Freeman, *The Political Process: Executive Bureau-Legislative Committee Relations*, revised ed., Random House, New York, 1965. Cater cites as an example the "military-industrial complex" and Freeman, Indian affairs. Livestock grazing is treated as a "subsystem" by Philip O. Foss, *Politics and Grass: The Administration of Grazing on the Public Domain*, University of Washington Press, Seattle, 1960. See also Arthur Maass, *Muddy Waters*, Harvard University Press, Cambridge, Massachusetts, 1951.

The Office of Education became the executive branch focal point for higher education policy and grew very rapidly when it was given administrative responsibility for the higher education programs authorized in the late 50s and 60s. The development of higher education as a policy arena in the executive branch was also signaled by the adoption of a new category in the federal budget titled "Assistance for Higher Education" in fiscal year 1963, replacing in part the earlier broad category of "Promotion of Education."

The higher education subgovernment attained institutional definition in the House of Representatives with the creation in 1957 of the Special Subcommittee on Education. This subcommittee, with jurisdiction over higher education, continues today under a new name, the Subcommittee on Postsecondary Education. Congresswoman Edith Green provided sustained leadership of the subcommittee from 1961-1972.

There are three other indicators of the emergence in the early 1960s of the higher education subgovernment in the House. First, the higher education components of President Kennedy's omnibus education proposals were split off and considered separately. Second, in 1961 the Special Subcommittee on Education launched the first systematic survey of federal activities related to higher education. Third, also in 1961, the committee chairman, Congressman Adam Clayton Powell (D-New York), appointed an ad hoc study group to investigate the needs of higher education. This group of five young members (including James O'Hara of Michigan, who later succeeded Mrs. Green as chairman of the Special Subcommittee on Education) produced a set of unanimous recommendations.[8] These three events signaled the emergence of a higher education subgovernment in the House that was distinct from elementary and secondary education.

Largely because the smaller membership of the Senate precludes as much specialization by subcommittees, the emergence of higher education as a subgovernment was not marked by institutional changes in the Senate comparable to those in the House. In the Senate all education bills were and continue to be considered by one subcommittee, chaired since 1969 by Senator Claiborne Pell.

Higher education institutions have been organized in associations for over a half century. However, it was not until the early 1960s that the six major associations had all established Washington offices. In 1962, the Secretariat composed of the executive secretaries of the major and several of the minor associations first met to exchange information and ideas on federal policy and political strategy.[9] Through the 1960s and into the 1970s, a rapidly growing number of specialized associations, universities and university systems established Washington offices.[10] Symbolically, the full fledged emergence of a higher education lobby can perhaps be dated from the acquisition in 1968 of a building, the National Center for Higher Education (familiarly known by its address "One Dupont Circle"), to house most of the higher education associations.

The case of the Education Amendments of 1972 amply demonstrates that the interactions among the actors in these executive, congressional and lobbying institutions were frequent and regular. Behaviorally they formed a sub-government. In addition, it is our judgment that these political actors perceived one another as the "significant others" in making higher education policy decisions. A variety of additional actors episodically appear and have an impact. But the day-to-day expectation and reality was interaction within the higher education subgovernment as we have sketched it.

In recent years higher education as a subgovernment has attained increasing definition. President Nixon's message to the Congress in March, 1970, "Higher Education," was the first presidential message to Congress devoted entirely to this subject. Previous higher education proposals had been included in presidential messages dealing with education at all levels or with health and education. In November, 1972, the House and Senate education committees published the first *Compilation of Higher Education Laws*. Higher education laws formerly were included in broader compilations.

In the 1960s and 1970s, the higher education policy arena became institutionalized, that is "relatively well-bounded," "differentiated from its environment" and "relatively complex."[h] The institutionalization of a policy arena is possibly a dimension for comparing policy arenas. For example, the comparison between a policy arena that has become less institutionalized and decayed, like civil defense, and one like higher education, which has become increasingly institutionalized, might prove instructive.

A Political Culture

A policy arena is also defined by a political culture. This term has been used largely to describe the political ideals and operating norms of a national polity as in Almond and Verba's classic work, *The Civic Culture*.[11] Or, it has been applied to homogeneous subnational populations having a unique history such as the French-Canadians of Quebec.[i] Our view is that there is also in each well-defined policy arena a fundamental consensus on goals for federal policy, the means that should be employed to attain those goals, and the nature of political relations through which policy making should occur. This political culture, the ideals and operating norms of the policy arena, sets the boundaries of legitimate

---

[h]On these definitional criteria, see Nelson W. Polsby, "The Institutionalization of the U.S. House of Representatives," *American Political Science Review*, Volume 62 (March, 1968), p. 145.

[i]For example, Louis Hartz, *The Founding of New Societies*, Harcourt, Brace and World, New York, 1964.

federal ends and means. It is the baseline from which new policy evolves. It is a reservoir of models to be emulated and a catalog of dangers and deviations to be avoided.

The political culture of a policy arena is not chiseled in stone, although some of the basic assumptions are more durable than others. In response to social change and historical circumstance, these assumptions are changing at different rates. Thus the political culture of a policy arena is a moving consensus.

Our examination of the historical role of the federal government in higher education yielded, in Chapter 1, five basic assumptions concerning federal policy making for higher education that can be characterized as the political culture of the higher education policy arena. The Education Amendments of 1972 were enacted within and reaffirmed this basic consensus as indicated in the discussion of the policy themes of the Act in the previous chapter.

The 1972 Act also indicates the direction of evolution in this political culture. The stress placed on innovation and reform in higher education and greater accountability from institutions of higher education suggests a broadening of the scope of permissible federal action at the expense of the primacy of the states. The adoption of the Basic Grant and the cost-of-instruction approach to institutional aid highlight the full emergence of equal educational opportunity as the principal federal policy objective in higher education. The institutional aid formula tentatively marks a movement from neutrality between public and private institutions to some special preference for the privates. Finally, the reorientation of the federal concern from higher education to "postsecondary" education and the creation of the National Commission on the Financing of Postsecondary Education indicates a quest for a more coherent federal policy.

Public Attitudes

A set of public attitudes also characterizes a policy arena. As reflected in polls of their constituents by Congressmen, there is generally a high level of public support for federal efforts in education. In 1973-1974, fourteen Congressmen asked their constituents whether they would recommend more, the same or less money for education.[12] The averages of the fourteen polls show that 42.3 percent of the respondents recommended more, 38.3 percent the same, and only 19.4 percent less for education. Thus education along with areas like health, pollution control, crime control and mass transit had a reservoir of public support for expanding or at least maintaining the federal commitment. This is in contrast to areas like defense, foreign aid, space research and welfare where the balance was clearly on the side of doing less.

On the other hand, when the general public is polled on the most important problems facing the nation, education ranks low. In three Gallup Polls in 1971, education ranked tenth and twelfth among the problems identified, mentioned by one or two percent of the public.[13] Thus there does not seem to be an urgency in public concern for education. This suggests that public opinion as it relates to policy making has two salient dimensions: Is X desirable? and Is X pressing? Our inference with respect to higher education is that it is seen as a good thing for the federal government to be supporting but not a high priority concern. By way of contrast, crime control, another area where there is support for more spending, is identified as ranking very high among the important problems facing the nation. There is thus a basically different environment of public attitudes for policy making in higher education and crime control.

Resources

There are also resource constraints in each arena. Viewed in the perspective of two decades, federal funding of higher education has been a bull market. In fiscal year 1959, the first year of full operation of the National Defense Education Act, higher education expenditures by the Office of Education amounted to $82.2 million.[j] In fiscal year 1973, higher education expenditures by the Office of Education were $1,710 million.[k] Thus between 1959 and 1973, while total federal expenditures tripled, OE expenditures for higher education grew almost 21-fold, or seven times more rapidly than total federal expenditures.[l]

Generalizations about the Process

The logical follow-up to the question, "Of what is this a case?," is the question, "What difference does it make that this is a case of X?" or more trenchantly "So what?" We have suggested some implications of the fact that this is a case

---

[j]This is the sum of the actual expenditures for the NDEA programs and for Land-Grant colleges in fiscal year 1959, *The Budget of the United States Government for the Fiscal Year Ending June 30, 1961*, Government Printing Office, Washington, D.C., 1960, p. 566.

[k]These are the actual outlays for fiscal year 1973 in the category "Assistance for Higher Education" in the budget of the Office of Education, *The Budget of the United States, FY 1975*, Government Printing Office, Washington, D.C., 1974, p. 310.

[l]This comparison obviously does not include expenditures for programs that might be included in the higher education policy arena but that are not administered by the Office of Education. The comparison is meant to be suggestive of the growth of the federal commitment rather than an exact measure of that growth. Public attitudes and resources are analogous to "popular demands" and "the economy" that Ira Sharkansky identifies as among the "determinants of public policy." Ira Sharkansky, ed., *Policy Analysis in Political Science*, Markham, Chicago, 1970, pp. 8-11.

of policy making in the higher education policy arena. However, to provide a satisfactory answer to the "So what?" question, it would be necessary to determine how much of what happens in the higher education arena is peculiar to that arena, and how much is attributable to its being a part of American national politics or American national domestic politics. Comparative case studies in several arenas of American national policy making would be required. This we have not undertaken, suggesting instead the terms for such comparisons in the concept of a policy arena. In addition, we offer the following generalizations drawn from this study, without being able to distinguish between those that are unique to the higher education policy arena and those that are characteristic of policy making across a number of policy arenas.

New policy choices were modifications and additions to existing policies, and where important departures occurred, current programs and arrangements frequently served as models. Federal policy making did not make its mark on a tabula rasa. New policies were reconciled with and embedded in what already existed. Policy-makers attempted to solve complex social problems by modifying and altering the myriad on-going programs.[m] Beginning with what existed as a baseline narrowed the options for new policy. There was a presumption against overturning wholesale the status quo. It was also difficult in practical terms to institute a major change in signals to the bureaucracy and to the programs' clienteles. Thus the assumption that new policy would be grafted on to the old tempered innovation and moderated the pace of change. The 1972 Act was quite appropriately titled the Education *Amendments* of 1972. The incremental nature of "normal" policy development was a fundamental characteristic of the process.

Even where departures were undertaken, the institutional mechanisms and basic concepts were frequently modeled on existing federal programs in related policy arenas. For example, the National Institute of Education was conceived as an analogue to the National Institutes of Health. The original version of the National Foundation for Higher Education proposal was drafted using as a model the National Science Foundation. The BEOG, a federally administered student aid "entitlement" program, was conceptually related to the G.I. Bill. Thus significant policy departures of the 1972 Act were far from unprecedented.

Policy making is incremental in three senses: It occurs within the limits of a slowly evolving political culture; it is built on and related to existing policy; and it draws from existing policy models. This does not imply that the status quo is forever frozen, but that policy development will be evolutionary rather the revolutionary. It also suggests that in the short run the broad outlines of future policy development are predictable.

---

[m]See Charles E. Lindblom, "The Science of 'Muddling Through'," *Public Administration Review*, Volume 19 (Spring, 1959); and Aaron Wildavsky, *The Politics of the Budgetary Process*, 2d ed., Little, Brown, Boston, 1974.

Policy making was conditioned by the basic calendar of American national politics. The rhythm of congressional and presidential elections, the yearly budgetary cycle, the sessions of Congress and the expiration dates of statutes all strongly influenced when action could occur and when it had to occur. For example, a higher education bill was approaching fruition in the House in 1970, a congressional election year and the year of intense student unrest. House members did not want to face the inevitable anti-student unrest amendments that would be offered on the floor, and they deferred action until the next Congress. Among other things, this delay meant that the sense of crisis supporting the passage of an enrollment-based institutional aid program dissipated.

The final consideration of the conference report took place in June, 1972, as the automatic expiration of most higher education programs approached. This enhanced the prospect that the conference report would be approved because rejecting it would leave little time to fashion a substitute.

There also seems to be a more general rhythm of innovation and consolidation. Between the breakthrough in 1965 and the Education Amendments of 1972, several pieces of higher education legislation were adopted, the most significant being the 1968 amendments. These policy changes were relatively minor. Between 1965 and 1972, the focus was on implementation and refinement of the 1965 Act. However, during this same period a backlog of new problems and new proposals for federal action accumulated. Thus in 1971-1972, there was a feeling that it was "higher education's turn" for another major thrust. Since many of the new programs enacted in 1972 are either yet to be implemented or have only recently been implemented, the 1965-1972 cycle may be repeated. As the Education Amendments of 1972 are reconsidered in the face of their expiration in 1976, it is likely that, as in 1968, most programs will be reauthorized with minor changes. Attention will probably focus on a few glaring problems, and major changes will be delayed until the next round (circa 1980).

The emergence of issues to the status of public problems was a complex social-political process. The timidity of this generalization reflects the fact that the least understood and perhaps least examined part of the policy-making process is its initial stage, the recognition of social aspirations and needs as public problems.[n] A few aspects of this process seem clear.

First, when the perceived interests of already politicized groups were threatened, they made demands on government for the restoration of the status quo or some other amelioration of their situation. The concern with the financial crisis in higher education can be understood in these terms. This issue was forcefully pressed on the federal government by the associations of colleges and universities.

---

[n]The most systematic effort addressed to this problem is Roger W. Cobb and Charles D. Elder, *Participation in American Politics: The Dynamics of Agenda Building*, Allyn and Bacon, Boston, 1972.

Second, when elites perceived that an issue affected their interests or was closely related to their ideological beliefs, it also attained a place on the agenda. With the 18-year-old vote, the interest of Congressmen in getting re-elected may have made them more attentive to the financial barriers and burdens faced by students. The fact that many policy-makers had attended private colleges may have helped to insure a prominent place on the agenda for the plight of the privates.

Third, social and political crises focused attention. In the case of higher education, the civil rights revolution of the 1960s made equality in general and equal educational opportunity in specific a salient public problem. The wave of campus disruptions not only attracted notice as an expression of dissatisfaction with America's foreign policy in Southeast Asia but also highlighted the need for innovation and reform in higher education. One spin-off of the Women's Movement was a concern with sex discrimination in higher education.

Finally, the boundaries of the political culture of the policy arena made some issues, like comprehensive higher education planning by the federal government, ineligible as public problems on the federal agenda.[o]

There were multiple and diverse sources of policy options. Once issues reached the national agenda, proposals to deal with them were advanced from many points within the federal government as well as the interested public. The Rivlin Report, Carnegie Commission studies and recommendations, Newman report, and Cheit study among others were all sources of policy thinking in the formulation of the 1972 Act. Clearly, no one had a monopoly on policy ideas in the formative stages of the legislation. Policy options came from the federal executive branch, congressional committees, the higher education associations, private foundations, and scholars.

The broad and diverse range of policy options was winnowed to a smaller number of "live options" through another complex screening process. Those in government in a position to act on public problems were searching for solutions. Those within and outside of government who were formulating proposals to deal with public problems were searching for sponsors among those who could take authoritative action. In some cases the search of the government policy-makers "mated" with the search of the policy proposers and live options were born.[p] Five factors seemed important in determining which policy options received serious consideration in the case of the Education Amendments of 1972.

1. Policy proposals that were supported by good data and lucid arguments were more likely to become live options. In the fascination with the political process, it is often overlooked that the merits of the case and the weight of the evidence strongly influence which ideas are taken seriously. For example, the persuasive arguments and evidence of the Jellema and Cheit studies that there

---

[o]See Peter Bachrach and Morton S. Baratz, "Two Faces of Power," *The American Political Science Review*, Volume 56 (December, 1962).

[p]The idea of "mating search" is developed in Richard M. Cyert and James O. March, *A Behavioral Theory of the Firm*, Prentice-Hall, Englewood Cliffs, New Jersey, 1963, pp. 52, 80.

was a financial crisis in higher education gained attention for institutional aid proposals. Conversely, when the data and analyses of these studies were later called into question, some of the liveliness went out of the institution aid bills.

2. The power and status of the source of a proposal also influenced the attention given to it. Policy proposals were not disembodied messages evaluated solely on their merits. They circulated in the policy arena carrying the names of sources with greater or lesser weight. The bills introduced by Representative Green and Senator Pell naturally commanded attention; bills dropped in the hopper by other Members, particularly those not sitting on the relevant committees, were usually taken much less seriously. Administration proposals automatically got a hearing. Policy advocates outside of government found easier entree if they carried status and name recognition. For example, substantial weight was attached to the recommendations of the Carnegie Commission because of the prestige of the Commission members who endorsed the reports.

3. Policy proposals that were inconsistent with the political culture of the policy arena had less chance of being considered live options. For example, a frequently voiced argument against enrollment-based institutional aid was that it seemed to imply that the federal government would assume a major share of the basic support of higher education, a responsibility traditionally left to the states.

4. The needs and interests of policy-making elites formed another mesh through which proposals were screened. Thus the Republican Administration resisted institutional aid because such a program promised a large, growing and inflexible new budgetary commitment. Senator Pell, facing re-election in 1972, was sympathetic to innovative and far-reaching proposals like the BEOG in part because such proposals with his name attached might grab the attention of his Rhode Island constituents.

5. Some policy ideas fell by the wayside for fortuitous reasons. For example, the recommendations of the White House task force on higher education chaired by James Hester had little impact. In 1969, fifteen task forces including the Hester group were established at the instigation of White House Counselor Arthur Burns to chart the policy directions of the New Nixon Administration. When these task forces reported the following year, Burns had left the White House to become Chairman of the Federal Reserve Board. In the absence of their powerful White House sponsor, most of these task force reports, in particular Hester's, languished in obscurity.

Decision making was pluralistic. The decision-making process was pluralistic in three senses. First, there was no single locus of choice. Instead, beginning at the sub-bureau level in the executive branch and at the subcommittee level in the Congress, there were numerous points at which decisions were made. Moreover, the number of decision-making points is compounded by the existence of a budgetary and appropriations process parallel to and largely isolated from the authorization process. Second, there was a broad distribution of political resources. Major actors at each stage were capable of significantly shaping the outcome. Third, the major actors at each of the decision-making points frequently differed in their policy preferences.

The criteria of choice tended to vary at each stage. Depending upon the actors and the decisions involved, the lenses through which policy options were viewed might be tinted with presidential politics, congressional district concerns, legislative-executive competition, enhancing the status of the Office of Education, or serving the interest of higher education institutions.

Decision-making was continuous and tentative. It is occasionally helpful to think of the policy process as having an end, for example, when the President signs his name to a bill or when policies have their intended (or unintended) impact. However, as noted in the previous chapter, the process has been continuous. Following enactment of the law, administrative regulations were drafted and debated, budget recommendations were formulated yearly, and Congress voted appropriations and amended the law. The social context in which policy had its impact changed and with it the impact and the nature of the policy itself. New actors and old actors in new contexts and with new preferences have continually remolded policy.

One implication of the continuous nature of the process is that policies are not inevitably doomed to stagnation. With frequent and regular opportunities to modify previous decisions, adaptive change is possible. In addition, knowing that there will be future opportunities to modify policy tends to mute conflict among policy-makers. The process is like a boxing match with a practically infinite number of rounds. You do not have to make an all-out effort for victory in any one round because there are many more to come.

In addition, policy decisions are seen as tentative. In the foreseeable future, most issues will return and another effort can be made to handle the substantive and political problems when better information is available and when clearer or easier political choices are presented.

The quality of decision making was uneven. A high quality decision is one to which the decision-makers give their systematic attention in rough proportion to the importance of the decision and where all of the relevant and accessible information is brought to bear. It is a conscious and informed choice. High quality decisions are also more likely to be good in the sense that the consequences of the decision are both desired and anticipated by the policy-makers. In the case of the Education Amendments of 1972, relatively little attention was given to a number of important decisions and only fragmentary and impressionistic information was relied on. For example, in the conference committee, the needs test for the Guaranteed Loan Program was discussed for about thirty minutes in the early morning hours of the last session. The most persuasive bit of data was Congressman Quie's red Corvette story. On the other hand, an issue like the institutional aid formula was the subject of extensive hearings and debate, and there were efforts to generate additional intelligence.

The uneven quality of decision-making was largely attributable to the massiveness of the omnibus bill. The decision-makers simply lacked the time, energy and intellectual capacity to give every issue the attention it merited. Some issues just "fell between the cracks."

Within each stage of the process as well as at different stages, which issues were dealt with effectively was due mainly to the mix of interests, beliefs, perceptions and resources operative at that stage. Thus the pluralism of the process led not only to the application of different criteria for choice at different stages, but also to variations in the quality of decisions. Not only did policy-makers at different stages answer the same question with a "yes" rather than a "no," they also sometimes reacted to the same question with a "don't care" rather than a "do care."

The intensity and magnitude of input from the outside also focused the limited time and attention of decision-makers. For example, the raging public debate over school busing forced the House-Senate conferees to give careful scrutiny to the busing amendments. In contrast, the low-key role played by the Administration during congressional consideration of the legislation meant that important questions related to the administrative feasibility of various programs slipped through without sufficient consideration. The squeaky wheels got the grease. Chance also played a role. The attention received by a squeaky wheel depended on when it squeaked, who heard it, and whether he had a grease gun or a monkey wrench in his hand.

Policy outcomes were significantly shaped by circumstantial factors. Things happened not only because of big causes but also because of many small and medium-sized causes peculiar to this case. The variety of circumstantial factors was almost endless and many have been noted in the narrative.

The personal and political skills of leaders is an important circumstantial factor. Current scholarship conceptualizes leadership in terms of the relationship between personal traits and the situation. Depending on the match, both formal and informal leaders influenced whether there was action or inaction and the nature of the outcomes when action occurred. They influenced whether disagreement in a group decision context was constructive or acrimonious. Chairman Perkins' conduct of the House-Senate conference is a clear example.

The federal courts were another circumstantial factor. Most actors in the policy-making process marched to the same drummer, the basic political calendar of elections, budgetary cycles and statutory expirations. The federal courts marched to their own drummer. They took and decided cases guided by their own schedule and their own logic. Court actions had important consequences for the policy-making process, but the timing and impact of these actions could not be predicted by other actors. The courts were uncycled, and, from the point of view of other policy-makers, a random variable that intruded at unexpected times in often unexpected ways.

In June, 1971, the Supreme Court handed down its decision in *Tilton v. Richardson*, injecting a constitutional issue into the institutional aid debate.

That same spring the Court in *Swann v. Charlotte-Mecklenburg* found busing acceptable "as one tool of desegregation." As a result, the Education Amendments of 1972 became the vehicle for a legislative remedy on the busing issue and enactment of the law was delayed and imperiled.

Notes

1. Arend Lijphart, "Comparative Politics and the Comparative Method," *The American Political Science Review*, Volume 65 (September, 1971), p. 691.

2. William Zimmerman, "Issue Area and Foreign-Policy Process: A Research Note in Search of a General Theory," *The American Political Science Review*, Volume 67 (December, 1973), p. 1204.

3. Stephen K. Bailey, *Congress Makes a Law*, Columbia University Press, New York, 1950; Joseph M. Jones, *The Fifteen Weeks*, The Viking Press, New York, 1955; Eugene Eidenberg and Roy Morey, *An Act of Congress*, W.W. Norton, New York, 1969; and Theodore Marmor, *The Politics of Medicare*, Aldine, Chicago, 1973.

4. Theodore Lowi, "American Business, Public Policy, Case-Studies, and Political Theory," *World Politics*, Volume 16 (July, 1964).

5. James Rosenau, "Foreign Policy as an Issue-Area," in *Domestic Sources of Foreign Policy*, James Rosenau, ed., The Free Press, New York, 1967; Theodore Lowi, "Making Democracy Safe for the World: National Politics," in Rosenau, ed.; Zimmerman, pp. 1205-1209; Robert Salisbury in Ranney, ed., pp. 163-174; Lewis Froman, Jr., "The Categorization of Policy Contents," in Ranney, ed.; and Aaron Wildavsky, "The Analysis of Issue Contexts in the Study of Decision-Making," *Journal of Politics*, Volume 24 (November, 1962).

6. Cimbala, pp. 154-155.

7. The National Commission on the Financing of Postsecondary Education, *Financing Postsecondary Education in the United States*, Government Printing Office, Washington, D.C., 1973, p. 106.

8. Lawrence K. Pettit, "The Policy Process in Congress: Passing the Higher Education Academic Facilities Act of 1963," Ph.D. dissertation, University of Wisconsin (1965), pp. 138-39.

9. Lauriston R. King, *The Washington Lobbyists for Higher Education*, Lexington Books, D.C. Heath, Lexington, Massachusetts, 1975, Chapter 2.

10. Ed Willingham, "Nation's Colleges, Universities Set up Offices to Deal with Government," *National Journal* (April 17, 1971).

11. Gabriel Almond and Sidney Verba, *The Civic Culture* (Boston: Little, Brown, 1965). On the concept of political culture in general, see Lucien W. Pye, "Political Culture" in David L. Sills, ed., *International Encyclopedia of the Social Sciences,* The Macmillan Co., New York, 1968.

12. "Second Annual Report on Congressional Opinion Poll Results," *Congressional Record*, daily edition, October 16, 1974, p. E6535. The questions related to education in general rather than higher education in particular. However, there seems to be no reason to believe that support for higher education expenditures alone would be significantly different.

13. George H. Gallup, *The Gallup Poll: Public Opinion 1935-1971*, Volume 3, Random House, New York, 1972, pp. 2292, 2311, 2324.

Afterword

Cynicism about the motives and competence of public servants pervades the mid-1970s. The story of the Education Amendments of 1972 is not one of heroes in the classical mode, but it does suggest a more balanced appreciation of the skills and intentions of policy-makers as well as the crosscurrents and constraints of the political setting in which they work. While human efforts may be puny in stemming the tides of history, political men can channel those tides, not to produce any result they want but to produce a result more in keeping with public goals as they perceive them. Not everything is possible, but it takes political skill and tenacity to get what *is* possible.

"Every statute. . .has a numerous progeny," Wilson wrote. The lineage of the 1972 Amendments is yet to be written, but new legislation is stirring as we conclude this work. The basic charter established in 1972 is being reviewed and debated in the recurrent cycle of policy making. Policy-makers will again weigh principle and politics in elaborating the national commitment to the support of education beyond high school.

Index

About the Authors

Lawrence E. Gladieux is currently Director of the Washington Office of the College Entrance Examination Board. From 1967 to 1969, he was Legislative Assistant to Congressman John Brademas of Indiana, and, from 1969 to 1971, he served on the staff of the Council on Federal Relations of the Association of American Universities. He received the B.A. from Oberlin College and M.P.A. degree from the Woodrow Wilson School at Princeton University (1967).

Thomas R. Wolanin is currently on leave from the Department of Political Science, University of Wisconsin-Madison and is Staff Director of the House Subcommittee on Labor-Management Relations. He formerly taught at Oberlin College and was a Congressional Fellow in 1971-1972 on the staff of Congressman Frank Thompson of New Jersey. He holds the B.A. from Oberlin College and the Ph.D. from Harvard University (1972). His study of Presidential Advisory Commissions has been published by the University of Wisconsin Press.

They have authored or coauthored articles in the *Journal of Law and Education, Yearbook of Politics and Public Policy, College Board Review, Journal of Politics, AAUP Bulletin,* and *Public and International Affairs.*